PRAISE FOR TEACHINGLAND

"This is a fun, fast-paced read that is all about using teamwork to improve the educational experience. Whether you're an educator in the traditional classroom or an instructor in corporate training, you and your students will benefit from the unconventional strategies and tactics this book offers to navigate the darkness of antiquated educational practices and emerge into the light of an improved pedagogy."

—Mat Chacon, CEO, Doghead Simulations

"We are too serious about education. But it's a serious business—literally saving lives. What Amanda Fox and Mary Ellen Weeks have done with the pure fun of applying the zombie genre to education is nothing short of brilliance. Their pure glee of 'slaying' the zombie problem to save kids and teachers is educational magic. Hard work can be fun. I remember a wide smile on my face learning the rules of zombie survival from *Zombieland*, and Fox and Weeks have successfully ported that feeling to the craft of classroom leadership in Teaching. I love this book!"

—Jon Corippo, executive director of CUE, author of *The EduProtocol Field Guide*

"A totally unique approach to professional development that stands out from every other teaching book I've read. Essential reading for educators striving to ensure their learning environment doesn't end up resembling a zombie movie!"

—Steve Bambury, head of digital learning and innovation, JESS Dubai

"What Amanda Fox and Mary Ellen Weeks have done in *Teachingland: A Teacher's Survival Guide to the Classroom Apocalypse* is to distill many great practices into a fun, highly useable manual for achieving amazing results in the classroom. These Jedi teachers know their stuff, and they offer insight into using powerful, passion-based practices to *really* reach and motivate learners. Make no mistake, this is a masterwork and a priceless tool for every classroom teacher!"

—Kevin Honeycutt, educational consultant

"For every teacher who has ever felt like they were constantly battling the sitting dead in their classroom, this is your survival manual! From practical ways to supercharge your classroom management to creating a culture of empowerment for your students, this book will challenge you, stretch you, and make you laugh out loud while doing it!"

—Steve Dembo, consultant, speaker, and author of
Untangling the Web: 20 Tools to Power Up Your Teaching

"It's human nature to get worn down by situations, and education can be no different. But this deadly book from Amanda and Mary Ellen has the perfect antidote: the equally human response of playfulness, humour, and creativity. As society moves to a fully digital and automated era where the most human intelligence or literacies are becoming more and more valuable, this is not only a smart move, but an absolutely key one if we are to truly survive. I'm confident that this book takes us even beyond that to also give an ability to thrive—first by understanding the recent past, and then via its incredible collection of practical tips and resources. I fully endorse *Teachingland* for the zombie-died among us as well as the still warm and red-blooded teachers who are out there every day making a difference."

—Jonathan Nalder, teacher, futurist,
digital trainer, and founder of FutureWe.org

"If you could only choose one book, then *Teachingland* should be it. It is full of actionable steps, great strategies, all the information you need to survive a classroom apocalypse and to create an authentic, engaging, fun classroom that students, other teachers, and administrators will all want to be a part of."

—Rachelle Dene Poth, foreign language
and STEAM teacher, edtech consultant

"Zombies! It's such a fun horror genre to see, but I never thought anyone would take that fun and apply it to the education world. As I read Amanda and Mary Ellen's book, I realized that comparison was just right. I have always believed that educators should not take themselves too seriously, and Amanda and Mary Ellen use the fun of the horror genre to talk about some serious issues in education. It's easy for students and teachers to get into a rut where it feels like they are education zombies, and this book is the perfect survival guide to get them out of it."

—David Lockhart, educator, presenter,
maker, Bigguyinabowtie.com

"I applaud Ohio University alumna Mary Ellen Weeks and her coauthor Amanda Fox for writing a creative and valuable resource for the newest educators in the field who will shape the future of children for decades to come. There is a lot to be proud of in public education, and I appreciate the authors' perspective of positivity and hope and their inspiring message of being the remedy and a leader of change. It is true that in the land of teaching, procedures, policies, and long hours can deflate even the best of teachers. It is also true that each day in this noble profession adds up to a lifetime of precious memories and impactful moments. While clever and entertaining, this book can help new teachers navigate the challenges, be a role model to others, and ultimately 'rise up to be the change' they want to be."

—Renée A. Middleton, PhD, dean of
Ohio University's Patton College of Education

"While I hate to admit that surviving the early stages of teaching might be like surviving the zombie apocalypse, I do appreciate that these seasoned, sensitive educators have framed this resource this way. This text allows new teachers to stay above ground despite the threats to their early careers and is a no-nonsense survival guide that can help keep teachers in the job and happy about it."

—Anna Nolin, superintendent of schools,
Natick, Massachusetts

TEACHINGLAND

A TEACHER'S SURVIVAL GUIDE
TO THE CLASSROOM APOCALYPSE

BY AMANDA FOX & MARY ELLEN WEEKS

Teachingland

This book is available at special discounts when purchased in quantity for use as premiums, promotions, fundraisers, or for educational use. For inquiries and details, contact the publisher at books@daveburgessconsulting.com.

Published by Dave Burgess Consulting, Inc., San Diego, CA
http://daveburgessconsulting.com

Editing and Interior Design by My Writers' Connection

Library of Congress Control Number: 2019931203
Paperback ISBN: 978-1-949595-16-1
Ebook ISBN: 978-1-949595-17-8

First Printing: May 2019

THIS BOOK IS *DEADICATED* TO ALL TEACHERS WHO RISE EVERY DAWN TO SHARE THEIR INFECTIOUS PASSION FOR TEACHING AND LEARNING.

INSIDE

A Fight for Survival

There is a universal fascination with the living dead. There is more to a zombie story than a bunch of corpses attacking the living. The real power of such a story lies with the undercurrent of hopelessness compounded by a very real instinct to survive.
—Julie Ann Dawson

The real horror of most zombie films isn't about the brain-craving, flesh-eating creatures that plague the world but how people respond to each other and work together in a time of crisis. When the stakes are high, and survival is at the forefront of our consciousness, good people do their best to make it through the night to the dawn.

With this book, we seek to shed light on an apocalypse currently unfolding right before our eyes by exploring the plight of educators fighting to survive and thrive in the current educational landscape. It is no easy feat. Trends in technology, pedagogy, and assessment are constantly evolving, and social media is setting the educational world on fire; meanwhile, schools and districts are struggling to keep up with the demands of statewide and federal accountability mandates, and many innovative educators are caught between wanting to do what they know is best for their students and yielding to the pressure to conform. Amid that chaos, those who choose to remain in their classrooms and schools and continue to teach are faced with a monumental task that cuts to the heart of this profession: raising up the next generation of leaders.

Our educational system is in a state of crisis, plagued by a virus characterized by excessive standardized testing, antiquated approaches to education, and expectations that value compliance and accountability over innovation and student engagement. Classroom teachers are at the battlefront, fighting hard to save their students from an educational world on the brink of outbreak. In *Teachingland*, we offer rules of survival, a mindset, a remedy, and a planning guide to equip you with stellar strategies and prepping frameworks to weather the outbreak.

But first, who are we? And why zombies?

Find a Kick-Ass Partner

We are Amanda Fox and Mary Ellen Weeks, two educators who met in 2016 through the Young Educator Network, a professional learning network (PLN) within the International Society for Technology in Education (ISTE). In 2015, Mary Ellen received an Emerging Leader Award from ISTE and went on to be president of the PLN. In 2016 Amanda also received the Emerging Leader award and went on to become incoming president the same year my term was ending. We both had specific ideas of what education should look like, and though our approaches are quite different—Amanda with guns blazing and Mary Ellen a little more pragmatic—we complemented each other and formed a perfect writing relationship.

You'll soon learn more about why we went with zombies, but for those of you not familiar with the cult classic *Zombieland*, our editor suggested just a bit of set up so you're not wandering around lost. We love *Zombieland* so much that we borrowed a few elemental rules to help cement the parallels between teaching and the zombie apocalypse and to make this book just a bit more fun. We selected the aliases Savannah and Columbus, because we are from Georgia and Ohio, respectively, and that's how the protagonists in *Zombieland* get their nicknames. Whether you are well versed in "zomnoculars" or not, we will provide enough context to drive our comparisons home, but feel free to watch the movies and tv shows that inspired us.

Amanda Fox, a.k.a. Savannah

I love music, and when I say I love music, I mean I love all genres. To me, music is magic. It inspires. It motivates. It provides solace in melancholic melodies. It summons thoughts of home, growing up, and Spanish moss-laden streets. Music breaks the constraints of this world and sends me time traveling with the help of a few harmonious notes strung together in perfect accord. It opens portals to other worlds long faded. Because of this magic, I have leveraged music in my classroom to reach students, engage them with content, build rapport, and explore deeper meanings. The true beauty of music is that it connects people. I have my own private radio that is permanently on shuffle, my mind the DJ who drops the needle on life's playlist. I also have a literal playlist, my "zombie writing music" playlist, that I listened to while writing this book. It inspires me when my mind fails to summon words or exude the creativity needed to push on. Fox, dance party of one—unless you count my DJ, Alexa, and she is pretty rad.

When it comes to my music collection, I like to think of myself as eclectic but not a real connoisseur. I mean, how can I take my musical library seriously when I have Hannah Montana and one-hit wonders like "What Does the Fox Say?" (Hey, my last name is Fox!) on the same playlist as jazz legend Louis Armstrong, guitar wizard Carlos Santana, and lyrical genius Lin-Manuel Miranda? Sometimes it's the music that reaches deep into my bones, and other times it's the lyrics that get me moving.

The phrase, "When words fail, music speaks," adorns one of my favorite T-shirts, which was given to me by a dear colleague. (My nerdy T-shirt game is strong.) I was born in the 1980s and came of age in the 90s, and in those pivotal decades of development, music spoke to me. It became part of who I am. Melodies become woven into the fabric of our DNA. My fabric also happens to be didactic. A teacher's blood courses through me, and it's through that lens that I view life.

In addition to music and teaching, I possess an equal love of film. Using video to tell a story and carefully storyboarding each shot with intentional meaning makes my nerd flag fly so high. Films hold so much more than stories; they hold histories. They act as mirrors, reflecting social constructs, policies, and even the fears of a nation. Films become time capsules meant to be poked, prodded, and dissected. And if you are lucky, you get to make your own or teach others to become part of the cinematic fabric of their generation.

I was able to do just that while teaching film to middle schoolers. But long before I was a teacher of film, I would create little scenarios in my mind. If this were a movie right now, what song would I play in the background? What is my soundtrack? How can I enhance the mood of the moment?

What is your soundtrack? Is it upbeat? Is it melancholy? We have playlists for all walks of life, but your teaching playlist should be inspirational! If it's not, that might be something you need to work on. You might be doing it wrong.

My scenario game continues:

If this were a zombie apocalypse, what is my best exit strategy? Where do I hide from a mob of undead? And I'm just walking into Wal-Mart, people! If this were the zombie apocalypse, at least I know I would have bucketloads of Twinkies and hopefully a kick-ass partner in crime like Tallahassee from Zombieland. My teaching partner in crime would definitely be Tampa—the Latin teacher in E-2 during my time at The STEM Academy.

So on film, music, and teaching…

By this point, you are probably wondering where I am going with this. I'm getting there! These two loves, music and film, along with my teacher lens intersected to create the ripe conditions to write this book. It's been in the making since 2015. Really, since the first year I started teaching when I was handed a copy of *The First Days of School* by Harry and Rosemary Wong. A lot of the advice in their book is centered around classroom management and procedures for the first days of school, whereas I feel rapport, team building, and focusing on getting to know your students is a much more valuable use of a teacher's time. The world has changed. The classroom landscape has changed, and the way we teach must change with it. Still, the Wongs' book inspired me—not to spend my days implementing better strategies but to write a book that speaks to this generation of teachers. A book with edge. A book that calls out the unacceptable and brings about a paradigm shift. A book that guides teachers to embody that paradigm shift. To become a catalyst that *fans a spark into a flame*. To build a legacy that I *can* plant and see.

> WHEN YOU'RE IN A DARK PLACE, YOU SOMETIMES TEND TO THINK YOU'VE BEEN BURIED. PERHAPS YOU'VE BEEN PLANTED. BLOOM.

One of my favorite film genres to teach is the horror genre. It provides a rich context for nonlinear writing, themes, insight into human fear and psychology, and how the body processes all of this scientifically—looking at the amygdala—in the brain, of course. And while teaching students about soundtracks, ambiance (or "zombiance"), lighting, the many subgenres, antagonists, and fears that go into crafting a horror story, I looked around at the current state of education and played my fun scenario game. It went something like this: *If the teaching profession were a horror movie, what subgenre would it be?*

It was a no-brainer (pun intended). A zombie one!

And so my research of the undead began, and as I wove it together with education with the needle of metaphor, the pages of this book on teaching and zombies grew. (So did my playlist. You can't embark on epic adventures without an epic playlist!) While investigating the parallels between zombie films and the teaching profession, I discovered one common denominator: the extreme need for hope in a time that breeds hopelessness.

At many times in my career I have felt immobilized by hopelessness; it would take hold and infection would spread and infect my mindset and actions. I would become overwhelmed by the weight of endless tasks and the dichotomy between being a teacher and being human. It is a dark time for our profession as accountability trumps trust; our very safety is threatened as we are asked to don weapons while wage raises and summers off are questioned. Morale can plummet if we let politics get the best of us. But unlike the victims of an apocalypse, we chose this role not for money, not out of pride, and not out of martyrdom, though some have sacrificed their lives at the hands of the unjust. We went into teaching to change the world for the better and to breed hope. To make passion and kindness the viral currency of this generation. In that spirit, I hope this book—with its rules, the speculative historical context on how we got here, and all the content within—proves to be a beacon of light, provides you with practical strategies, and becomes a fun guide for survival. I hope the words I have planted bloom in the hearts of the weary and that you hope along with me for a better world.

Mary Ellen Weeks, a.k.a. Columbus

Reading Savannah's bio makes me smile. It is so very her. She and I could not be more different. When she tells you she loves playing out zombie apocalypse survival scenarios in her head, she's being absolutely serious. She is all over the place (in a good way), but I am much more pragmatic and type A. The thing we share, though, is a passion for facilitating a love of learning in students at every level, and interestingly enough, our philosophy on how to do this is largely the same. This shared passion is what lead us to coauthor this book.

Coming out of high school in Zanesville, Ohio, if I had been asked if I was going to be a teacher, I would have laughed. My journey to becoming an elementary principal in one of Ohio's first STEM designated elementary schools and writing this book has spanned two states, fifteen years, a few dead-end jobs in other industries, some serious personal tragedies, and some amazing principals who trusted me to do what I felt appropriate to engage my students.

Unlike Savannah, I started my career in Natick, Massachusetts, under a principal who believed that students would grow if they were engaged. While we were expected to use data to inform our instruction, it wasn't our primary focus. In my second year of teaching, she gave me the tremendous opportunity to participate in a blended-learning pilot program that would be started in the eighth grade and scaled to the high school the following year. It was an incredible experience that allowed me to make the paradigm shift from teacher with all the answers to a facilitator of learning.

Two years later, when we moved back to Ohio for more family support because we had two babies, I was horrified to walk into my new classroom to find a tape recorder on my desk and a dinosaur desktop "4ewq1As" that must have been at least a decade old. I went to another teacher and asked if I could throw it away, and she abruptly informed me that I absolutely could not throw it away because it was a teaching tool. I knew then and there that this was not going to work. My principal, impressed with my background, left me alone to do the best I could with the limited resources I had and said nothing when the majority of the "teaching tools" from my classroom ended up in the hallway for the custodian to take away. My saving grace was my team, a group of teachers who were awesome and would try just about anything. Towards the end of the year, Gabby, the teacher next door and a fellow "techie," as the Luddites sometimes not-so-lovingly called us, and I started lobbying to pilot a 1:1 program with Chromebooks. My principal agreed to give us a Chromebook cart and make us a dyad. Gabby ended up taking another position, and I started begging other colleagues to try this pilot with me. No one agreed.

At the end of that summer, I spent the first part of the year on maternity leave. Toward the end of my leave, my assistant superintendent called me and asked me to take on a fully blended, 1:1 multi-age classroom with a part-time coteacher. This classroom was meant to be a catalyst classroom, one that anyone could observe at any time. I agreed and returned early from my leave, anxious for this new challenge. My coteacher, Dan, and I were completely self-contained, so we had the latitude to thread computer science and transdisciplinary problem-based learning into the curriculum. We also engaged our students in Genius Hour. Our classroom was like nothing these students had ever experienced, and they thrived. We built a television studio in our classroom, and my students fell in love with film. We had several teachers come in and say that all the reasons they thought that our classroom would not work were proved wrong.

The next year I was recruited to be an instructional coach in a neighboring school district, and now I am the principal of one of Ohio's first STEM designated elementary schools. My staff is incredible, and it is a privilege to lead this work.

Field Guide Layout: How to Use This Book

This book was written to serve as a field guide for surviving what we see as the era of the classroom apocalypse. We use a zombie apocalypse metaphor to shed light on the darkest parts of the education profession while also embracing humor to dissect the system from policy to classroom instruction. This includes caricatures of various stakeholders and their roles, pedagogy, mindset, assessment, and professional learning discussed using a tongue-in-cheek approach.

We have created our own zombie tropes or *zomnacular*—see what we did there? The tropes are present throughout the entire book, but they are defined contextually. There is a helpful glossary in the front of the book, which you might want to preview prior to reading to set the zombiance. In the glossary, we define what the virus is, what a zombie is, and how the disease spreads as well as other terms that are useful to decode our *zombigogy*. You should venture into this book with the awareness that no one is immune to this virus. We have even been susceptible at times. If you follow our survival rules, you might be lucky enough to survive your first year (and beyond).

The next section, Pride, Prejudice, and the Classroom Apocalypse, provides a speculative historical context and timeline of when the classroom apocalypse began and the multiple variables that led to the perfect conditions for not only an infection, but an outbreak running through classrooms all over the United States. Its tone takes a more somber approach, highlighting the first bites into the system and our response as a society. It was written by Amanda Fox and Tim Childers.

Chapters 1 through 10 are titled after pop-culture zombie movies and television series. Drawing parallels from the screen in each chapter introduction, we explore each show's theme and zombie metaphor to fit our educational context. Some of our favorite zombie films are adaptations from comic books and graphic novels, so at the beginning of each chapter, illustrations will depict the chapter's central message.

At the end of each chapter, we feature Tales from the Trenches: authentic, personal accounts written by teachers who have survived their first years and beyond. We share several of our own experiences in this section but also offer varying perspectives. After surveying bunkers all over the country, we compiled accounts that resonate with the content of each chapter and offer practical advice to help teachers make sense of the educational landscape. Each Tales from the Trenches contributor will be referenced by where they are from and the year the story comes from, and names and Twitter handles are listed with permission.

Chapter 1 lays the groundwork for each subsequent chapter with our Teachingland Survival Rules delivered through bitmoji, which are lovingly and loosely borrowed from Zombieland. (If similar rules can keep Tallahassee and Columbus alive during an actual zombie apocalypse, then they are good enough for us!) In *Zombieland*, the rules for survival were humorously listed during a time of loneliness and despair. *Teachingland* is no different. We have devised thirteen rules and adapted them to fit our context, with Chapters 2–9 unpacking each rule in greater detail. As most field guides go, this book can be read in one sitting, or you could read the chapters that address your most immediate concerns. Either way, we hope you learn not only how to survive the ever-changing landscape of the classroom apocalypse but emerge from your trench as a leader.

Augmented Reality Easter Eggs

As technology rapidly evolves, so do the augmented reality tools available. As Charlie Fink, *Forbes* journalist and VR guru, wrote in the beginning pages of his book *Convergence*, "This book is out of date. It was out of date the day it was written." Sorry, Charlie, I'm stealing those words. Because this book uses AR technology, it will likely be dated before the ink hits the page. But that hasn't stopped us from including what currently exists. Our book is augmented with HP Reveal (the online studio is being phased out in July 2019, although the app will continue to be supported, for... how long? Who knows?). We have also used Thyng and Artivive. Download each of those apps and prepare for an epic AR scavenger hunt by scanning any images to unlock digital content. For information on current AR platforms utilized in this book, supporting docs, and tech tutorials please check our website, TeachinglandTheBook.com. As tools of today dissipate into the ARVerse graveyard, new tools will emerge. We vow to evolve and update and try to keep our AR content alive.

Check out these tools:
- HP Reveal
- Thyng
- Artivive
- Metaverse

In our Brain Stretchers section at the end of some chapters, we have included a Metaverse QR code. Metaverse is an augmented reality app that can be downloaded on your phone, tablet, or Chromebook. You can scan the Metaverse QR code with your camera to launch the app or take you to the app store to download it. If you scan from within the app, click on the scan me now arrow at the top and scan the QR code to start the experience. When you complete the experiences you earn Teachingland Digital Badges.

We also hope you will create your own Teachingland Metaverse experiences and add them to our collection. Want to make an AR experience on one of our chapters or concepts? Use the Metaverse Teachingland Collection code to add your experience our AR arsenal made by #wifiwarriors all over the world!

Collection code: xczaza

Glossary

ANTIDOTE: Strategies to cure and prevent infection.

BITE: Moments that spread the disease either through drill and practice or killing the love for learning; students can bite each other through learned dead behavior.

BLUE-TAPE THINKING/TEACHING: A teacher who is in the trenches being innovative, integrating PBL (problem-based learning), design thinking, and creative ways to engage students.

#BRAINSNAP: An adaptation of Tara Martin's #BookSnaps but customized to #Teachingland. Taking a picture of our book, annotating it, then posting it to social media.

BUNKERS: Schools.

CLASSROOM APOCALYPSE: Damage to classrooms all over the world on a catastrophic scale due to a global movement in overtesting and impossible teacher/student expectations based on shallow/snapshots.

FLATLINE: An infected student or teacher on the verge of a zombieism from the feeling of hopelessness brought about by a broken system.

LUDDITE: Either a new teacher to integrating edtech, a teacher apprehensive about integrating technology, or a seasoned teacher that refuses. Luddite is usually used in the latter situation.

OLE PEDAGOGY PLAYERS (O.P.P.S): Cognitive scientists, learning scientists, educational philosophers, and practitioners who have contributed immensely to the classroom apocalyptic landscape. If you are gonna use other people's intellectual property, I would start here.

RED-TAPE THINKING/TEACHING: Recycling the same lesson plans year after year, teaching to the test, drill and practice, not integrating technology, and making excuses to not rise up and reclaim our art!

R.E.M.E.D.Y.: Our acronym for good pedagogy: Reach, Engage, Make, Evaluate/Empower, Demystify, and Yearn.

SANCTUARIES: Conferences, Edcamps, and learning communities to share ideas and antidotes!

SAVAGE FAILURE: Failure that stops trying or failure that doesn't end in learning.

TRICKLE DOWN ZOMBIENOMICS: A top-down, policy-driven solution posed as a cure but really an infection to the whole system. **VIRUS:** The sickness plaguing the nation's education system characterized by overtesting, outdated thinking, and excessive focus on compliance and accountability that leads to burnout and disillusionment among students, teachers, parents, and members of the community.

VITALS: Feedback from assessments to show that students are learning.

WARM BODIES: Students who have been brought back from the brink of zombification through phenomenal, innovative teaching strategies. This extends to teachers who have been brought back!

ZOMBIE: An infected person in the classroom apocalypse.

ZOMBIGOGY: The art of channeling excellent culture-changing teaching and guiding disengaged students back to warm-bodied lovers of learning. This also refers to teachers as adult learners continuing their craft through professional development. This involves creativity and triage.

ZOMBIE ZIPS: Ziploc bag challenges that can be completed in a forty-five-to-sixty-minute class period.

FOREWORD
by Carl Hooker

Anyone who knows me knows that I am a HUGE fan of zombies. I've personally spent countless hours investigating every zombie movie that Netflix has in their collection. I regularly participate in meaningless blogs and Reddit posts around things like the White Walkers from *Game of Thrones* to the zombie virus in *World War Z*.

I've used this lore and love of zombies many times over in my role as an educator. From multiple blog posts to even mentions of the undead in my books, it's something I can't limp away from. In 2014, I created a talk called "Surviving the Digital Zombie Apocalypse." While the talk was meant to be tongue-in-cheek, it ended up being impactful in creating awareness around devices and how we use them in classrooms and everyday life.

I realized quickly that the draw to the zombie theme was palpable. Attendees wanted to fill their braaaaaains with ideas around effective technology integration in the classroom. So with the help of a make-up artist, I decided to kick things up a notch. The next time I gave the talk (here locally at SXSWedu in Austin), I was in full zombie getup. White contact lenses, torn and bloody coat, scarred green face, you name it, if it was zombie-related, I had it on my body.

While this was meant to garner an emotional response from those watching the talk, what I realized was there were some unintended consequences from going "full zombie":

People don't look at you when they pass in the hallway—It became an interesting psychological experiment to see how many people would look away versus how many would stare and smile.

Little kids thought I was real—as I was "ambling" back to my car, I noticed a school bus passing by full of kids. I decided to chase after the bus a bit, to which they started jumping up and down screaming, "ZOMBIE!!" When the bus stopped, I ran the other direction for fear of ending up in the newspaper.

It wasn't just little kids who thought I was real—Texas is an "open-carry" state, which means anyone can walk around with a gun. I encountered a young man on the streets after my talk who quickly grabbed for his firearm, which made me jump out of character pretty quickly shouting, "NO! I'm not really a zombie! Don't shoot!"

I tell you this back story for two reasons:

1. You can go too far with an idea.

2. That is NOT the case with this book.

When Amanda and Mary Ellen contacted me and requested that I write a foreword for their book, I was a little internally torn (Ha! Another zombie pun!). I've been such a fan of the analogy of the undead in education, my bias would show regardless of the content. As I read through this book, my fears of bias were quickly diminished.

These talented ladies have poured tons of resources and research into the development of *Teachingland*. They take an engaging and entertaining approach to tackling the use of technology in classrooms and bring forth meaningful ideas and strategies that are of value to any teacher trying to survive.

There's something in this book for every educator out there from the first-year teacher to the highly experienced one. While I don't want to spoil the ending, some of my favorite components to this book are the listing of archetypes that we face in day-to-day teaching and their "Tales from the Trenches," which contain inspiring stories from teachers in the field.

I won't give away much more, but I'll let you know you are in store for a page-turner that will "infect" your thinking in a good way going forward...enjoy!

EDITOR'S NOTE

> *Carl Hooker has been a part of a strong educational shift with technology integration since becoming an educator. From his start as a teacher to his current district technology leadership, he's always had one common belief: The kids need to drive their own learning. He realizes the challenges in our current public educational institutions and meets them head on. His unique blend of educational background, technical expertise, and humor make him a successful driving force for this change.*

Carl is the "Godfather" of LearnFestATX (formerly iPadpalooza). This learning festival has grown into a global phenomenon over the years, impacting schools and teachers from all over the world.

Carl has recently authored a six-part book series titled *Mobile Learning Mindset*. These books focus on a different stakeholder and the role they play in a successful mobile learning initiative. Aside from his work as an author and district leader, Carl also works as a keynote speaker and consultant through his company HookerTech, LLC as well as an advisor on multiple edtech start-up companies. He's been named *Tech & Learning Magazine*'s 2014 Leader of the Year and is a member of the Apple Distinguished Educator class of 2013.

Follow Carl on Twitter @mrhooker and his blog: http://hookedoninnovation.com

CHAPTER 0

Pride, Prejudice, and the Classroom Apocalypse: The Historical Context That Bred the Virus

Written by Tim Childers with Amanda Fox

Our concern, however, goes well beyond matters such as industry and commerce. It also includes the intellectual, moral, and spiritual strengths of our people which knit together the very fabric of our society. The people of the United States need to know that individuals in our society who do not possess the levels of skill, literacy, and training essential to this new era will be effectively disenfranchised, not simply from the material rewards that accompany competent performance, but also from the chance to participate fully in our national life. A high level of shared education is essential to a free, democratic society and to the fostering of a common culture, especially in a country that prides itself on pluralism and individual freedom.
—"A Nation at Risk," April 1983 report from
the U.S. Department of Education

Most people don't believe something can happen until it already has. That's not stupidity or weakness; that's just human nature.
—Max Brooks,
*World War Z: An Oral History
of the Zombie War*

Pride: Intro

There are many days that I (Savannah) leave the classroom high on the success of having taught a kick-ass lesson during which students got excited about content, and we created amazing artifacts that made me proud. Then 3:05 p.m. comes, and I realize I still have a mountain of non-instructional-related tasks to complete, which quickly leaves me feeling deflated. Hopelessness infects, spilling into my personal life and consuming even my dreams in a nightmarish fashion. We are a generation of teachers who grade by computer light—luminance for the classroom apocalyptic romantic.

As I listen to students' Flipgrid videos on the historical context of the Holocaust, I wonder how we got here. And I'm not talking about the bottom of a bottle of wine or the grading. I mean, when did our education system get here—to this point where teachers are undervalued, overworked, underpaid, and not trusted as professionals? How can we survive the many hats that we must wear? You know what I'm talking about....bear with me as Tim Childers and I lay out the historical context and educational policy that has influenced today's classroom landscape. It might sound boring, but we will try to do our best to get you laughing while we describe the conditions that have allowed our system to become infected.

The Virus

To understand the present apocalyptic state, we must revisit the past. The first signs of infection came in April 1983 with "A Nation at Risk: The Imperative for Educational Reform", a landmark report released by the U.S. Department of Education. Were we at risk for a zombie outbreak? No, not quite. But our government and business leaders had decided that the sex-drugs-and-rock-n-roll mindset that emerged during and after the Vietnam War had left our country without a mission. (And we had just gone to the moon. Yes, all you conspiracy theorists out there, it really did happen!) So that year, in addition to *Reading Rainbow*, Michael Jackson's moonwalk, and the first mobile phone network, "A Nation at Risk", was born. While parents across America talked on gigantic mobiles and their children moonwalked and watched LeVar Burton (Take a look. It's in a book!), the government was making a serious educational diagnosis and comparing the United States to other industrialized nations around the world. According to this report, academic standards were too weak, students had too much freedom in the classes they could choose towards graduation, teacher preparation programs were not producing qualified classroom teachers, colleges were required to offer too many remedial courses to bridge the gap in student knowledge, and SAT scores had been on a steady decline from 1963 to 1980. The list of problems with our educational system seemed endless.

That same year, in 1983, technology was just beginning to make a strong impact on the economy across nearly all industries. Computer science was on the horizon as a new and necessary skill for all students. (Savannah actually had a college instructor in her undergraduate program who used air quotes every time she said the word *Internet*. We digress.) Without computer science, we would begin to lag behind other countries at an even more alarming pace; in fact, "A Nation at Risk" issued this dire warning: "Each generation of Americans has outstripped its parents in education, in literacy, and in economic attainment. For the first time in the history of our country, the educational skills of one generation will not surpass, will not equal, will not even approach, those of their parents."

Almost as an aside, the report included a disclaimer that the average citizen was more literate than the average citizen of a generation before. But the average high school graduate was not as equipped as the average graduate from the previous generation. The central message was that the educational system of the United States was sick. It needed an antidote for the pervasive illness that was about to destroy our nation from the inside out. As a result, the inoculations began in the form of future policies like NCLB (No Child Left Behind) and Race to the Top, and we started down the path to the Classroom Apocalypse without anyone even realizing it. After all, we were the best country in the world, right?

The recommendations of "A Nation at Risk" were well crafted, thoughtful, and clear. They centered on six core areas: content, standards, time, teaching, leadership, and money.

Here are just a few items of note put forward in the report:

- Five new basics of curriculum—English, math, science, social studies, and computer science—should be taught to all students.

- Grades should have meaning to demonstrate mastery of a subject while colleges should raise their academic requirements for entry.

- Standardized testing should occur at major transition points along the education spectrum.

- Students in high school should have far more homework than they have now.

- Administrative burdens on teachers should be reduced.

- Teachers should be on an eleven-month contract with pay raises that make them equitable across other similar industries.

- State and local governments should bear the weight of paying for the education in their state.

- The Federal government should be limited in its control of education and act primarily as the body that decides the why of education in our country.

For years, "A Nation at Risk" was discussed and debated among educators and legislators alike, but no one attempted a cure for what it claimed ailed our education system, and no one would ever guess that what was to come would exacerbate the problem. States were left on their own to make sense of it.

Some states threw money at the problem, while others languished in a morass of, "We're doing OK. We will continue doing what we have always done!" But we were not OK. Years later, the problems outlined in "A Nation at Risk" were still mostly there. Many of the report's recommendations had gone wholly unheeded. Our nation's pride became a chink in our armor. It wasn't the diagnosis that weakened us but the cures that were attempted later.

Prejudice: No Child Left Behind (or for Dead)

In 2001, while Savannah was in high school and Knox was entering his first year of teaching, President George W. Bush attempted the first real inoculation against this virus diagnosed by "A Nation at Risk." While everyone had their eyes on the Twin Towers falling and the start of the war on terror, the government quietly passed No Child Left Behind into law.

Savannah remembers her teachers muttering, and mocking NICKEL-B, as they pronounced it, calling it "No Child's Behind Left." State and local governments clamored for ways to prove test results were improving, while terms such as adequate yearly progress and accountability entered the common vernacular, and drill-and-kill became routine. As Savannah was blaring Destiny's Child's "Survivor" from her Walkman, teachers were trying to survive the new pre-testing, mid-testing, and post-testing culture—including Knox. This is also when trickle-down zombienomics manifested, with an entire industry springing up to help teachers test their students, which caused the moans and groans to only grow louder.

Savannah remembers telling her friends not to call during certain time windows in the evenings, so she could use AOL to dial up the internet (Air quotes!) to study. Thanks, Dr. Stone. She would drill herself on vocabulary words in preparation for the SAT, as fear of low scores and not getting into college became her primary motivation. Oh, the frustration of watching the little running man about to connect, only to have a phone call interrupt the connection! This generation will never understand the anticipation and frustration of America Online—well online if no one was calling us. Who knew then that using a phone and browsing the internet would be so easy in the future—and something we could do while on the go! In the meantime Knox was trying to survive these new expectations and test prep culture.

By the dawn of the twenty-first century, the classroom became devoid of any excitement for learning, with teacher's, like Knox passing from creative freedom and more autonomy and going firmly into survival mode. Savannah remembers sitting quietly doing worksheets in cemetery-row seating, unaware that an outbreak was in full swing and would continue to infect the U.S. education system well into her own teaching career. In local schools, teachers' workloads grew, laughter was drowned out by groans, and recess was slashed for bunkering down in the name of test preparation.

So where was the prejudice in this wide-scale inoculation? NCLB offered parents the choice to send their children to higher-performing schools, causing the gap between various demographics to widen. Consequently, rations from the already failing schools were given to the schools that were compliant. Meanwhile, trickle-down zombienomics increased the divide while lining the pockets of businesses colluding with government. This so-called cure spread through urban and rural America faster than the original plague.

We were a nation at risk, and testing was the answer.

Except that it wasn't. And the classroom apocalypse was now upon us on a pandemic scale.

The Apocalypse: Strain Race to the Top

In 2009, when Savannah joined the ranks of Knox and entered the classroom as a teacher for the first time, with her so did President Barack Obama's R2T. (No, not R2-D2. That would have been much cooler, though now you can get him as a Sphero!) R2T was "Race to The Top," a $4 billion initiative that was supposed to turn NCLB on its head. It didn't. Race to the Top included some of the recommendations from "A Nation at Risk" that No Child Left Behind failed to address—more teacher accountability, for one. But nothing got any better. Both Knox and Savannah's students continued to suffer, and the infection spread to teachers as they scrambled to cover every single standard by the end of the school year and prepare kids to move from bubble sheets to next-generation questions. The apocalypse worsened.

While NCLB was largely an unfunded mandate for school improvement across the nation, Race to the Top offered funding. Hundreds of millions of dollars were available to individual states via grants for school improvement, but the price was steep. Race to the Top mandated every state to increase the rigor of their standards, instruction, and testing.

Rigor, as defined by Merriam-Webster, is "a harsh inflexibility of opinion, temper, or judgment." It basically means "stiffness" and is often tied to mortis, which means "in death." To a great degree, this infection of overtesting and intense focus on teacher and school district accountability was causing the rigor mortis of creativity and engagement among students and teachers across the United States. The groans of our youth being tested to death echoed in the hallways of our schools, and the Classroom Apocalypse continued.

As teachers, we were tasked with not just testing students but monitoring the growth of each child from one year to the next. This incomprehensible statistical model differs from state to state, and it predicts how a student will score on this year's test based on how the student scored on previous the year's test. A higher score indicates the teacher did a great job while a lower score means the teacher is ineffective. Nothing in this value-added model takes into account factors such as students' home lives, parental support, food security, or health status that might impact their learning. All accountability for students' test performance rested squarely on teachers' shoulders.

Students also suffered because many of the things that enrich students' educational experiences such as fine arts programs and recess were suddenly at risk. Fortunately, Savannah taught

English/language arts and Knox had risen to the ranks of administration, so their jobs were safe, but many of their colleagues who taught electives worried about the security of their positions.

The accountability aspects of Race to the Top that demanded increased rigor over engagement infected the heart and soul of education: the joy that comes from learning. We have become a nation of zombies. We are the walking dead seeking higher test scores to indicate that we are doing a good job.

The Antidote

Thankfully, there now appears to be another turning point in our system that is coming from the bunkers and trenches themselves. Teachers, administrators, and parents are tired of the race, and are disrupting the status quo. Problem-based learning is replacing drill and kill strategies used to prepare for the test. Traditional grading systems are morphing into standards-based indicators of progress. States are putting money back into the arts, foreign languages, and even computer science instruction. There are classrooms thriving in this apocalyptic landscape thanks to grass-roots movements and learning frameworks such as Design Thinking.

For the first time in decades, there is hope.

This book attempts to shine the light of that hope on the still-dark corners of our education system. There are programs that are working and breathing life back into students, and it's teachers who are making the difference. Those independent and innovative teachers are the cure. Their perspectives, their instructional practices, and their strategies are the antidote for the virus that has plagued our society for far too long.

You might be asking, "What can I do to combat the zombie apocalypse and provide a cure for students?" The answer is real-world problems. Life connections. Empathy. And yes, technology used correctly in ways that can spark the imagination back into children. Read on to learn the rules of Teachingland, and how you can not only survive but be the R.E.M.E.D.Y. Be the disruptor. Be the hero of your own narrative.

PART 1
What You Need to Survive

Visit TeachinglandTheBook.com to access the links and resources in this chapter.

Scan me

CHAPTER 1
Teachingland: Survival Rules

You have completed your internship, earned your diploma, and tossed your apple-embossed graduation cap up into the air. At your new school, preplanning sessions are underway, you're getting to know your team, and your classroom is Pinterest perfect. Everything is going wonderfully. Everyone loves you. Students arrive on the first day lining your desk with apples and the shelves with Kleenex and Lysol wipes. They happily announce that they finished all their summer reading, and they seem so eager to learn that your heart is filled to overflowing, and you just know you picked the right profession!

Yeah. That's lovely, but it's not quite how most first days go, let alone first years. (It wasn't how ours went.)

In reality, you graduate, interview, and land a teaching job. If you are lucky, your new colleagues will be as excited as you are to have you join them. If that luck holds, you might be assigned a mentor, or some of the veteran teachers might share their twenty-year-old materials with you. Oh, joy. During the first couple of weeks—that honeymoon period when you and your students are getting to know each other—things go pretty well. Then you start diving into curriculum, and you quickly realize from the glazed-over look in your students' eyes and their strange behavior that they are showing signs of infection. What are you doing wrong? You are covering all your standards, but you can't escape this overwhelming feeling that is consuming you. You are drowning in procedures, policies, grading, and all the other wonderful extras that come with being a classroom teacher, and your shoulders are only so wide. This is called the bait and switch.

Here's the truth: You go into the field of education to change the world with your passion for teaching, but decades of plague have rendered Teachingland a harsh, sometimes dangerous environment, and if you're not prepared, the dismal conditions can crush your spirit. To get prepared, you must learn the rules of Teachingland.

Introduction to Teachingland Survival Rules

Welcome to *Teachingland*, boys and ghouls. As Little Rock and Wichita go up and down on the Pacific Playland amusement park ride, you too will at times have highs and lows and feel like you are about to be eaten alive. But it is possible to survive this apocalypse unscathed (mostly, anyway) and with your sanity and passion intact. The key is knowing the rules. Rules typically restrict certain behaviors, but our rules of survival also stipulate the behaviors necessary for positive interactions, conflict resolution, professional growth, and a culture of creativity. For the diehard *Zombieland* aficionado, these rules do not follow the same chronological order as in the movie, but they have been adapted to fit the context of saving teachers from the classroom apocalypse. While largely unwritten, our Teachingland Survival Rules are no less effective for being somewhat unofficial. It might even serve you well to keep this list handy as you navigate this perilous landscape; in fact, we invite you to add your own tried-and-true rules to the list!

Rule #1: Buckle Up, Buttercup

Young teachers coming out of universities are armed with theory and best practices as their professors know them, but rarely are they prepared for the reality of the modern classroom. The best thing you can do to prepare for your first year of teaching and beyond is to strap in, take a deep breath, follow the rules that have been laid out in this survival guide, and expect the unexpected. So buckle up, buttercup. There will be highs, and there will be lows. 'Tis a 180-day roller coaster. That's just how it goes!

Rule #2: Beware of Break Rooms

In *Zombieland*, you had to watch out for bathrooms because zombies are all about attacking when you are most vulnerable. Luckily, you are not as likely to be bothered in the bathrooms of Teachingland, but the undead do sometimes congregate in common areas such as the break room. You can read more about the archetypes of the apocalypse in Chapter 2 and arm yourself with knowledge so you'll know what to expect. While break room banter can be a lot of fun, it can quickly turn sour, and you might need a good escape plan or a need to stand up and not spectate.

Rule #3 Cardio: Rule of Two Feet

To survive in Teachingland, you must know when to run—the "cardio" rule in Zombieland. More specifically, what to run from and where to flock. You have two feet, right? Use them. We're serious, people. Walk, run, or dubstep (We prefer the dubstep!) with great speed away from teachers who have been infected by the system. They're not hard to spot. They'll be the ones spewing negativity and red-tape thinking, shutting down innovative ideas and bashing colleagues. They typically like to horde in the teacher workroom, so it's smart to get in and out as fast as possible. If you think you want to stick around and battle it out, make sure your brain is up to the task.

Rule #4: Brain Stretch (Be Flexible)

So you have decided to stay and engage in the Battle of the Brains! When the banter turns into complaining, colleague bashing, or sabotaging innovative strategies and initiatives being implemented on a school-wide or classroom basis, be prepared to stand your ground. Some examples of break room banter are Luddites relentless in their steadfast commitment to resisting change, or EdTech Hipsters trying to sell you on a tool solely for the sake of the newest fad. To stay quick on your feet, try limbering up on twenty-first-century pedagogy and engaging student-centered strategies that work while also not being afraid to try new things. Been running from the break room for a few days? Ready to make contact? Read Chapter 4 to get down with O.P.P.s, the Ole Pedagogy Players of the apocalypse. You should know them!

Rule #5: Bare Hands

In a sea of worksheets and canned digital curriculum parading as personalized learning, your most effective and engaging materials are most likely the ones you and your students build yourselves. Take everything you learned while limbering up and begin applying it in your trenches to increase student agency. Hopefully, the R.E.M.E.D.Y. in Chapter 5 will protect your students from an outbreak and encourage others in the bunker to take the same precautions. For more ideas about how to keep your students warm-blooded, check out Chapters 6 and 9!

Rule #6: Double Tap: Formative before Summative!

And no, we are not talking about a Snapchat replay, although #BookSnaps are a great way to showcase learning. In Teachingland, you should never assume what a student does or does not know. It's important to take the pulse of individual students before applying an automatic defibrillator to the entire class. Some students might have a steady pulse rate on a topic, while others might need triage on an individual concept. In addition to taking individual vitals, you should design meaningful taps, as drill-and-practice may leave your trench vulnerable to outbreak and low on passion. IXL (https://www.ixl.com/) can be a great tool to take the pulse of students when used correctly but should never be a babysitter! Knowing the hearts of your students and meeting them where they are will lead to more authentic and personalized learning experiences. To explore better ways to engage your students, check out Chapter 6. To learn more about authentic assessments, read Chapter 7.

Rule #7: Always Check the Backseats...in the Trench

When it comes to our students, we need to make sure the entire trench is healthy and engaged. Remember, there is more to Teachingland than content and assessments. We are teaching the whole child—heart, hands, and head! So what's the plan when you discover that a few are "riding in the backseat" or have little to no pulse? How can you learn to identify the infected masquerading as healthy students? Building rapport and developing good trench management are some of the tools you need. Read Chapters 3 and 6 to learn how to build camaraderie!

Rule #8: It's a Marathon, Not a Sprint (No, It's a Sprint as Long as a Marathon!)

In the day to day (180, to be precise), education is definitely a sprint as long as a marathon! It can feel like we are always sprinting to get students to meet standards while meeting our own deadlines and adhering to curriculum maps and pacing guides. In the meantime, we are constantly having to adjust when we realize some of our students have flatlined. We plan for daily, weekly, quarterly, and yearly learning goals, but sometimes our best laid plans are ambushed by infected colleagues, our students, bad policies, or even our own missteps. With constantly revamped pacing guides, content and grade-level moves, and changes in curriculum, it's not just first-year teachers who are only a day ahead of students, and that is OK. For more on surviving this exhausting 180-day journey and bugout bag, skip to Chapter 5.

Rule #9: Break It up and Shake It Off

While we have established that curriculum maps, pacing guides, and lesson plans have their place, their use must be flexible, and sometimes you must adjust on the fly to meet the needs of your learners. Make sure you are tapping your students often to ensure they are not showing signs of infection. If they are getting glassy eyed, you have no choice but to switch things up, chunking activities into bite-sized pieces that address standards while still accommodating your students. The constant adjustment can be tiresome, but it's vital that you shake it off and figure out how to reach students to avoid infection. When our plans bite the dust, we must rise like the phoenix from the ashes of those plans and sprint to the finish line. Failure is not fatal if we iterate and improve. Fail forward and fail fast. Model this intentionally to build grit! To read more about picking yourself up and dusting yourself off, check out Chapter 5. Or skip to Chapter 10 for my Teachingland Manifesto.

> FAILURE IS NOT FATAL IF WE ITERATE AND IMPROVE.

Rule #10: The Buddy System: Have a Mentor!

It's important that teachers take the initiative in Teachingland. Everyone should have a "teaching idol" or someone who embodies who you want to be as an educator. Unfortunately for many new teachers, mentorship programs are nonexistent or ineffective. Sometimes the person you're paired with tries to suck the life out of you with their decades-old worksheets! Don't fret. Wisdom can be imparted across a two-way street even in the oddest of pairings. You did just come out of college with fresh strategies! If, however, your mentor is slacking, reach out to your networks, ask your administrator to let you observe someone who matches your core values, or cozy up to that teacher you have been wanting to learn from—even if the relationship has to be virtual. The best mentorship programs involve having more than one mentor. We suggest building a crew—I mean this is the classroom apocalypse and survival is in numbers-the more brains the merrier! Dying to find your own Tallahassee and build a virtual PLN or idea/support army? Need some tips on learning on the run? Head to Chapter 8 and become a legend in your own right.

Rule #11: Ziploc Bags: Zombie Zips

While Ziploc bags might not have made the final cut for *Zombieland*, we can't get enough of them in Teachingland! Ziploc bags are not just for holding yummy sandwiches. They can also hold all kinds of things for STEM, STEAM, and Maker activities. We call them Zombie Zips, because as students build and create with items in the bag, their brains are stimulated and creative juices are flowing! They come in sandwich, quart, and gallon sizes. Zip on over to Chapter 6 to learn how to exploit these little plastic engagers!

Rule #12 Enjoy the Little Things

It is important in Teachingland to celebrate all successes—no matter how small—even if it's that first sip of coffee in a quiet classroom before the students arrive. Whether it is the impact we have on one student, a nice email from a parent, a lesson that goes well, or a leadership opportunity among colleagues, savoring these moments can be the fuel we need to get us through to the next dawn! These moments are the ones we reflect on in our times of struggle and the ones we share with our colleagues as exemplars of success. Stories like these are found in the Tales from the Trenches at the end of each chapter. Even in failure, we can find lessons to take away.

Rule #13: Don't Be a Hero

This is, technically, two rules rolled into one. Let's face it—some rules are made to be broken. You are the protagonist of your trench, and your students' survival starts with you. It's a tremendous responsibility. Embrace the role of hero and make sure your students become the hero of their own narratives. How can you be the hero *and* change the zombie culture to a warm-bodied love of learning? By being a

> EMBRACE THE ROLE OF HERO AND MAKE SURE YOUR STUDENTS BECOME THE HERO OF THEIR OWN NARRATIVES.

lifelong learner yourself, connecting with like-minded educators, and advocating for the professional development you need. When you model leadership by sharing with other colleagues and learning beyond the bunker, students will also feel empowered.

Your Trench, Your Rules

The classroom experience can sometimes feel like a real horror film if we're ill prepared, but when we use our heads, create with our hands, and teach with our hearts, we rise up and stand strong against the forces working against us. Make sure you keep these rules close and refer to them often if you plan on surviving and thriving in Teachingland. And while the list is a fantastic start to helping ensure your survival, it is certainly not comprehensive. What rules fly in your trench? We encourage you to add your own to the list or adapt some of the other *Zombieland* rules that make sense in your classroom apocalyptic landscape. Share your rules with us using the hashtag #teachinglandrules, and if you are feeling extra lively, create a poster illustrating your rule or add it to our #gridrules Flipgrid and share it! The Twittersphere is a safe space for communicating your rules and strategies with colleagues of the apocalypse, and they will be grateful for your contributions to ensuring survival.

Tales from the Trenches

Welcome to the first set of Tales from the Trenches! This is where we will highlight journal entries from real teachers in real trenches, sharing very real stories from their bunkers.

@AmandaFoxSTEM
Savannah
c. 2012

Savannah here. My first year of teaching was in rural Georgia. It was definitely an adventure, and the book I was given to help me make sense of the trenches was Harry and Rosemary Wong's *The First Days of School*. While the book had a bunch of good advice about classroom management, the thing that stuck with me the most was what I considered to be bad advice and went against my very nature. "Don't smile until after Christmas." I mean, really? Aren't we supposed to be cultivating positive relationships with students? Instead of taking the Draconian approach to classroom management as suggested by the Wongs, I decided to manage through high expectations, words of support and encouragement, and following my heart, which led me into this profession in the first place. This method has served me well over the years, and I feel like my students have respected me more for treating them like humans and co-conspirators in this learning journey—not a horde of zombies. Sometimes our mentors or those who are deemed experts on a topic don't always have the best solutions. Learn early to challenge the status quo and know that it's your trench, your rules. When the door closes, do what works best for you and your students.

In addition to being advised not to smile (Wong's advice), there were many other instances that mottled my first bunker with apocalyptic symptoms—my school issued a ban on students using cell phones even for learning, red-tape thinking, and a Luddite culture; then, during the week of preservice, the unthinkable happened. It was a first-year teacher's biggest fear—my mentor and grade-level counterpart was indeed a Luddite—what I defined to be the opposite of myself. To be clear, Luddites aren't zombies. They can be worse. They churn out infection from their trenches with airborne range. There I was, wide-eyed and iPad-clad with dreams of students asynchronously posting brainstorms in real time on Padlet, and I was met with resistance! To add insult to injury, in addition to my mentor being a Luddite, I was told that I had to teach the same thing—the same way on the same day—so our students would get the same style of teaching, and if I didn't, I would receive a poor evaluation. She was a seasoned teacher of more than twenty years, and my ideas of integrating technology were halted by her generous trips to the copy machine to make color-coded worksheets and handouts for both our classes.

I remember most of the month of September was spent staying in the bunker until six o'clock at night. On the days it was my turn to make copies for both our classes, I found myself wishing I could just create a Google Doc or be a little greener and use the iPad cart and Edmodo to distribute an assignment. An overwhelming hopelessness came over me. Though I was a first-year teacher, I had very clear ideas about what my style of teaching looked like, and it wasn't the antiquated practice I was being forced to adopt. I mean, I did go to college, and technology integration is something I have always understood and been passionate about. But here I was in my first year being told that policies like "bring your own device" were not allowed, because "cell phones are distractions." Ten years prior, in the same building, I was banished to I.S.S. for possession of a cell phone my junior year, and the same practices were still in place (although we had moved way past Nokia bricks without keyboards for iPhones with qwerty keyboards that processed inquiry faster than page turning). I wished all my students were in possession of a cell phone.

What does a teacher do in a situation like this? I will tell you what I did. Mentorships are often confused as a relationship where knowledge is transferred from one person to another, but it should go both ways! Once I realized I had knowledge that was valuable to share with my mentor as well, specifically assuaging her fears of using technology, we worked on a symbiotic coteaching structure where she let me teach all our students the technology aspect of the lesson, and she taught the content skills. Though a Luddite, she brought a knowledge of pedagogy, structure, and frameworks to the table that was valuable and made me a better teacher.

Ultimately, I learned that we must choose to see the best in people and highlight their strengths. I wasn't doing that the first part of the school year. What we eventually came up with was using iPads and Storybird as a tool for students to demonstrate their knowledge of dialogue and punctuation. We even had students from her class collaborate with students from mine! Both of our trenches were full of great stories of origin authored by students, and the groans and moans that came with worksheets and drill and practice were replaced by cheers and reviews by peers.

Takeaway: Know your value. Stand your ground. Choose to highlight the good in others— and don't be afraid to speak up when you have good ideas! If I had spoken up sooner, it wouldn't have taken us until February or March to find a system that worked for us and benefited our students. Just present your ideas respectfully and always strive to appreciate the strengths of others. It goes a long way in building a positive climate among colleagues and a creative culture inside your bunker. We all have things we excel at, and the same truth goes for areas we need to improve in.

Want to incorporate Storybird into your classroom? Check out our resource page for Chapter 1!

Mary Ellen Weeks
@Mrsmeweeks
Natick
c. 2010

I was fortunate enough to land my first teaching job in a very innovative school district in a suburb of Boston, Massachusetts. It was my dream job. It was a privilege to work in a beautiful building under a visionary principal who gave me the space to be innovative and do what I thought was best for kids. I had a kick-ass partner, we did amazing things together, and I quickly realized that I had found my calling.

The problem was that I did not know all the rules. I sailed through my first two years, but I treated my new career as a sprint, not a marathon. My principal had me teaching two subjects, and I was good, but I wasn't passionate about teaching world history. In fact, I knew nothing about world history and relied completely on others in the department. I really wanted to switch to teaching language arts only, and instead of just waiting patiently for my turn to make a move, I pushed. Hard. I felt entitled, and if I am being honest, I became sort of insufferable when I didn't get my way. Eventually, my negativity and inflexibility got the best of me, and that situation, along with my being overwhelmed with two small children at home, was enough to convince me and my husband to move back to Ohio.

Shortly after we moved, I realized I had completely dropped the ball. It has worked out, and Ohio has been good to us, but I promised myself that I would never, ever make the same mistakes again. Hopefully, by being armed with the Teachingland rules, others can be saved from becoming the colleague of the apocalypse that everyone fears is hiding out in the break room!

BRAIN STRETCHERS

1. What rules do you find most applicable to surviving the classroom apocalypse in your bunker?

2. Have you ever broken one of the Teachingland rules? If so, how did you cope?

3. Do you have any rules that you would add to this list?

Visit TeachinglandTheBook.com
to access the links and resources
in this chapter.

CHAPTER 2
Land of the Living: Colleagues, Parents, and Apocalyptic Culture

Set your life on fire and seek those who fan your flames.
—Rumi

Mike: They're pretending to be alive…
Riley: Isn't that what we're doing? Pretending to be alive?
—*Land of the Dead*

A Romero Zombie by Any Other Name Would Still Smell…Not Sweet

As teachers and students, we all have days where we feel like we are pretending. Whether we are teachers pretending to be alive when the stress of the job is killing us or students pretending and going through the motions of learning. Whether we are pretending we know what we are talking about, pretending we are learning, pretending we are busy, pretending to get it, pretending to not get it, pretending to be someone we aren't…pretending is often a self-defense mechanism. We want to be liked. We want to fit in. We want to be valued. The quote above is from Romero's *Land of the Dead*.

Any true zombie aficionado is familiar with the work of George Romero, the father of modern zombie tropes and a major contributor to the subgenre earning its separate categorization within the larger horror genre. *Night of the Living Dead, Dawn of the Dead, Day of the Dead*, and *Land of the Dead*, are all movies in which, when stripped of their zombies, we still find clever commentary on various aspects of society that through Romero's eyes were broken. For those of you who may not be familiar with the impact his films have had on the genre, let me break a few down and highlight their cultural relevance.

In *Night of the Living Dead*, Romero tackled the topic of racism, as it's woven into the social dynamics of the film. The African-American protagonist, Ben, survives the undead, only to be shot by the living, presumably for the color of his skin, and this is long before Brown's shooting in Ferguson. *Dawn of the Dead* addresses commercialism and consumerism, with the setting of a mall the idyllic backdrop where horror unfolds. And then, of course, there is *Day of the Dead*, which Romero himself says is about how important communication is to humankind. And last but not least, *Land of the Dead*, which tackles the disparity between the socioeconomic gaps in society and critiques the ruling class. In *Land of the Dead*, for instance, the various archetypes aren't quite living in a world of harmony, as they fight for survival and equity. As a commentary on social class, capitalism, and materialism, we see a vast array of archetypes and their interactions, demonstrating that human behavior can be more dangerous and contagious than a zombie or the virus. Differences wedge deadly conflict, and ultimately lead to the downfall of Fiddler's Green, the walled-in fortified city where the wealthier humans take residence. The takeaway from *Land of the Dead* is that we are all human even if we think some of our colleagues are masquerading as living. But these differences don't have to lead to conflict; they can enhance our bunker and lead to greater success!

While the social commentary on the themes of racism, equity, communication, and commercialism through the lens of zombies are all valid topics and translate into the educational landscape, what we find even more significant is Romero's zombie reinterpretation that changed the zombie archetype forever. Say the word *zombie*, and a bluish, greenish corpse and Romero's zombie walk will probably manifest in your head. But if there is one thing we have learned from Romero…it's that archetypes can change. So can our archetypal perceptions of others, how we are perceived, and how we perceive ourselves. In this chapter we introduce teacher and parent archetypes. Some of the teacher and parent archetypes that are introduced in this chapter have been around forever. Some are fairly new. But most importantly, which you will learn as you read, they are not permanent, as most things aren't, and you will probably find yourself reflected in some of them—maybe most of them throughout your teaching career.

Introduction to Teachingland Archetypes w/ Peter Ulrich

There you are, minding your own educational business, when someone suddenly sparks something inside you that can't be ignored. Or wait, is that the burrito from lunch? NO! It's the longing to change the way you have been teaching and let go the reins of testing-oppression that have bled you dry. Who is this inspiration? A superhero? An anti-hero? An administrator? NO!

It's a colleague! An actual, honest-to-goodness education colleague who cares about the same things you care about! It's like karma or kismet or Krispy Kreme—something! But wait… how did they get here? Is there a sanctuary nearby? Can they help you navigate the swirling numbness that has become your daily existence? YES! And these educators who make us feel instant sparks are the ones we often migrate to first because they share similar values and interests. They fan your flame!

But in the land of the living, there are also colleagues who are different from you, those who don't share your view of technology and innovative teaching strategies the same way (Luddites) or maybe those who wave their edtech flag high (the EdTech Hipster)! Sometimes these different values or approaches to teaching can put us off from starting conversations or kindling collaborative relationships, and the worse-case scenario can lead to conflicts. As previously mentioned, the real problem in a zombie movie isn't the actual zombies but the humans and the relationships we build during a time of stress and survival. And relationships are hard.

It's vital to familiarize yourself with the different archetypes of teachers that exist in the bunker and how to work in harmony. This chapter will present you with at least fourteen, and these are just the few we have identified! Remember the adage, "Friends help you move; real friends help you move bodies." In your zombie-filled life, that is more important than ever. You are responsible for the daily move of bodies. If you know how to find common ground and approach colleagues with the conscious decision to see their inner strengths, no matter how different they are from you, you are sure to find a friend and at least an ally. While we don't expect you to be besties with everyone in the bunker, it is good to establish a rapport with your colleagues that is positive, inviting, and collaborative.

I (Savannah) believe it all hinges on how you listen and communicate. Columbus and I initially pegged each other as our polar opposites and never in a million years thought we would ever collaborate on a book! When looking at our catalogue of archetypes—though we both identified as EdTech Hipsters—I am more of a Showboat, while Columbus takes the quiet, pragmatic approach of an Aspiring Leader who has risen in ranks. Sometimes your kick-ass partner will surprise you, and you will find a best friend in someone you would have deemed as the unlikeliest ally. Give everyone a chance. Just because you have different dreams of how something should look, at the heart of it, you are both still dreamers, and different perspectives can be refreshing.

> GIVE EVERYONE A CHANCE. JUST BECAUSE YOU HAVE DIFFERENT DREAMS OF HOW SOMETHING SHOULD LOOK, AT THE HEART OF IT, YOU ARE BOTH STILL DREAMERS, AND DIFFERENT PERSPECTIVES CAN BE REFRESHING.

In this chapter, we are going to explore different teacher and parent archetypes in education. These are the two most important stakeholders you will interact with on a frequent basis. When you tread thoughtfully and nimbly with purpose and passion, you are sure to contribute to a bunker culture of innovation and collaboration.

TEACHER ARCHETYPES	PARENT ARCHETYPES
The Innovator	The Helicopter Parent
The Pinterest Prince/Princess	The I'm-a-Really-Big-Deal Parent
The Aspiring Administrator	The Super Mom or The Super Dad
The Newbie	The Earthy-Crunchy Parent
The Worker Bee	The Teacher Parent
The Hand Wringer	The I'll-Call-the-School-Board Parent
The Minion	The Unresponsive Parent
The Showboat	The Nervous Nancy
The Hoarder	The Sports-Are-Everything Parent
The Solo Silo	The Cool Parent
The Island	The Tiger Mom or The Tiger Dad
The Luddite	The Not-My-Baby Parent
The EdTech Hipster	The When-I-Was-in-School Parent
The Trench Totalitarian	The I'm-Not-That-Parent Parent

Colleagues of the Apocalypse Explained

As we previously mentioned, the undead aren't the only things you have to be cautious of during a zombie apocalypse. Your biggest allies and competitors come in the form of other humans: your colleagues. Your coworkers can either push you to achieve greatness or snuff out your passion depending on the kind of relationships you cultivate. It is our hope that as you read this chapter you will put aside the innate human instinct to compete with others and replace it with collaboration. If you compete, compete to be the best version of yourself you can be.

Always remember that you are the hero and leader of your own classroom narrative, but you are also expected to collaborate with others who are also the hero of their own narrative—we can all be heroes! On this journey, you will find a vast array of teacher archetypes to interact with. When working

> KNOWING THE DIFFERENCE BETWEEN WHEN TO SHINE AND WHEN TO SUPPORT GOES A LONG WAY IN FACILITATING A CULTURE OF INNOVATION AND SYNERGY.

in group situations, sometimes your role will be to lead, and other times you will have to let your colleagues have the spotlight. True educational leaders understand they aren't always the experts and that there is value in learning from their colleagues. Knowing the difference between when to shine and when to support goes a long way in facilitating a culture of innovation and synergy.

To help foster positive interactions and put your best foot forward, we have compiled a catalogue of archetypes that will probably seem very two-dimensional and static. Over the span of your career, not only will you recognize these personalities among your colleagues, you might see them in yourself. While our archetypes are oversimplified and hyperbolic, the reality is that there is nothing more complex than the inner workings of human motivation, psychology, and response to internal and external stimuli.

Before we discuss how to foster harmony in the bunker, let's take a look at the many different colleagues you're likely to encounter:

THE INNOVATOR

Innovators are willing to do just about anything to engage their students. They understand that their role in the classroom should be that of facilitator rather than the all-knowing giver of knowledge. They leverage student-centered approaches to instruction and classroom setup to maximize student success and autonomy.

THE PINTEREST PRINCE/PRINCESS

These two love the glitter and the glam, and they prefer their surroundings to look amazing all the time. Walking into their trenches—full of colorful posters and perfectly positioned pocket charts atop beautiful and creatively relevant backgrounds—can immediately bring on feelings of deep inadequacy. Their accessories, in coordinating colors and patterns, are in such good shape it's hard to believe children ever use them. Either way, their organization skills are on fleek!

THE ASPIRING ADMINISTRATOR

Aspiring Administrators are often in a leadership program or have plans to enroll in one very soon. They have already started to practice flexing their managerial muscles, especially if they have started their internship. They are often found in close proximity to the principal, which makes everyone around them nervous about speaking freely. Whenever questions are raised about a new initiative, their response is sensible and politically correct. They're also adept at providing their colleagues with explanations in a way that makes them wonder why they even raised the question in the first place.

THE NEWBIE

Newbies are in their first few years of teaching. They can appear scattered, are almost always overwhelmed, and sometimes require a lot of support from their more experienced colleagues. They usually have great ideas that they learned during their college coursework or from their student-teaching experience, but they need guidance and time from a kick-ass partner to implement these successfully. That said, they are generally highly motivated and passionate, eager to engage their students, and willing to try almost anything.

THE WORKER BEE

Worker Bees are not your typical idea people, but they understand the importance of staying close to those who are and work their tails off to do what is best for their students. Whether helping kick off a new initiative or partnering with someone on a classroom activity, they are fabulous with logistics, planning, and bringing projects to fruition. These teachers are detail oriented, and they don't stop until they see things through. They can often be found in their trench burning the midnight oil.

THE HAND WRINGER

Hand Wringers wear their hearts on their sleeves and worry about all there is to worry about in every situation. Their greatest asset is their empathy, which is stuck in overdrive, but this can also be their greatest downfall because they tend to stick to strategies they know are safe and avoid taking too many risks. Sometimes they are referred to as Negative Nancies, but they are really just consumed with worry, which comes across as negative. Hesitant to allow students to struggle or experience discomfort, they stand ready to rescue at the first sign of confusion or frustration. Consequently, opportunities for engagement can pass them by.

THE MINION

Minions are followers to a fault. They can often be found goose-stepping behind someone else, sometimes an administrator and sometimes another teacher. They will do whatever it is they are told without questioning or considering whether it fits the needs of their students. Whenever questions are raised about an activity or initiative, they can regurgitate verbatim the official rationale or explanation provided by the powers that be.

THE SHOWBOAT

Showboats love the spotlight. Unlike the Innovator, whose priority is engaging and doing what is best for students, these colleagues are all about what makes them look good. That is not to say that the projects and lessons they believe will make them shine are never good for kids. Sometimes they can quench their thirst for glory while also engaging their students, but their primary goal is usually self-serving.

THE HOARDER

Hoarders keep everything. Literally. They can be found trolling the bunker during summer vacation looking for materials and furniture others have discarded. Need a relic to help you teach a lesson on the history of just about anything? The Hoarders can hook you up! If they have ever used it or just thought they might use it someday, chances are they still have it.

THE SOLO SILO

Solo Silos go it alone. They have teaching figured out. They are self-contained, independent, and usually great teachers, but they aren't fans of the sharing-is-caring mindset. A crossbreed between an Innovator and a Hoarder, The Solo Silo also hoards ideas, strategies, and new tech finds. They can be reserved or a showboat. Maybe you can negotiate some information sharing, but only if you offer an olive branch first.

THE ISLAND

Islands are often easy to spot because they are the only ones to teach a specific kind of content in the entire building, and they usually see every student in the school over the course of the school year. They are the single expert in their niche area and usually have no one around to collaborate with. It's lonely on the island.

THE LUDDITE

Luddites bring a wealth of experience to the table, but they often have a strong aversion to innovation and change—even when it is in the best interest of students. Mid-to-late in their career, they often are fond of cemetery-row seating and filing cabinets and binders full of lesson plans they have used year after year. Aside from their usual moans and groans at the mere mention of a new initiative, they can often be heard using phrases such as, "I don't have time," and, "That won't work."

THE EDTECH HIPSTER

Whether a new or a seasoned educator, The EdTech Hipster is always online and scrolling Twitter for a new tech nugget to implement in their classroom. They often spread the gospel of new apps, platforms, and gadgets and can often be found saying, "Hey, have you heard about or seen (insert new app)?"

THE TRENCH TOTALITARIAN

Rules are rules are rules. And rules are meant to be broken, right? No! Not in this trench. Whether a student violates dress code by wearing a brown belt instead of black, arrives ten seconds late to class, or gets caught chewing gum, you can bet there is no infraction that isn't met with consequence. While Trench Totalitarians might have classroom management down to a science, their black-and-white view of the world is highly limiting. It makes for a gray and gloomy classroom where rapport and relationships tend to fall by the wayside

Strategies for Finding Harmony in the Bunker

While interacting with all of the various types of colleagues can be frustrating, don't lose heart. There are ways to cope and even maximize your colleagues' strengths to make life in the trenches to run more smoothly. Here are some tips to ensure your survival:

TIP #1: SEEK FIRST TO UNDERSTAND, THEN TO BE UNDERSTOOD

In any interaction with colleagues, especially if its challenging and opposing perspectives are in play, it's vital to try and understand the other person's point of view before you seek to be heard. If you can understand why the other person is doing what they are doing, you can find empathy and respond in ways that make all parties feel heard, thereby making it easier to collaborate on solutions and find common ground. This can be done in a nonthreatening way through asking clarifying questions and using "I wonder" statements. Always speak from your heart and center while trying not to speculate.

TIP #2: ASSUME POSITIVE INTENT

In any disagreement with colleagues, it's easy to believe your way is the right way, but it's important to realize your colleagues also believe their way is right. While this type of situation can easily become a disaster of apocalyptic proportions, casualties can be avoided if all parties are able to realize that everyone is coming to the table with the intent to do what's right by students. Even if your colleagues' suggestions sound completely ridiculous to you, if you can assume that they believe their idea is what is best for students, you can ask clarifying questions and find common ground that works for everyone.

TIP #3: COLLABORATE IN WAYS THAT LEVERAGE EVERYONE'S STRENGTHS

One of the things we can choose to control is how we view our colleagues. We can choose to see only the two-dimensional archetypes and all their faults listed above, or we can look deeper at the strengths each individual brings to the table. All the colleagues of the apocalypse discussed above have strengths. In creating learning experiences for students, we tend to seek out colleagues that match or complement our own style. But you can't always choose who you are teamed with, and having to collaborate with someone who is so completely different from you can feel like an absolute nightmare. The key to making this work is focusing on the positive aspects of what that person has to offer.

For example, while the Luddite and Innovator might not gravitate towards one another for collaboration purposes, it can work when they appreciate the knowledge and skills the other person brings to the table. The Luddite might bring a wealth of experience in classroom management and parent communication, while the Innovator can offer out-of-the-box thinking that will engage students in modern ways. If the Innovator can use active listening skills to understand the Luddite's misgivings about whatever it is they are working on, and the Luddite can appreciate the authentic, modern learning experience the Innovator is trying to create for students, this unlikely pair can reach common ground and even learn something new from each another.

Meet the Parents of the Apocalypse

Aside from your colleagues, parents will be some of the most challenging stakeholders you will encounter. Teaching is the hardest job that everyone thinks they can do because they went to school, and no one struggles with the paradigm shift of student-led learning more than parents. If their students aren't bringing home ten spelling words to work on or nightly homework on a regular basis, many parents will panic and wonder if their children are learning anything. We will talk about ways to forge strong relationships with parents, but first let's take a look at some of the parent archetypes you might encounter.

THE HELICOPTER

Helicopters are commonly found hovering around their children at all times. While sometimes overbearing, they do believe they are doing right by their kids, and they stand ready to confront anyone who they believe is not.

THE I'M-A-REALLY-BIG-DEAL PARENT

I'm-a-Really-Big-Deal parents are skilled at letting everyone know how vastly important they are. They make it clear, in no uncertain terms, that they are willing and able to leverage their position of perceived power to their advantage if their child shows any sign of discontent or if they disagree with how you are running your classroom.

THE SUPER MOM AND THE SUPER DAD

Super Moms and Super Dads are the parents you watch with envy as they make it all look so easy. They volunteer for everything from the PTA to room parent to coaching their children's sports teams, are perfectly put together (as are their children), and never seem stressed.

THE EARTHY-CRUNCHY PARENT

These parents are all about their children's physical and emotional well-being. Their primary concerns include the use of chemicals as cleaning agents, including antibacterial soap, hand sanitizers, and wipes in the classroom as well as the type of energy your classroom management system brings to the learning environment. While they can be over the top with trying to ensure that all classroom snacks are free of Red Dye #40, these parents will be in your corner with authentic learning experiences and student-led learning.

THE TEACHER PARENT

Teacher Parents are teachers themselves and therefore will have lots of ideas about how your classroom should run. Chances are, if their children are in your school, they specifically asked for their kiddos to have you, so expectations run high. This type of parent struggles to avoid offering advice when you are telling them about their child's performance or struggles, but generally they will understand what you are saying, even if they do not want to hear it.

THE UNRESPONSIVE PARENT

Do you have a parent you've called three times this week, sent four Class Dojo messages to, and emailed twice—all with no response? You are probably dealing with The Unresponsive Parent. These kinds of parents can be particularly frustrating because, even though it might not be true, it can feel as though their child's education isn't a priority.

THE HAND WRINGER

Hand Wringer Parents are seemingly always worried about everything from whether their child is making friends—and who those friends might be—to their child's academic progress and the safety of the playground equipment. They demand a lot of time, attention, follow up, and reassurance, but once trust is established, they tend to calm down and back off.

THE SPORTS-ARE-EVERYTHING PARENT

Sports-Are-Everything Parents are far more concerned with their child's potential future as a professional athlete than they are with their education. Their children will often show up at school tired, having been out late at practices, and their primary concern with their grades surrounds their eligibility to play sports.

THE COOL PARENT

Cool Parents are primarily concerned about their friendship with their child. They struggle with discipline and follow through at home because they can't stand for Johnny or Suzie to be upset with them and will look to you to parent their child for them in the classroom. While they will relate to whatever struggles you might be having with their child in school, they will usually be at a loss for a solution.

THE TIGER MOM AND THE TIGER DAD

Tiger Moms and Tiger Dads do more than support their child in homework or big projects like science fair. They take it to the next level. Their children come to school with suspiciously excellent projects that just might have been done by…um…an adult. The Tiger Mom and The Tiger Dad want their student to excel and make an A—even if they have to do some of the work to make that happen.

THE NOT-MY-BABY PARENT

Not-My-Baby parents are some of the most challenging to deal with. These parents are unwilling to accept that their children are anything but perfect, so do not expect support from this parent if you need to call home to discuss problem behavior or substandard academic performance. It is likely the blame will be put back on you or other students.

THE WHEN-I-WAS-IN-SCHOOL PARENT

When-I-Was-in-School Parents know how a classroom should be run. When they were in school they got math homework every night, and they want to know why their kid doesn't have math homework. When you give their children math homework, they don't like the way it is currently being taught, and they make sure they tell you how ridiculous the new methods are. If you do something that is different from how they were taught, they will likely compare it to their superior educational upbringing.

THE I'M-NOT-THAT-PARENT PARENT

The I'm-Not-That-Parent parents usually start off by saying they're not The Helicopter Parent or The Hand Wringer Parent, but the next thing that comes out of their mouths totally blows their cover. So they are, in fact, this other parent, but they are sailing down their own special river of denial.

Tips for Forging Strong Relationships with Families

Not unlike the teacher archetypes, these parent archetypes are meant to be two dimensional. While these were created in jest, it's important to be careful because if you can't find empathy for the parents of your students, it is easy to categorize people in this way and assume you understand them when you actually have no idea what their situation is. While dealing with parents can be a challenge, there are steps you can take to build strong, trusting relationships with the families you serve.

TIP #1—REMEMBER THAT PARENTS WERE THEIR CHILD'S FIRST TEACHER

From the time children are born, their parents are their primary source of guidance until they start school. Even if their child goes to daycare, parents continue to play a huge role in teaching them to walk, talk, get along with others, be safe, and navigate the world around them. Assume parents love their kids and want what is best for them. For many parents, it's hard taking a step back and letting go—even a little—while their child is at school. While it might feel as though they are overbearing, that is not their intent. If you can understand that their inability to let go is not about you and find ways to make them an active participant in their child's learning and classroom experiences, your interactions with some of your more challenging parents will be easier because they will feel engaged and in the loop.

TIP #2: SEEK FIRST TO UNDERSTAND, THEN TO BE UNDERSTOOD

Parents will get upset with you. It's something that happens to teachers all the time, and it can be really uncomfortable when it happens. When you experience this, your first inclination might be to push back or get defensive. Before you do that, first try to understand why they are upset and remember to not take it personally. Sometimes the initial issue they are lashing out about isn't the real issue at all. When a parent calls you and they are upset, try taking the following steps:

Listen: Hear them out. Listen quietly to what they have to say without interrupting.

Repeat for Understanding: Repeat back to them what they have said; for example, "So what I hear you saying is . . ."

Confirmation: Give them an opportunity to confirm what you understand their concerns to be. Let them tell you if you understand them correctly. If not, repeat the first three steps again until they confirm that you understand what they are upset about. You can't address an issue unless you properly understand it.

Perspective: If the parent confirms that you are understanding them correctly, offer your side of the situation if it's appropriate. Keep it short, sweet, and to the point; focus on the facts.

Feedback: Give them an opportunity to offer feedback on your side of the situation.

Solution: Thank them for bringing their concern to your attention (even if you are not feeling thankful). If you have a solution, propose it. If you do not have a solution, ask them if they have any ideas on how the two of you can resolve it. This is where it makes sense to do some negotiation to come up with something that works for everyone.

Find Answer/Follow Up: If you and the parent were able to agree on a solution, great! Let them know that you will be following up to tell them how it goes and get feedback from them (and make sure you do). If you were not able to agree on a solution, let the parent know that you will talk to an administrator or a mentor and come back to them with some ideas. Make sure you follow up as quickly as possible.

TIP #3: MAKE LEARNING VISIBLE TO PARENTS

Most parents have gone to school, so that is their frame of reference for what school should look like. Consequently, many parents, unless they are in the education field themselves, expect their child's school experience to look like theirs did. After all, they turned out OK, didn't they?

The best way to deal with this mindset is to give them access to what and how their child is learning in your classroom every day. There are many ways you can do this. One way is through a learning management system that parents can access and have 24/7 access to the curriculum. If you have your students turn in their work this way, they will even be able to see how they are performing. Columbus's school uses Seesaw, which is free for teachers and notifies parents (at the teacher's discretion) when their student has posted an assignment and allows them to give their child feedback. You can also set up a classroom blog, encourage parents to follow you on your professional Twitter (which should be completely separate from your personal account), send home a weekly newsletter, and invite them to participate in the learning environment. When Columbus was leading a blended-learning catalyst classroom in a community that was somewhat leery of change, she invited parents and other teachers in for playdates with the technology. It was a huge success, and parents and even some of her more Luddite-like colleagues saw the value in this type of learning environment for students.

Check out this flowchart on how to communicate with students made by standtallsteve.com.

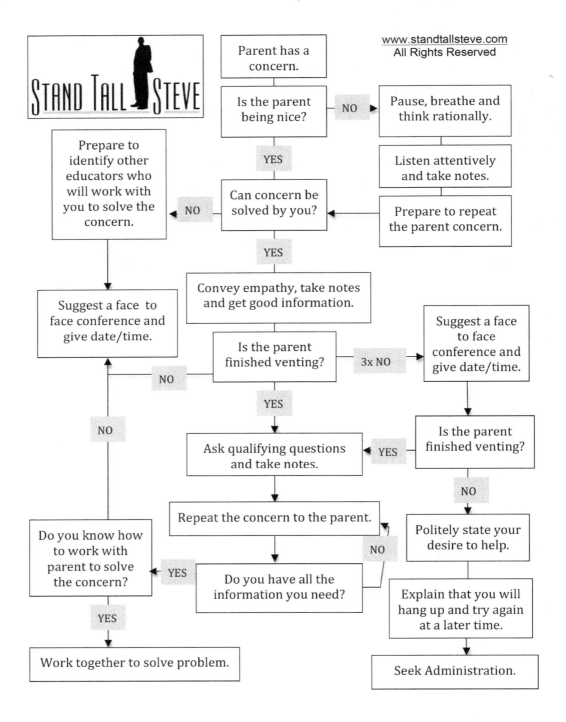

Tales from the Trenches

A note to leaders: Summon the Epic

@AmandaFoxSTEM
Savannah
c. 2013

In a building full of different archetypes, personalities, and diverse backgrounds, how can we forge a culture that is collaborative, innovative, and positive? I have walked into many buildings over the years, and I can usually feel within five minutes what kind of energy the school has. Whether it's body language, laughter, or conversations, good vibes aren't a product of happenstance. They are intentionally summoned.

During the summer of 2013, I was hired to teach social studies at a new STEM school. In truth, there was nothing new about the building, but the concept was new to our district. At the time, Peter Ulrich, the school's principal, was probably the only person who had a clear vision of what STEM might look like. He had hired me and several other educators to implement that vision, but most of us didn't know what STEM was or why it had been chosen as a curricular framework for our entire school.

Before the school year started, Ulrich held a face-to-face meeting for teachers and staff—most of whom didn't know each other—to get acquainted and discuss what STEM might look like in our school. We essentially met to demystify the acronym and dig deep to devise a framework for the year ahead.

As I walked into that first meeting, I heard music from *Man of Steel* playing in the background. The music did a strange thing. It changed my nervousness to curiosity and set the tone for the entire planning session. Pushing through those doors, I knew I was heading into what would be an epic, monumental time in my life. That musical score was the perfect tool to inspire me and empower me. In that moment, thanks to Ulrich, the possibility of our STEM-filled future formed in my soul.

As the years passed, I experienced many other moments where Ulrich summoned the epic at meetings. He just had this way of making every new journey seem like we were sitting inside a theater waiting for the show to start, only to find out we were part of the show.

Looking back, I realize I didn't just meet my colleagues and discuss our vision of STEM that day. I also learned that a good leader must summon the epic and invite all stakeholders to the table to successfully unleash the full potential of innovation and camaraderie. No matter the differences that exist, when people are invited to the table to create a sustainable idea, class, or program, they become a part of something larger than themselves. You must invite stakeholders to share in the molding of what that program is going to look like. This sharing of visions extended to our students and their parents as well, because that is what was modeled. Good leadership trickles down; unfortunately, so does the bad leadership. At that first meeting, the music might have bonded us and alluded to greatness ahead of us, but the fact that my colleagues and I were invited to help shape what STEM was and looked like gave us accountability, pride, and buy-in.

Ulrich is now the director of governance of middle schools in Savannah, Georgia. Many leaders move on, and their initiatives dissipate or even disappear overnight. The STEM Academy still operates using many elements of his vision. It was planted in the hearts and minds of each teacher and through daily cultivation and contributions went from a singularity to a collective reality.

Jonathan Coker
Tampa
c. 2016

As the resident Latin teacher, I was constantly talking to my middle school students about various gods, heroes, and monsters. I even had my students take a "Which Jungian Archetype Are You?" online quiz to pique their interest for one of my mythology lessons. After taking the quiz myself, I got back the result of "mother goddess." In one class, the moniker quickly became my new nickname—one that led me to understand something about how students perceive their teachers. I realized we are probably not the heroes of our students' stories, because most students see themselves as the heroes of their stories.

But all teachers have those days when they need to feel like heroes. They need to grab a colleague, close a door, and vent. So to this day, when another teacher comes into my room to talk, I strive to listen to them as if they were the hero of their own story. In that way, maybe my middle schoolers were right. I was playing the part of a mother goddess not only to my students but my colleagues too, nurturing and supporting them through their struggles, celebrating when they figured out the answer to their problems and guiding them in unexpected ways.

If a man in his mid-thirties could be a mother goddess, then perhaps we all can play various archetypes in each other's lives This type of thinking is a paradigm shift for schools because it requires us to work cooperatively rather than competitively. Teachers would not be competing for the best scores but instead finding ways they can learn and grow from each other. Students could lead the classroom learning rather than sitting passively. Principals could be caregivers rather than rulers.

Isabel Bozada
@IsabelBozada
Beavercreek
c. 2015

When I was hired for my first teaching job, I was introduced to my new team in an email and told that I was going to be in Room 19 and teaching third grade. Within twenty-four hours, a teacher named Angie called to tell me that we were actually on a team together, and I would be teaching math while she was teaching reading. She invited me to come in the next day so she could show me around. From there on out, Angie seemed to know everything about teaching at Herbert Mills.

I was a total EdTech Hipster and a classic Newbie—totally scattered, overwhelmed, and requiring a lot of support. Angie was a Worker Bee who tirelessly burned the midnight oil and worked her butt off to do what is best for students. I also had the perception that she was a Pinterest Princess due to her flawless rock-star themed room. She was pregnant with baby #2, due in February—right as the scramble of testing season was to begin. Our partnership was a constant struggle. She was entering her third year in a row of having different teaching partners because she was such an effective mentor. I came into my new school with way more ideas than I had the skills to implement. We had different approaches to almost everything, but our students had to learn in both of our rooms.

When Angie went on maternity leave, I was left alone with an incompetent substitute, the responsibility for all forty of our third graders, and the sinking suspicion that I needed her a lot more than I thought I did. I realized all the little things she did every day that helped me out—reminding me to send papers home, creating resources for our science and social studies units, thinking of the easily overlooked little things. I also realized how important strong classroom management skills were, and I started to hone my own to make up for what was not happening with her substitute. The day she came back from maternity leave was the happiest day of my first year of teaching.

Today Angie and I are no longer a teaching team, but we are true partners, using our unique talents to work towards being Innovators in our school. Angie helps me organize my thoughts and gives structure to my off-the-wall ideas. I push her to try new things that will help not just our students but all the students at Herbert Mills. When Angie wants to expand her teaching practice, she calls me to figure out a new tech tool to use. When I am struggling with how to get my literacy block to be more efficient, I observe Angie's classroom and borrow some of her excellent management ideas. As we learned more about each other, we realized that our initial perceptions were only a small part of who we were as teachers and as humans. Along the way, we have made the conscious decision to recognize and use each other's strengths. Although we approach the world in different ways, we are allies for our students and for our school.

BRAIN STRETCHERS

1. Which teacher archetype do you identify with? Why?

2. What archetype is most prevalent in your bunker? How does that impact the culture?

3. Which teacher/parent archetype do you find that you are most compatible with? Why?

4. Which teacher/parent archetype do you find the most challenging? How can you effectively manage a relationship with them?

5. How do you plan to involve parents in your classroom?

Visit TeachinglandTheBook.com to access the links and resources in this chapter.

CHAPTER 3
Cooties: Tricking Your Trench and Managing the Horde

You remember in Commando *and every other suiting-up scene where there was a suiting-up scene? Well this is that scene...they have us outnumbered, outgunned, and outnumbered...but there is one thing we have that they don't. The drive to win.*
—Wade Johnson in *Cooties*

If there is any movie that parallels what classroom management—or lack thereof—could look like in Teachingland, it would definitely be *Cooties*! It didn't take a huge leap for us to connect the two, as its setting is an elementary school. Classified as a Zomb-B film, (ba-dum-bum tsss) it chronicles a group of teachers who report to teach summer school, only to find themselves in the middle of a zombie apocalypse! Patient zero is a young girl who eats a contaminated chicken nugget (We were always told to beware of cafeteria food!), and as her behavior changes, she quickly infects other students until the entire school is consumed in chaos. The quote at the beginning of this chapter references actor Rainn Wilson's pep talk to his colleagues as they prepare to take back control of the school. But how do we as educators suit up and prepare for the pandemonium we are sure to encounter in our trenches?

In the classroom, the truth is not too far removed from what happened in the movie, but the source of the outbreak might not be as obvious as a contaminated chicken nugget. It could be a disengaged student who disrupts your lesson and quickly gets other students to join in, an ineffective delivery of your lesson plan, or the kind of rapport you have with your students. The catalyst can take various forms, but just like in the movie, mark our words, it will result in chaos. And we're not talking about pleasant, organized chaos, which is totally OK! It's important to put a plan in place in the beginning so you don't find yourself doing trench-wide triage on the daily. Because even with the best plans, there will still be urgent situations that require reactive intervention.

Classroom management is, hands down, one of the most challenging but also one of the most important parts of surviving the classroom apocalypse. Because of its multifaceted nature, it should be proactively approached as a vaccine to a virus that could infect the horde. The vaccine includes student and parent buy-in, engagement, rapport, classroom layout, and healthy boundaries. Your vaccine is essentially your blanket approach, but your daily interactions and strategies might vary from class to class, year to year, and even student to student. And even if you have given classroom management your best shot, it doesn't mean all your students are safeguarded from distraction, disruption, or disengagement—the DisTrio, as in, "Don't you tri-dis in my trench!" Hundreds of books have been written on this topic, but we are going to stick to the basics of how to manage your horde and trick your trench environment in a way that promotes student learning.

Reach and Rapport

The most important component of managing your trench is relationship building and defining your classroom culture. Positive rapport can be an invaluable asset in trench taming. In the movie *Cooties*, rapport was nonexistent, and teachers seemed to be absent from the moment or simply self-absorbed during most interactions with students. The result was a disconnect and the dehumanization of both parties in the eyes of the other.

While it's critical that you get to know your students, it's also important that they get to know you. Even the youngest learners want to know who you are and what makes you excited. If you and your students can find common ground, it will be much easier to build strong relationships. For the past two years, Columbus's school has held STEMcation Day right before winter break, in which teachers engage students as they rotate through STEM activities that are rooted in the personal passions of their teachers. On that day, in a building with a high-needs population, there is rarely a single behavior problem because the students are truly engaged and get to see their teachers for who they are.

> IF YOU AND YOUR STUDENTS CAN FIND COMMON GROUND, IT WILL BE MUCH EASIER TO BUILD STRONG RELATIONSHIPS.

Framing Your Trench Culture: Packing the Theater

Opportunities such as open house and curriculum nights exist to allow you to begin connecting with students and families before they ever enter your trench. With social media and communication tools, you can reach out and start building relationships long before students ever set foot in your bunker. Ask yourself, *What will their first impression be?* To evoke curiosity, excitement, and wonder at the beginning of the new year, you need to reach down inside yourself and summon the epic (refer back to Chapter 2's Tales from the Trenches). What can you do to make students feel like they are being summoned to the beginning of an epic journey? How can you make students excited to come to your classroom every day?

One way is to design an online space that students can check out prior to the open house or the first day of school. It allows them to become familiar with the content and can build suspense about what lies ahead. Dynamic newsletters that start before the beginning of the school year and continue as the year progresses is another great strategy to help pack your open house and make your students eager for the first day. Using iMovie or another video-editing app to create a trailer previewing the fantastic adventure to come is also effective at building excitement and setting expectations early!

Taking this movie concept to epic proportions, The STEM Academy in Savannah, Georgia, invited students to become part of an intergalactic adventure and become protagonists of the *Nevermore* trilogy! Each grade level literally experienced a story-centered curriculum and was invited to help rewrite each subsequent year or sequel with their teachers. Using videos and a Weebly site to host the storyline, students and teachers became part of something larger than a school. They became heroes of their own narratives, embarking on learning adventures at every turn. It's important to frame your own narrative and craft your own culture before someone else tells your story. This way you communicate a culture that embraces collaboration, creativity, and critical thinking. We even had an astronaut statue at open house that students were invited to take photos with!

Check out the video and website to learn more about STEM's Planet Nevermore:

http://planetnevermore.weebly.com/year-one.html

http://bit.ly/planetnevermoreintro

This storyline was woven throughout the year, and videos were also used to kick off a day of team building through the highly anticipated Nevermore Games: http://bit.ly/planetnevermorevid

You don't have to create something as large and fantastical as a trilogy to create a positive culture. It could be as simple as adopting a PBIS (Positive Behavioral Interventions and Supports) program such as Love Your People, crafting mission statements for all stakeholders, or finding another common thread to weave positivity throughout your culture.

Another example of creating an intentional culture is the L&N STEM Academy in Knoxville, Tennessee. Taking the concept of Moonshot Thinking (the act of problem-solving in education using radical ideas and technology), L&N pushed even further and created Mars Shot Narratives for their stakeholders. Tim Childers, former assistant principal, says, "Well, we have already been to the moon. Now we are shooting for Mars, so Mars shot thinking is what we expect from our students."

Framing expectations in the form of narratives provides those involved with the context or vision of the role they play in school culture. Here are examples of the Mars Shot Narratives:

OUR STUDENTS' STORY

Students at the L&N STEM Academy are a little bit different. They're curious, ambitious, digital natives, and that difference, that curiosity and ambition, has brought them to our school. Students come to the L&N looking for opportunities they won't find anywhere else: boundless opportunities to explore STEM subjects and careers, opportunities to belong to a community of similarly curious, ambitious students, and opportunities to change the world.

But they may not know how vast their STEM opportunities are. They may be unsure of how to belong and contribute to a community. And they don't know—yet—just how they're going to change the world. If they don't learn these things now, during these critical years, they'll miss those opportunities to learn, to belong, to contribute, and to change.

Fortunately, at the L&N STEM Academy, students engage with caring teachers, administrators, librarians, STEM professionals, and counselors who help them discover the expansive array of STEM opportunities before them. They collaborate with similarly motivated students who simultaneously accept them as they are and challenge them to be more than they ever thought possible.

And these students discover how they can—and will—change the world through human-centered STEM principles grounded in empathy, through professionalism and collaboration, through innovation and design, through inquiry and critical thinking.

When our students are successful, they will be empowered to indulge their curiosity and achieve their ambitions. They will not only seek opportunities, they will seek to create opportunities for others; they will not only be part of a community, they will create communities; they will not only change their world, they'll change our world in boundless ways.

OUR TEACHERS' STORIES

Teachers at the L&N STEM Academy are looking for ways to lead students in STEM thinking and careers in a way that is without limits. They know this is what sets our school apart from others in our district and our state. They understand that failure to lead our students into boundless STEM opportunities means we will be like every other high school, and our purpose for existence will be gone.

In order to reach this Mars Shot goal, they must overcome the problems of space, time, and an uncertain future. To do this, our teachers work with students, community stakeholders, industry leaders, teacher collaborators, and visionary administrators. With these guides, our teachers will learn to overcome the problem of space by taking their instruction outside the walls of our school both physically and digitally. They will overcome the problem of time by offering instruction in ways not limited by the hours in a school day. And they will tackle an uncertain future in STEM career paths by never being complacent in the ways—and content—they teach.

When they are successful, our students will embrace empathy as the starting point to all problem-solving, engage in more than one approach to possible STEM careers, take classes both synchronously and asynchronously online, avail themselves of multiple early postsecondary opportunities, seek out internships in STEM fields, and find themselves pursued by colleges and universities.

L&N STEM Academy also separates students into houses like Harry Potter. This builds culture and instills pride and camaraderie. What does your school do to set expectations and build culture? What is working? What can be improved upon?

Tricking Out Your Trench

A popular meme on Twitter shows a government-funded classroom versus a teacher-funded classroom, and the difference is astounding. The first is a sterile environment, easily dismissed and not at all inviting. We can remember walking into our first classrooms, and outside of desks, filing cabinets, and whiteboard, (maybe even a chalkboard and a little bit of mold), they were pretty plain and resembled that government-funded classroom. But with a little imagination and a lot of elbow grease, we were able to design spaces that enchanted our students and set them free to shine.

When you tackle tricking your trench, it should embody fun, collaboration, creativity, innovation, wonder, and everything else you want your kids to feel when they come to learn. The look and feel of a particular space can be a powerful variable in creating an environment conducive to learning. Gone are the days of cemetery-row seating where students are required to sit in a desk. Your physical space should be reflective of the type of activities students participate in. Social construction of knowledge is an important aspect of learning, and so our trenches should be laid out in a way to facilitate collaboration. So how can you ditch the cemetery-row seating and upgrade your government-funded trench and ensure your design matches your purpose?

SEATING

While some students are perfectly fine to sit and do their work, some students need to move, while others prefer to stand. Having a variety of seating options available to students, as well as places for them to stand, can go a long way in optimizing the learning environment for maximum student success. The seating arrangement is just as important as seating variety. Creating themed station areas in your classroom also helps with arranging materials and assigning purpose and function. Sounds expensive, right? It doesn't have to be.

In Columbus's school, some teachers use ironing boards as standing desks. Kids can be found lounging in a repurposed church pew or atop cushions typically used for outdoor furniture. Duct taped pool noodles anchor exercise balls for students who need to bounce, and TV trays allow students to work on the carpet if they are so inclined. Some teachers have traded desks for standard school-issue tables, and one teacher removed the legs from a circular table and used books to elevate it just enough that students can sit crisscross around it. Because the standard, brown school-issue tables aren't real wood, students write directly on them using dry erase markers and use stray socks (clean, of course) and mittens as erasers.

In Savannah's film classroom, she mounted monitors on the walls and centered tables around them as presentation spaces. Each table was an editing team, and little thinker dolls (plush dolls of scientists, philosophers, and artists) were assigned to the tables. The Karl Marx table was where students "capitalized" on good ideas. The Andy Warhol table had the tagline, "Where your ideas pop." Students love to fidget with the dolls while editing and also learn about historical figures. To expand classroom space, Savannah had green screens lined up all down the hallway outside her classroom. Her school utilized every space in the building for learning. In the corner of the room, a stop-motion animation station was available, and locker stands were used as iPad tripods. Finding creative and inventive uses for items inspires students to do the same. Savannah has often been called an EdTech Swiss Army knife, finding new uses for common classroom items.

While Pinterest can be a tricky place to find good curriculum materials (see Chapter 9 for details) it is a great place to find DIY strategies on the cheap to trick out your trench on a budget.

While flexible seating areas are a great option, there is also a time and place for students to be seated at their tables or together on the carpet for whole-group mini-lessons or activities. The goal is to find balance while manipulating space to achieve your objectives.

To summarize, you should take the following into consideration when tricking out your trench:

- Is your space inviting, warm, and safe?
- Is it reflexive to the learning objectives?
- Does it provide opportunities for collaboration and communication?
- Is it conducive to creativity?
- Does your design match your purpose?

Banding Together to Manage the Horde

As a teacher, you play an integral role in raising up your students to be effective communicators, strong collaborators, and responsible citizens of your school and classroom community who are perseverant in their endeavors—but your plan needs to be part of a larger picture.

Your trench should reflect bunker-wide expectations, and a handbook is a great place to define what your classroom culture should look like. Pulling in bunker-wide approaches to address procedures, management, behavior issues, and consequences will ensure there is continuity in practice to yield the best results no matter where a student is in the building.

Prior to the start of the school year, faculty should decide on a holistic approach to management, clearly articulating core values, student expectations, and consequences. If you are team teaching, it's critical that you and your teaching partners utilize the same classroom management strategies. A teaching team with completely different expectations and consequences is a recipe for disaster. You and your colleagues are guaranteed to learn a lot from one another if you are willing to leverage your strengths and present a united front to your students.

Additionally, make parents aware of classroom expectations and consequences as early as possible. Use Class Dojo, Remind, Bloomz, Classcraft (Savannah's Favorite) or even send good, old-fashioned notes home to keep parents abreast of how their students are doing in the classroom (flip to Chapter 6 for more on this). Taking a proactive approach to communication can lay a positive foundation for the school year. Just as students need to know you value and care about them, parents need to know you care about their children. Send parents positive feedback and notes about their kiddos every chance you get. This will help build trust and mutual respect, which will be critical to gaining their support if you must relay difficult or negative information about their child.

Circle Circle, Dot Dot, Now I Have My Cooties Shot

You have summoned the epic, begun building rapport, designed a Pinterest-perfect classroom, and the big day is finally here! The students are coming. While you are off to a good start, the real work of building a positive classroom culture is about to begin. Going back to the *Cooties*, before Clint Hadson, portrayed by Elijah Wood, ventures out into the student zombie horde to get a sugary snack from the teacher break room vending machine to save a diabetic kid (We told you to beware of break rooms!), one of the uninfected students looks at him and says, "Circle circle, dot dot, now you have a cooties shot," while motioning with her finger on his arm. Unfortunately, protecting your trench from cooties—or a zombie-producing virus—requires more strategizing than a childhood incantation or simply wishing for good vibes. Like a healthy and vibrant school culture, effective classroom management doesn't just happen; it's the end product of careful, strategic, and creative planning.

Part of that planning is recognizing that you and your students are going to be spending a great deal of time together over the course of a 180-day school year. Outside of their homes, your students will likely spend more time in the bunker than they will in any other place. At an average of seven hours of school each day, that's

> AT AN AVERAGE OF SEVEN HOURS OF SCHOOL EACH DAY, THAT'S 75,600 MINUTES. THINK ABOUT THAT FOR A MOMENT. AS TEACHERS, YOU HAVE 75,600 OPPORTUNITIES TO MAKE A DIFFERENCE IN THEIR LIVES.

75,600 minutes. Think about that for a moment. As teachers, you have 75,600 opportunities to make a difference in their lives.

One way to make a difference, even before day one, is to celebrate their individuality. All your students want to feel welcomed and valued, and it's important to start getting to know them long before you dive into content. You can begin to build rapport through team-building activities, questionnaires, asking them to write about themselves, design challenges, or leveraging video. We go deep into strategies and edtech tools to reach students personally and academically in Chapter 6 as part of our R.E.M.E.D.Y. approach to the apocalyptic classroom. While we list a few tools to help forge relationships, the possibilities are truly endless.

A good strategy is to identify a few edtech tools you plan on integrating throughout the year. Have students create personal artifacts, biographies, and timelines with these platforms. Having taught film, Savannah used iMovie to create a video about herself so her students could learn about her. After modeling the use of technology, students then created videos. This was not only a great way to assess where student skill levels were coming into the class and beginning an ipsative baseline, it also allowed her to get to know her students. Introducing new tools with fun subject matter allows students to focus on developing a new skill rather than new content, and from what we know about Spencer's theory of cognitive load, it is important not to overload students with too many new things at once.

Here is Savannah's ME video (project adapted from Don Goble's "I Am" assignment). drive.google.com/file/d/0B2nCLoAACqatMDJmbnQzbWZyM0E/view?usp=sharing

SET EXPECTATIONS EARLY

Classroom management is so much more than getting students to adhere to a set of rules. It is a culture of respect and high expectations you set with your students as soon as the year begins. If students don't play an active role in creating that culture and don't have a voice in setting classroom norms and expectations, they will not buy in. On the very first day of school, ask students what they need in order to feel safe in their learning environment and then decide together what expectations need to be in place in order to attain that classroom culture of respect where students can be who they are, and risk-taking is valued.

It's also vital that you set the bar high. Even the youngest children are extremely perceptive. The expectations you communicate to students have the capacity to become a self-fulfilling prophecy. In other words, students will rise (or fall) to whatever expectations you set for them, so expect students to be their best selves every day.

TRENCH PACTS

Instead of going over prescribed rules and procedures, coauthoring a trench pact with students provides the opportunity for students to become stakeholders in their classroom contracts and opens the floor for rich discussions around why certain rules are important. Having students sign the pact and posting it year-round in the room functions as an accountability reminder through the year. Classcraft, a gasified learning management system (LMS), has a hero pact that students sign before commencing in game play and creating their characters and teams. This exercise reinforces student accountability.

CREATE CONSISTENCY

Once you and your students set norms and expectations, make sure they are posted. I (Columbus) have also found it's a good idea to have norms for various classroom situations that can lend themselves to off-task behavior or conflicts; for example, many teachers assume students come in knowing how to collaborate. The truth is, many adults struggle with effective collaboration, so this skill needs to be explicitly taught, and it makes sense to have norms around this so everyone understands what is expected. I did this in my classroom when I realized some students were being left out, and some were taking over. As a class, my students came up with a set of norms surrounding effective collaboration, we filmed good examples and bad examples, and we posted these norms whenever collaboration was occurring, so expectations were always clear. I have seen teachers establish, post, and review situational norms for everything from putting away Chromebooks to walking in the hallway.

When these expectations are in place, regardless of the situation, make sure that you are consistent in enforcing them. If you set norms for collaboration, revisit those norms every time your students are expected to collaborate and hold them accountable for their behaviors. The same holds true for classroom expectations. Students need to be able to predict the consequences for their actions. If consequences and expectations are inconsistent, students will not know what to expect and thus will be more likely to act out. This will be frustrating for both you and them. Below are eight ways to be proactive with managing your trench.

8 Proactive Strategies for Managing the Horde (In No Particular Order)

Countless books have been written about classroom management strategies, but here are a few we think will be most beneficial:

1. Practice Routines and Transitions

It is not enough to tell them your expectations for routines and transitions; you have to show them. In the first few days of school, model procedures and practice them. Allow students to rate their performance and offer suggestions for how they can improve.

2. Praise Positive Behavior

This one speaks for itself. The more often you praise students and build them up, the more it will be reinforced that you value and care about them. This will go a long way in building up relationships and creating a warm, safe classroom culture of high expectations that is more likely to be free of infection.

3. Maintain Students' Dignity Always

There will be times when doling out consequences is unavoidable, and when this happens, it is crucial that you maintain a student's dignity in the process. Avoid humiliating students in front of their peers. It is very difficult for a student to make good choices when you amp up their emotions by embarrassing them in front of their friends. If they don't see a way out of the situation, they are likely to continue to escalate.

4. Offer Choices

As adults, there are times when certain tasks seem daunting for one reason or another, and we avoid them because sometimes we just can't even....The same goes for your students, which can lead to acting out and other avoidance behaviors. If you offer students choices on which tasks to complete or even how to show you what they have learned, they will be more engaged and more likely to follow expectations.

5. Use Proximity

Don't forget Teachingland Survival Rule #7 (Always Check the Back Seats). Move around your trench as you teach. Do you have a student who suddenly seems disengaged or is chatting with a friend? You don't have to say a word. Just walk over and stand next to them.

6. Craft Creative Attention Getters

Sometimes the same call-and-response techniques get old and tired. Try and switch these up and get students involved in helping you create new ones. As is the case with anything, if students are active participants in creating these, they are more likely to respond positively and appropriately; for example, whole-brain learning uses a set of verbal cues to transition students or grab attention such as a teacher saying, "Class, class," and students responding, "Yes, yes."

7. Model Empathy

We all have shortcomings. Maybe you have an acute fear of public speaking, or you tend to call out in faculty meetings. Perhaps you struggle to sit still for any length of time, or you have a hard time switching activities once you get in the zone. Share with students the things you struggle with and talk about how you manage your own idiosyncrasies. Be relatable and show your students the same empathy and compassion you want others to show you.

> BE RELATABLE AND SHOW YOUR STUDENTS THE SAME EMPATHY AND COMPASSION YOU WANT OTHERS TO SHOW YOU.

8. Collaborate with Students on Ways They Can Show You They Need Help

Many times when students act out in the classroom, it is because they have a need that is not being met. Work with students to come up with ways to show you that they need help when they are too embarrassed to ask for it or when it is not an appropriate time for them to tell you verbally. If you can help them meet their needs, they are more likely to engage appropriately and productively in the classroom environment. (Check out our backchannel strategy in Chapter 6.)

Trench Triage: Negative Nuggets

Even though you have put all these wonderful management strategies to work, there will be times when you will have to address individual unwelcome behaviors. Earlier in the chapter, we mentioned that while strategies can work to manage the horde as a whole, sometimes we can't plan for individual circumstances that arise: the independent contaminated nuggets thrown in our direction, like the one that turned students into zombies in the move *Cooties*. Check out our 6-pack of frequent misbehaviors and how to address them for trench tranquility.

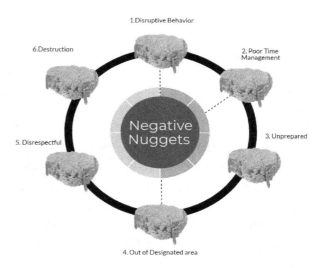

Trench Triage Traits

1. Disruptive Behavior
2. Poor Time Management
3. Unprepared
4. Out of Designated area
5. Disrespectful
6. Destruction

Negative Nuggets

The graphic above can be broken down into three main reasons for misbehavior: Disruption, Disengagement, and Distraction. From there we identify six common negative nuggets that occur, that, if not corrected, can spread quickly to the rest of the trench. In the table below, we list our solution sauce for solving some management issues.

BEHAVIOR	SOLUTION SAUCE
Disruptive Behavior	Offer choices, figure out if there is a need that is not being met and address it, allow the student an opportunity to leave the situation and calm down
Poor Time Management	Visual schedule, checklist, timer, preferential seating in front of a clock, frequent check-ins

Unprepared	Checklists, whiteboard with what students need to be prepared posted outside of the classroom, alternate (less-preferred) set of activities for students who aren't prepared
Out of Designated Area	Take away flexible seating privilege, visual boundaries (i.e., tape on floor to show student boundaries)
Disrespect of Staff and Peers	Figure out what need is not being met and address it, offer choices, allow the student an opportunity to leave the situation and calm down
Destruction of Property	Loss of item(s) that are being damaged, offer choices, allow the student an opportunity to leave the situation and calm down, when calm have the student participate in repairing the damage if feasible

Technology

In the classroom apocalypse, in addition to bringing learning back to life, we must make sure that students are keeping their technology alive during the school day as part of being prepared. With technology integrated more seamlessly than ever into trenches all over the world, it is important to address procedures regarding its use, storage, and treatment—including its charging. Usually school-wide or district policies address actual device use and online interactions, but what about how and when students charge their devices in your classroom? Access to power outlets in older buildings hasn't quite caught up to 1:1 environments. In my (Savannah) trench, students were expected to arrive with devices charged and ready to rock and roll. Charging times were permitted before and after school, at lunch, and during break. Any classroom became a charging station, and stations were also located around the school. If your students are heavily using devices, you may want to consider what technology procedures are needed to make your trench run smoothly.

Additionally, if the technology that students are using remains in the classroom and does not go home with them, what are the procedures for returning the technology? Is there a space or charging cart they are required to return devices to? In my school (Savannah), we have a set of Oculus Go headsets. The headsets hold a short charge of about two hours, so it is imperative after each class use that they return the headset and the controller to a charging station. The controllers only function with the specific headset they came with, so initially there was a problem with class time being wasted on pairing headsets and controllers. To prevent this loss of instructional time, I labeled the headset and controller with a number system to easily identify which one matched. You may want to create a value system or naming system for your tech and have students sign out devices to keep them accountable for taking care of technology and following use policies.

Tales from the Trenches

@AmandaFoxSTEM
Savannah
c. 2013–2014

Managing a body of faculty is not quite the same as managing a classroom, and in my career, I have seen various approaches to school-wide management. During the 2013–2014 school year, I accepted a new position as a sixth-grade social studies teacher at the first STEM school in Savannah, previously having taught my first full year in rural Bryan County as an English teacher. I found myself in a new school, teaching a new subject, surrounded by new people, and it has been one of the most amazing experiences personally, creatively, and professionally while at the same time the most daunting.

At this new place, my dreams of having the freedom to try new innovative practices were not only encouraged, failure was not viewed as an ending point or fatal; instead, my principal, Peter Ulrich, prompted us to return to the drawing board, constructively highlighting the pieces of my work that held merit and discarding approaches that didn't quite fit our collective school vision or just didn't work. He proved to be one of the most valuable resources I have had in my career: A leader who led by encouraging us to try new things. A "yes" man! A principal who didn't micromanage but trusted us as professionals to do right by our students, stepping online to intervene to lift us up after a misstep—a leader who led through inspiring. It was liberating.

One of the things Ulrich said that has stuck with me after all these years is, "Dreamers should all be together." He hired a staff of dreamers that challenged the status quo; further, he invited us to the table to sit in on the interviews. After all, we would be the ones elbow-to-elbow in the trenches together! His encouragement was accompanied by trust, and failure was greeted with compassion instead of the all-too-often finger pointing and consequences.

Because of the common finger-pointing scenario, teachers sometimes are afraid to admit to failure. We have societal pressures of delivering perfect instruction partnered with fallacies of being the expert in the room. We are expected to be innovative while finding a balance between traditional methodologies so our teaching is still recognizable to the adults in society from when they were in school. Fortunately, "O Captain! My Captain!" has his eyes set on the future and tomorrow's classroom and recognizes the process of change. Ulrich trusted me as a professional who was well equipped to lead tomorrow's generation while remembering that I'm a person at the same time.

Depending on who your leader is, teaching can be empowering or dehumanizing. As much as we like to flaunt "Teaching Is My Superpower" T-shirts, it can also feel like the weakness in the armor when we do deal with failure, usually privately. This helps whom?

Working under a leader who inspires, acknowledges we are all human, and creates a culture where failure is OK has helped me become that same kind of leader for my students. Principals and other school leaders have the power to model the kind of heroes teachers can be for their students. They have the power to set the tone for the entire building, which includes the tone within individual teachers' classrooms. Classrooms that invite students to the table to take part in learning design. Classrooms that are compassionate and recognize our students are human and prone to failure. Classrooms where teachers inspire, let students fail, and then parachute in to pick them back up so their love of learning doesn't crash into a failing end. Failure is not finite, and micromanaging is not leading.

I am the teacher I am today because I had a Blue-Tape Leader (refer to Chapter 4) constantly pushing boundaries and constraints. He never micromanaged my classroom. He believed in me. He led by letting me lead and was more concerned with helping me get to where I was going. True leaders raise people up. And when you raise people up, you create a community that makes the impossible possible. And I became that Blue-Tape Leader for my students.

Ken Doyle
@historymrd
Natick
c. 2012

My first teaching job was as a permanent substitute for an eighth-grade social studies class in April 1999. I was hired to replace a veteran teacher who was given early retirement. It was the week after April vacation, and as I was to start this new experience, I was told the kids were miserable and had no desire. What I learned in those brief three months and my reflection afterward taught me more than any course I have ever taken.

I had decided a year and half earlier to leave the private sector and follow my passion: working with kids. As I started this journey in 1999, I found that I was at a great disadvantage with the students. Despite the fact that they knew who I was and what my responsibilities were, teaching just didn't seem to flow. The students were hostile and incredibly reluctant participants in their own education. No doubt some of this was due to the lack of structure they were forced to endure for much of the previous year. Upon reflection, however, I came to the realization that what I lacked with the students was just as important as structure and routines. I lacked any sort of relationship with these kids. I was viewed as an outsider, and the students didn't respond to me academically as a result.

Since then I have made great strides in building strong relationships with the students I have had the pleasure to work with every day. I greet each student at the door, and I make an effort to get to know their outside interests. If the student is in the play, I make an effort to attend. If a student plays a sport, I try to attend at least one game. Those gestures, which really take just a little bit of my time, pay off huge dividends with the students. They know you care through your actions. It doesn't have to be attending after-school functions; a conversation about the weekend can go a long way in building the relationships some kids crave. Of course, I can't reach every kid, but I do

THEY KNOW YOU CARE THROUGH YOUR ACTIONS.

reach some. While building those relationships, it's also important to understand, whether you like it or not, you could be filling a void in that child's life. How you react to that is up to you. That became very clear to me five years ago with one student in particular.

I had a student who came to my eighth-grade class with a reputation of being difficult, reluctant, and incredibly disruptive. Her father had passed away two years earlier after a completely avoidable accident. Her mother, although she wanted what was best for her daughter, struggled to consistently manage her behavior. I communicated with this student in a positive manner on a daily basis. I talked to her about her outside interests. I never raised my voice to her, but I always held her accountable. I soon realized that I was filling the role she needed. Eventually, she would excel in the eighth grade. She made honor roll and because of this, realized she could be successful. The pain she suffered still has not gone away, but she is now a college student and looking forward.

I understand that I am a small part in the success of my students, and every adult in their life plays a role. The importance of relationships is underscored by the fact that I still meet with my former students, guiding them in some of life's decisions after high school and college. I know my role will always be as their teacher, and with that comes a responsibility. I will always see them as my students, and none of this would be possible if I hadn't made the effort to build relationships when they were only in the eighth grade. After twenty years, I'm still teaching in the same school in the eighth grade and thankful for the opportunity to experience so much joy in my professional life.

@TomParr4
Dallas
c. 2006

Survival. That was all I could think about in my first year as a middle-school teacher. It didn't matter that I had experience working with kids. It didn't matter that I had previously found success in my field before deciding to teach. Survival was all I could think about or hope for, and I wish I could say that I succeeded. But that was not what happened to me and so many other teachers before me and after. We simply don't make it. The walls close in, the horde catches up, and you find yourself yelling in your head like the all-too-loud audience member in a horror movie, "Don't do that!" "It's right behind you!" "Don't go in there alone!"

I lasted three years, which is two years below the average. But that was not the end of my story. Three years later, I would get another chance. A chance to right the wrongs I committed in my first attempt. I was stronger, wiser, and much humbler.

I had to realize where I had made my first mistake. Classroom management. I owned *The First Days of School* by Wong and read most of it, but I wasn't prepared for the students. Most of these kids came from families where everyone worked. They worked hard and all the time. These kids went home and worked in their families' businesses or had duties at home that I never dreamt of dealing with at the age of twenty-five, let alone at the ripe age of thirteen. They were cooking, cleaning, and raising their younger siblings. So when I would show up and talk about being silly and putting on plays, all I got back were blank stares.

They didn't care about Greek history. They didn't want to know about the intricacies of design or play development—but they did want to play. About six months before the end of my first teaching job, I finally had a moment of enlightenment. I stopped caring so much about how to manage the perfect classroom and started to do things differently.

I wish I could say it was a planned moment of genius, but I was just grasping at straws. As my class was once again out of control and not listening to me, I sat down at my desk. I grabbed a small hand puppet (a bear) from a prop drawer. I put it on my hand. I slowly took off my tie and wrapped the tie around the bear forming a sort of kimono look. I then started talking to it. Slowly the class stopped talking to one another and began wondering just what in the world I was doing. Eventually the room went silent as "Samurai Teddy" and I began to have a conversation.

I'm sure many of them thought I had finally lost my mind, but I didn't care. I had their attention. Teddy and I talked about the importance of stories. Why every story holds an importance. A passing of knowledge from one to another. When class was finally over, I put Teddy back in the drawer and the students begged to have him come visit again. The same students that previously had been too cool to participate in class wanted to know more.

One class told another, and by the end of the week, Teddy and I had taught what turned out to be the best week of teaching in my life. I don't think it was the lesson; it was the puppet. It was the idea of play. The idea that someone could completely believe the puppet was real. As I indicated before, these kids didn't have the luxury of growing up with *Mr. Rogers* and *Sesame Street*, so when the moment to be kids presented itself, they bought in. They were hungry for more. More ways to tell their stories. They created their own puppets, began designing and building costumes, and eventually wrote fully realized scripts to share their hopes and fears. These puppets freed them.

Over the last few months of school, Teddy would only make appearances about once or twice a week, but each time the classes would sit, ask questions, and generally love class. We would even have guests come into the class to be interviewed by Teddy.

It may seem weird and nontraditional, but it worked. It freed me too. I was able to think outside the box. My classes and student relations emerged from stagnancy and blossomed into new life.

When I was given the opportunity to teach again three years later, I didn't need the puppet. But I used every lesson he had taught me. Connect to the students. Find a way—any way—to allow them to dream, to participate, and to appreciate a good story. The classroom no longer had to be managed; instead, I was the guide on a path to discovery.

> CONNECT TO THE STUDENTS. FIND A WAY—ANY WAY— TO ALLOW THEM TO DREAM, TO PARTICIPATE, AND TO APPRECIATE A GOOD STORY.

Tom Wolken
Louisville
c. 2019

Do you feel like rapid advancements in classroom robotics leave you with zombie technologies? They move, respond to stimulus but don't get your heart beating. When so-called past prime technology has much to offer, using it in your classroom is not a dead end. Why? Coding fundamentals are common across most platforms, languages, and even device generations. This is my story of finding and raising an army of undead robots using the tech that was handed down to me. Sometimes, our budgets don't allow for the best and newest, but we don't always need the latest robots or tech to teach relevant skills.

I recently took a position teaching robotics and coding. The first order of business was inventorying the school's robotics resources. Like a shuffling slack-jawed hoard, several Lego Mindstorms NXT kits were lurking in a closet. Their beams, wires, and brains scattered among several boxes like so many limbs and tendons. I could hear their moaning. No, wait that was me. Were they infecting me with their malaise? Codeveloped with MIT and released nearly a decade ago, Lego Mindstorms NXT set the standard for educational robots. Yes, mine had been buried and were, literally, a little grimy. Why were they still a relevant teaching tool?

Similar to zombies in their simplicity, I began to contemplate the value of raising them from dead:

1. They don't require lots of resources—No PC or tablet costs. The NXT brain, also call the brick, has a stand-alone programming system built into it.

2. They're not complicated—Programming is icon based, written directly on the brick's LCD display and intuitive for all ages.

3. Their senses are still keen—Sensors are robust, easily connected and little hands friendly.

4. They just keep going—Mature firmware. You won't waste time chasing and downloading upgrades. It just works.

5. They focus on one thing—Class time is programming centric because building the robot takes less than 30 minutes.

What can you do with it? Just, introduce the sequencing, debugging, fundamental coding structures, and sensor inputs and outputs. Not to mention the creativity, problem-solving, and cooperative learning! A zombie has a simple brain; pursuing flesh, eating flesh, repeat. Similarly, the NXT brick programming is limited to five commands. As a teaching platform, that brevity is a strength. Sequencing is what a student does to make sure the program executes in the correct order; i.e. the robot must drive forward before turning left. While five commands doesn't sound like a lot, it's my experience that it's enough for students to make sequencing errors. On the other hand, with so few commands, a little experimentation gets it right.

That brings us to debugging or identifying errors in code. Debugging is not haphazard, it's a process. Students review their short list of commands and map them to the robot behavior. I found it helps to pair students. One reads the commands aloud while the other acts as the robot. As the 'robot' physically moves thru the five commands, errors quickly become evident. Encourage a mistake-friendly environment because it develops their skills and confidence.

Students use conditional and looping structures while coding the NXT brain. The brick presents if…then statements as sensor input code blocks. The program execution pauses until the sensor condition is true; i.e. If the touch sensor is pressed then play a sound. In every NXT program the fifth and final block is either Stop or Loop. Students choose to end the program after running once or run continuously. Ending with Loop emphasizes the importance of proper sequencing. Students will tell you the only thing cooler than making a robot "go" is programming it to react to "stuff." With its variety of sensor inputs, programming the NXT won't disappoint. There are light, color, sound, touch, and ultrasonic sensors. Sensors return easy to understand values like distance and color names. Like the limited number of code blocks, the short list of the return values let students focus on best practices for sensors; which sensor is most suitable for a task, appropriate placement on the robot chassis and validating the returned values.

NXT programs use sound and motion as outputs. There are block commands that play one or two notes and blocks that control motor direction and duration. Use these limited choices to teach students how outputs perform two essential functions. Foremost, providing user feedback; i.e. the user knows the touch sensor was pressed because a sound was played. Secondly, helping debug programs; i.e. where is the programming stopping before it reaches the play sound block?

Unlike the "real" undead, these zombie bots have sharp senses and a very fine brain. They are a great addition to your robotics classroom. And they won't bite your students!

Check out chapter 3 resources page online for a link to the robot programming guide Tom used.

BRAIN STRETCHERS

1. What edtech tools do you plan on using during the year, and how can you leverage them in the first few days of school to learn about your students?

2. What are your non-negotiables for students in terms of their behavior?

3. Does your organization have classroom management strategies implemented on a school-wide basis? If not could you implement some?

4. How do you plan to hold students accountable to your expectations?

5. What are three ways you plan to establish rapport with students?

6. What are three ways you plan to establish rapport with families?

Visit TeachinglandTheBook.com to access the links and resources in this chapter.

Scan me

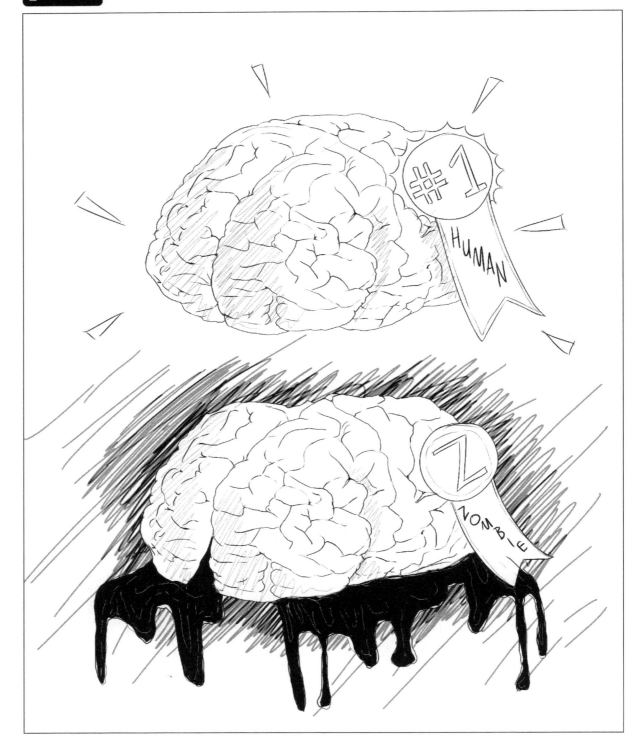

CHAPTER 4
The Walking Read: Arm Yourself with Learning Theory and Pedagogy

You still don't get it. None of you do! We know what needs to be done and we do it. We're the ones who live. You! You just...plan and hesitate. You wish things weren't what they are. Well you wanna live? You want this place standing? Your way of doing things is gone...
—Rick Grimes, *The Walking Dead*

As teachers discuss best practices through attending conferences and professional development training, there are those that swear by traditional pedagogy vis learning theory and theorists, while others are more inclined to shrug off theory and jump straight into emphasizing practice and hands- on training. When this happens a gap occurs between modern practice, and how it evolved out of learning theory and cognitive science. As teachers, we know what needs to be done, and we do it, but sometimes we don't give thought to the theories that birthed our modern way of doing things. The above quote from Rick Grimes really resonates well within education.

In the *Walking Dead*, Grimes says "Your way of doing things is gone...,' and while it may be true in a zombie apocalypse, the only way to survive in the classroom apocalypse is to be able to link modern practice back to learning theory and cognitive science to become part of the Teachingland Walking Read. While both are dealing with brains, the science behind the way we learn is an important guide to the way we practice and teach. In this chapter we talk about the pedagogical landscape today, and how we can create e a symbiotic relationship between the era of rapid technology development and integration (modern components), with traditional, old-school theory. Essentially, we hope to equip you with resources and theorists to explore the "how we learn" so when it translates into how you teach, you have a better understanding of why you are electing to utilize the strategies and edtech tools you do.

Pedagogy

Effective cognitive theories and innovative pedagogical frameworks combined with effective use of technology are the best weapons you have in the Classroom Apocalypse. Teachingland Survival Rule #4 is about the best way to protect your brain. To do that, you must understand how the brains of the walking "edudead" function. More importantly, you must know how to keep the brains of the living engaged in authentic ways that do not lead to zombieism. Vaccinations are always better than triage!

We have compiled a list of Ole Pedagogy Players (O.P.P.s) of the apocalypse, some of whom you might have studied in your teacher-preparation programs or in professional (dead)velopment. Whether that was last year or a decade ago, when you've got the O.P.P.s in your back pocket, and you're using their theories to inform your practice, you can bet that you are equipped with one of the primary components of zombie prevention and survival. Our Ole Pedagogy Players stat cards will give you a quick strategy check when time is of the essence. To dig deeper, download the entire deck from our website. (This is highly recommended for preservice teachers!) We have presented our O.P.P.s as playing cards and used the comicbook app to create them. We are also slowly augmenting them with digital content! Check out our chapter 4 resource page online for more information. You can even try this strategy with your students when introducing new concepts, historical figures, or scientists.

Ole Pedagogy Players

These thought leaders, cognitive scientists, and educational philosophers have contributed greatly to modern pedagogy and therefore deserve recognition and further exploration. These are sixteen learning theorists who have influenced our practice. Don't see your favorite listed? Create your own stat card and give your O.P.P. a shout-out on Twitter using #teachingland #O.P.P. hashtag. We will add it to our website. Now, without further *ado*, meet the Ole Pedagogy Players:

John Dewey	Experiential Learning, Teacher Facilitator
Seymour Papert	Digital Making, LEGO Mindstorms, and CS education for all
Lev Vygotsky	Social constructs and learning through community
Jean Piaget	Schemas, Learning Development Stages
Marc Prensky	Digital Natives, Digital Immigrants, Gaming
William Glasser	Choice Theory (What a person wants or needs)
Maria Montessori	Individualized Education
Margaret Bancroft	Special Education
Abraham Maslow	Maslow's Hierarchy of Needs
Benjamin Bloom	Bloom's Taxonomy (six levels of complexity)
Howard Gardner	Multiple Intelligences
Jerome Bruner	Three Modes of Representation
B.F. Skinner	Behaviorism and Operant Conditioning
John Sweller	Cognitive Load
Charlotte Mason	Home Education and "living books"
Madeline Hunter	Instructional Theory-into-Practice Model

Check out our website resources for Chapter 4 for a downloadable link to our augmented O.P.P. playing cards.

A Pedagogical Stagnation

We believe the nation's educational system has for several years now existed *between para-digms* or in a time of pedagogical stagnation. Simply put, our pedagogy—the ways we teach and instruct and the ways we think about teaching and instruction—has failed to keep up with our technological innovations, contributing greatly to the current Classroom Apocalypse. Consider John Dewey and the other O.P.P.s—what would they say if they woke up in one of today's classrooms? In some ways, not much has changed, but the technological landscape has moved light years ahead of Dewey's time. That said, cognitive research from his generation paved the way for today's innovations. Bottom line? Far too many teachers and educational leaders are reluctant to evolve and embrace change; furthermore, too few educators under-stand how to take relevant frameworks from yesterday and pair them with twenty-first-century tools to prepare learners for tomorrow's demands. Why is that? We believe many teachers and educational leaders are reluctant to disrupt what feels familiar, measurable, and safe even if that's what our students need to be successful in this new connected society. They suffer from generational pedagogy—a disconnected approach to engaging and reaching youth in which they teach in the same way they were taught.

In all fairness, what are teachers to do when all their hand-me-down strategies are torn and tattered, and they're struggling to survive a widespread and brutal Classroom Apocalypse? We believe our dear friend, Brett Salakas, co-founder of #AussieEd, just might be on track to a solution. Brett is always talking about creativity, and he loves to discuss the work of Sir Ken Robinson—specifically his ideas for the new paradigm surrounding twenty-first-century educa-tion. Robinson maintains, "The answer is not to standardise education but to personalise and customise it to the needs of each child and community. There is no alternative!" In his keynote speech at the 2018 Future of Tech Education Conference, Robinson spoke about how today's educational system "rewards conformity and compliance, but life is marked by diversity and collaboration."

Unfortunately, the need to survive our infected bunkers has left little time for collabo-ration, personalization, or diversity. Politicians, lawmakers, and government institutions in cahoots with testing monopolies have provided enough red tape to quarantine this epoch of educators through trickle-down zombienomics. In short, they have profited off the creation of unnecessary accountability products such as assessments, drill-and-practice workbooks, testing platforms, and test prep materials.

But the future is not entirely bleak. There are some brave souls out there who are fight-ing back and are getting good outcomes through innovation, creativity, and student-centered approaches. In classrooms where the educator makes the paradigm shift from all-knowing giver of knowledge to a facilitator-of-learning role while leveraging creativity, design thinking, and student agency to meet systemic requirements, hopelessness is replaced with hope. Columbus has a few teachers in her building who are allowing students to choose from a variety of learning activities to demonstrate understanding and build their skills. By putting students in the driver's seat, they are building student agency and seeing stronger outcomes because students are invested in their learning. These teachers are part of a grassroots movement that is disrupting education from the bottom up. What is their weapon? Creativity, perspective, and understanding that teaching is an art, and the arts are fueled by passion. And passion is more contagious than any zombie virus.

Mindset: Insane in the Membrane, Insane in the Brain

> *Often, a school is your best bet—perhaps not for education but certainly for protection from an undead attack.*
> —Max Brooks, *The Zombie Survival Guide*

When you think of the walking dead, what images come to mind? For us, it's abandoned buildings full of chain-locked double doors barely holding back a writhing mass of ravenous zombies as a few gray and decaying hands slip through the cracks.

The zombie hands trying to escape are synonymous with teachers that feel bound inside the box of standards and pacing guides. When these teachers allow them to be the sole driver of their instruction instead of viewing them as a baseline for what they should be teaching, it is easy to feel trapped. Though they long to get out, they feel chained to content, burdened by time constraints, and maybe don't know where to start. The scenario also speaks to being locked into tradition or the generational pedagogy mentioned earlier. The rest of the world is locked out, and they run crypts where time does not seem to faze their instruction that is perfectly embalmed in tradition. Sometimes our mindset—not the things we blame—can be what is driving us crazy. This scenario speaks to what Carol Dweck would call a *fixed* mindset.

When teachers view standards and pacing guides as *what* they should be teaching and leverage creativity and innovative strategies to make learning come alive, they are able to break the chains in the above scenario and throw open the doors for students. These teachers exhibit qualities of what Dweck would call a *growth* mindset. When teachers are demonstrating this type of mindset, they become creative problem solvers and do not allow themselves or their students to be restrained by any new mandate or constraint, and they don't view standards or lessons as barriers to innovation.

Instead of mindsets being a binary, where a person is either one or the other (we would all like to believe we have a growth mindset all the time), we see mindset as a spectrum. We believe teachers can fall in various places along this continuum depending on the situation. Perhaps when it comes to reinforcing reading strategies, a teacher has a variety of authentic and innovative activities that leverage student voice and choice to showcase learning. When it comes to working on reading fluency, however, that same teacher may believe that the only way for students to demonstrate their learning is to do repeated readings 1:1 at the teacher table.

The important thing to remember here is that no one has a growth mindset about everything all the time, but the goal is to always keep growing and working on your mindset to keep from getting trapped. Being a lifelong learner, being flexible, and always striving to improve are tenants of what we call Blue-Tape Thinking, which we cover in the next section.

Pedagogical Mindset and the Paradigm Shift Spectrum

In the Introduction, we slammed government policy for sucking the creativity out of classrooms all over America. But if we are being completely honest, the new, hefty load of accountability and testing is only part of the problem, and we would be doing a disservice to students if we didn't explore all the conditions that have contributed to the current outbreak. Equally harmful are some of the ways teachers and schools deal with trickle-down zombienomics. Some educators respond with Red-Tape Thinking, while others respond with Blue-Tape Thinking. As you read ahead, consider what is Red-Tape/Blue-Tape thinking, and where do you think you fall in the spectrum?

Our Classroom Apocalypse's Paradigm Shift Spectrum looks at Red-Tape and Blue-Tape thinking within the construct of a color spectrum. It shifts some of the responsibility of the problems within the educational system back to the teacher and is not meant to add more hopelessness through shared responsibility; rather, it's meant to liberate teachers from their shackles and lies primarily in perspectives.

The concept of Red-Tape Thinking is borrowed from the idiom of red tape—the excess of bureaucracy and rigid formalities or rules. Red-Tape thinkers view constraints (standards, pacing guides, and formalities or accountability pieces of the system) as barriers that immobilize them. We have both done extensive professional development with teachers on embedding innovative strategies into instruction, and too many times we have heard, "I don't have enough time for that," or, "How can I give time to the kids to complete those projects with all the content I have to cover?" This is the perfect example of Red-Tape Thinking. It's using the antiquated education system as an excuse to not change it, and even worse, believing the excuses.

On the other hand, Blue-Tape thinkers understand standards, pacing guides, and policies as WHAT they must teach and use their creativity and innovative strategies to meet these demands in a way that is meaningful for students. They are not hindered but empowered to use the art of innovative pedagogy to engage students in the content. One thing we notice about the teachers and schools that are thriving during the classroom apocalypse is the creativity harnessed when approaching content and lesson delivery. These teachers also tend to put students in charge of their learning through strategies such as making, critical-thinking tasks, design thinking, and problem-based learning as well.

What is the differentiator between these two? Perspective. Grit. Perseverance, and the ability to problem-solve.

The Color Purple

In between these two extremes, are those who are trying and fall into varying degrees of the color purple. I think most of us fall in this shade. They are experimenting. They are clawing their way out of the building to the world outside and slowly coming back to life through masterful teaching. They feel increasingly empowered as they creep from Red-Tape Thinking to varying shades of purples and ultimately blue!

Why Blue Tape? Because blue tape is the tape of Innovators. It is the tape that maker's don. It is the tape of painters, and it should be symbolic of the creative mindset and perspective with which we encourage our students to view the world. It is the tape of the classroom apocalypse. If there is one thing that is certain, it is that change is imminent. Today's barriers might not be the red tape of tomorrow, but if our perspectives and mindsets are flexible, creative, and viewing failure as a launch pad, we can find applicable solutions and are empowered to change—instead of being resigned to what is "out of our hands" or restricted by red tape.

Check out the Paradigm Shift Spectrum on our website. We have listed the two extremes but previously mentioned the varying degrees. Try plotting where you think you are along this spectrum on various goals you are trying to address. Are you a deep shade of purple? Lilac? Periwinkle? Most of us will find ourselves in some sort of shade of purple, save the dreamers, left-field thinkers, change agents, and leaders. They don a brilliant blue! This is a great activity to do with faculty or teams when approaching a new year, new technology integration, or really anything you want faculty to introspective about. You can find a copy of our Paradigm shift Spectrum on our website under Chapter 4 resources.

Teachingland Frameworks Abridged Version

Theorists and theories alone are not enough to survive the classroom apocalypse. They are instead the Rick Grimes' (the protagonist from *The Walking Dead*) in the land of the undead that guide us through the inner workings of the ways students learn. Theories alone can't offer a solution or cure to what is ailing out nation. From these theories, frameworks are born. Frameworks then have to be put into place, and in the twenty-first century are often facilitated by tech tools. The perfect trifecta to crafting high-quality instructional practices. Consider frameworks the strategic plan that guides us in the trenches and the technology tools the vehicles that drive them.

Depending on which bunker or trench you find yourself in, the frameworks you use may be top down, and you may be required to use a preselected one due to the nature of your school. Or you may find yourself in the position where you can choose your own framework. Either way, other factors, such as access to technology (in some cases), content area, and your own personal teaching style may also weigh in on your decision. And you don't need to use just one! There is no one cure in the way of a framework. Utilizing a variety of approaches, methods, and tech tools can be the most effective way to keep learning exciting and engaging for your students. Trying new things and new ways to engage students can also keep us passionate about teaching and learning as well. The craft is the combination of approaches that are perfectly tailored for the students that are in your room! Imagine each of these components as a lock on a lockbox that requires a combination code. Each piece you select contributes to unlocking learning!

Below, we have briefly summarized some popular frameworks and strategies, and we have included fun apocalyptic scenarios of them in action! There are links to external resources to explore if you choose to go deeper down any of these rabbit holes.

FRAMEWORK: Design Thinking

AERIAL RECON OVERVIEW: This is a nonlinear human approach to learning and problem-solving that involves identifying a problem, ideating, and designing potential solutions. In some cases it means creating a product, improving the design, and presenting solutions.

ZOMBIE APOCALYPSE SCENARIO EXAMPLE: Design a prototype for a tool that is going to help you survive the zombie apocalypse.

A GREAT PLACE TO START: •The Teachingland Design Cycle (Chapter 5)

•Stanford's D.School Framework dschool.stanford.edu/resources-collections/a-virtual-crash-course-in-design-thinking

•Within DBC Books: *LAUNCH*, John Spencer and A. J. Juliani

FRAMEWORK: STEM/STEAM

AERIAL RECON OVERVIEW: Aside from the obvious acronym for science, technology, engineering, art, and math (omit art for STEM), STEM is a pedagogy that involves an authentic, transdisciplinary project or problem-based approach to instruction. In a STEM/STEAM school, nothing is siloed, creating rich, engaging, twenty-first-century experiences for students.

ZOMBIE APOCALYPSE SCENARIO EXAMPLE: Research, plan, and design a way to grow a hydroponic garden to feed all the people in your bunker.

A GREAT PLACE TO START: •Check out these schools that are making it happen!

•Elementary Schools: Herbert Mills STEM and Summit STEM in Reynoldsburg, Ohio

•Middle School: The STEM Academy, Savannah, GA

•High School: L&N STEM Academy, Knoxville, TN, eSTEM & HS2 Academy in Reynoldsburg, Ohio

•They recommend these resources: stemx.us

FRAMEWORK: Maker Framework

AERIAL RECON OVERVIEW: The maker framework is a head-hands-heart approach to problem-based and project-based learning that is often collaborative and focuses on learning experiences as a method for solving authentic problems.

ZOMBIE APOCALYPSE SCENARIO EXAMPLE: In the zombie apocalypse, electricity is hard to come by, and cold food can be gross. Using the materials provided, make a solar oven to make survival a little more bearable.

A GREAT PLACE TO START: •Look at the work of Rafranz Davis and Colleen Graves

•Within DBCI Books: *LAUNCH*, John Spencer and A. J. Juliani spencerauthor.com

FRAMEWORK: Mobile Learning

AERIAL RECON OVERVIEW: Mobile learning is a pedagogical approach in which all instruction and interaction takes place online and can be accessed by the student via computer or mobile device.

ZOMBIE APOCALYPSE SCENARIO EXAMPLE: After students left the trenches, the teacher launched an in-depth conversation on geography, terrain, and the best pathways to travel, using Twitter.

A GREAT PLACE TO START: Carl Hooker, *The Mobile Learning Mindset*

FRAMEWORK: Problem-Based Learning

AERIAL RECON OVERVIEW: Problem-based learning is a student-centered approach to instruction and assessment that allows students to leverage the content they have learned in the classroom to design solutions to relevant, real-world problems. Problem-based learning makes the biggest impact when it is transdisciplinary, involves a high risk for failure, and a potential for multiple solutions.

ZOMBIE APOCALYPSE SCENARIO EXAMPLE: Are our bunker doors impenetrable? If not, how can you design a better door to withstand zombie hordes?

Leveraging measurement, research, and engineering and design standards, students use the design cycle to prototype and share their solution to this problem.

A GREAT PLACE TO START: Within DBC Books: John Spencer and A.J. Juliani, *Empower* stempblcycle.weebly.com

FRAMEWORK: Flipped Learning

AERIAL RECON OVERVIEW: Flipped learning is a pedagogical strategy where students are introduced to instructional content outside of the classroom, usually online. The real significance of the flipped classroom is how it transforms class time.

ZOMBIE APOCALYPSE SCENARIO EXAMPLE: Outside of the trench, students watch videos on how a compass works and functions. When they return to class the following day, they spend class time building one.

A GREAT PLACE TO START: •Look at the work of Jon Bergman, Aaron Sams, and Lodge McCammon

•Within DBC Books: *Ditch that Textbook*

FRAMEWORK: Personalized Learning

AERIAL RECON OVERVIEW: Personalized learning involves tailoring all aspects of pedagogy, instruction, and assessment to meet the needs of individual students.

ZOMBIE APOCALYPSE SCENARIO EXAMPLE: *Using voice and choice:* Students select presentation tools and choose to research postapocalyptic career choices based on parallels to the medieval period. *Path and pace:* Students choose a specific scientific advancement to research to inform their own prototypes. They work at their own pace to complete assignments.

A GREAT PLACE TO START: Within DBC Books: Alice Keeler, *50 Things to Go Further with Google Classroom* and *Google Apps for Littles* Joy Kirr, *Shift This*

FRAMEWORK: Blended Learning

AERIAL RECON OVERVIEW: Blended learning is an instructional strategy in which face-to-face instruction is combined with online learning.

ZOMBIE APOCALYPSE SCENARIO EXAMPLE: After a lesson on circuits to reestablish electricity in the bunker, students go online to a circuit simulator and practice creating circuits.

A GREAT PLACE TO START: •The Blended Learning Universe curated by the Christensen Institute

•Within DBC Books: *Ditch that Textbook*

FRAMEWORK: Inquiry-Based Learning

AERIAL RECON OVERVIEW: Inquiry-based Learning is a pedagogical approach that involves sparking curiosity through empowering students to pose their own questions about a topic, research solutions, and present what they have learned.

ZOMBIE APOCALYPSE SCENARIO EXAMPLE: A zombie outbreak has occurred. Where did it start? Who was patient zero? Students will formulate a hypothesis about how they think this particular virus was transmitted after reviewing interviews and anecdotes from witnesses.

A GREAT PLACE TO START: •Trevor MacKenzie, *Dive into Inquiry: Amplify Learning and Empower Student Voice (Volume 1)*

•Trevor MacKenzie and Rebecca Bathurst-Hunt, *Inquiry Mindset: Nurturing the Dreams, Wonders, and Curiosities of Our Youngest Learners (Volume 2)*

• Within DBC Books: John Spencer and A.J. Juliani, *Empower*

FRAMEWORK: Project-Based Learning

AERIAL RECON OVERVIEW: Project-based learning, like problem-based learning, is a student-centered approach to instruction and assessment that allows students to create real-world, relevant projects that are rooted in content.

ZOMBIE APOCALYPSE SCENARIO EXAMPLE: During the zombie apocalypse, food may be scarce, and being prepared is vital to survival. Leveraging nutrition standards, students must stock a pantry with a variety of foods that will not only keep, but will also make up a balanced diet so everyone in the trench stays healthy. They can create a model of their pantry, create a poster, or present it digitally.

A GREAT PLACE TO START: •The Buck Institute, bie.org

•Ross Cooper and Erin Murphy, *Hacking Project Based Learning: 10 Easy Steps to PBL and Inquiry in the Classroom (Hack Learning Series) (Volume 9)*

•A.J. Juliani, *The PBL Playbook: A Step-by-Step Guide to Actually Doing Project-Based Learning*

FRAMEWORK: Story-Centered PBL

AERIAL RECON OVERVIEW: Story-centered, problem-based learning presents students with curricular content in the form of problems contextualized within a plot or story to increase engagement and student motivation.

ZOMBIE APOCALYPSE SCENARIO EXAMPLE: The first outbreak for the zombie apocalypse has happened, and as an employee of the CDC, it is your job to inform the public of what to do if they come into contact with the infected. How should citizens respond to this outbreak, and what should they do to avoid infection?

Create a response protocol and pick a tool to communicate your ideas.

A GREAT PLACE TO START: •Look at The STEM Academy in Savannah, Georgia

FRAMEWORK: Game-Based Learning

AERIAL RECON OVERVIEW: Game-based learning, not to be confused with gamification, provides students with opportunities to learn content through high-tech, low-tech, or no-tech games.

ZOMBIE APOCALYPSE SCENARIO EXAMPLE: In an effort to understand how the zombie apocalypse could reach pandemic proportions, students study the yellow fever outbreak of 1793. The students play an online game like Plague, by Ndemic Creations, to understand how epidemics of diseases occur.

A GREAT PLACE TO START: •Lee Sheldon, *The Multiplayer Classroom*

•Within DBC Books:
Michael Matera, *Explore Like a Pirate: Gamification and Game-Inspired Course Design to Engage, Enrich and Elevate Your Learners*

Tales from the Trenches

@AmandaFoxSTEM
Savannah
c. 2013

In 2013, I decided to explore the flipped-learning model and began creating flipped social studies videos. If you haven't checked out Lodge McCammon, he is a fantastic resource for how to flip with no fuss. He subscribes to the Keep it Simple, Stupid (K.I.S.S.) philosophy, and I started using some of his kinesthetic lectures that aligned with my curriculum before venturing into making my own flipped whiteboard videos. We danced our way through sixth-grade history, learning about the five themes of geography and even World War I and World War II. At the end of the unit, my students did a flash mob in the cafeteria. (Some of my colleagues weren't too thrilled about this.) There is a chance you will get some backlash when you are trying something new and innovative, but hey, I didn't care! Using the flipped method freed up class time and allowed students to collaboratively work on creating their own artifacts. My planned destination for the end of the school year was to find myself sitting on an arsenal of flipped lectures that covered all sixth-grade social studies like a content queen; however, I ended up somewhere completely different.

As the year progressed, I learned about an opportunity to try out a beta gamified curriculum software for my classroom. One thing I can't stress enough is to seek out opportunity. Because of the anomaly of the creative environment I got to work in, I applied without second thought to have

> ONE THING I CAN'T STRESS ENOUGH IS TO SEEK OUT OPPORTUNITY.

my class participate in a beta group for a game called *Historia*—a game that highlighted the interconnectivity of all subjects through the fictional recreation of societies throughout history, including boss-battle simulations against the actual society of the time. (I know, it's a mouthful, right? And that description doesn't do it justice!) To my surprise, we were accepted.

NARRATIVE INQUIRY AND GAMIFICATION THROUGH *HISTORIA*

This was a turning point for me, and the opportunity pushed me to grow as an educator in ways I did not expect. It inspired me to do something a little different with my videos, which ultimately led to a change in perspective of how to flip my classroom and mostly in the amazing way my students responded. Instead of making whiteboard videos that just delivered facts and information, I began to create narratives involving time travel and the future.

Through a fictional storyline and green-screen videos, I elicited participation in the story crafting from students. We were studying the ancient civilization of Sumer, and in order to be part of the story, they had to research the society, historical context, and the contributions to civilization based on five pillars. I would leave them with a piece of the story and hook, then ask them to complete it; for example, I said, "If we are traveling back to ancient Sumer, are we time traveling or are we going into an alternate world, like in *The Matrix*? How do we get there?" They would fabricate rich stories and weave in actual elements from history. They had to know what the civilization was like when we arrived! The next day, we would share our ideas, and the best ones would become part of the classroom narrative we were crafting as a community.

Engagement soared, and my students were writing intricate and historically accurate plots. They even started going ahead of the content I assigned and independently researching parts of the civilization that would strengthen their stories because they wanted their voice to be included in the collective piece. They were becoming self-guided learners. The old saying, "You won't understand unless you walk a mile in their shoes," applied perfectly here. This game had my students doing that, and I don't really know what kind of shoes Sumerians wore, but I bet my students could tell you!

We use the words *authentic* and *personalized* a lot in the education world—authentic assessment, authentic engagement, personalized learning—but in this case, it totally fit. My students authentically engaged the content and personalized their learning based on interests and the types of stories they were telling. I provided the pace and path, but they were provided their choice and their voice. Combining gamification of *Historia*, narrative inquiry, and historical fiction proved to be a success. Through storytelling the students brought 3,000 B.C. to life and came to understand the societal pillars of that time—with a little help from their iPad.

I delivered the stories through videos. To start off, I made the videos after school. Within a few weeks, the students were making their own, and we were also collaborating on films in class! Check out this snippet below!

At the beginning of 2013, my goal was to sit on a mountain of grade-level curriculum videos I had made. My adventure into the flipped classroom led me down a rabbit hole, and like Alice, it opened up new worlds of adventures for my students and myself. I realized flipped lectures do not always have to be vehicles of instruction created by me. They can be creative, collaborative adventures that allow students to time travel to another epoch. I thought my flipped lectures made my classroom innovative, but until I changed the vehicle from a Prius to a DeLorean by traveling back in time, I was just delivering facts. By giving students a voice, a part, a "histopod" to communicate with the past, I was able to truly transform my classroom to a place where students were encouraged to learn fearlessly *with* me—not *from* me.

So instead of being at the top of a mountain at the end of that year, I was at the bottom of another one: a new journey of crafting a story-centered PBL framework—the one that you read about in this chapter. This was where it all started. Get used to mountain bases, my friend, because it is every year of teaching—if you are doing it right. Every year you grow. Push the envelope. You arrive at the end of a year realizing how much more you still need to learn.

Like Sisyphus, I start my journey of rolling a rock up the hill each August for it to only roll back down in May. The 2013–2014 school year, my journey went as far back as the Sumerians and back to the future.

Maybe in the next narrative of inquiry videos we will travel to the future, and by encouraging students to envision tomorrow, we will solve some of the problems of today.

BRAIN STRETCHERS

1. Which O.P.P. do you most closely identify with? Why?

2. Where do you fall on the Paradigm Shift Spectrum? Are you a Red-Tape Thinker or a Blue-Tape Thinker? Somewhere in between? Why do you think so?

3. Where does the majority of your bunker fall on the Paradigm Shift Spectrum?

4. How can you impact change in a bunker full of Red-Tape Thinkers?

5. What frameworks have you used in your classroom? What frameworks do you want to use in the future?

Visit TeachinglandTheBook.com
to access the links and resources
in this chapter.

CHAPTER 5
Preppers: Doomsday Planning and Preparation

Often, a school is your best bet–perhaps not for education but certainly for protection from an undead attack.
—Max Brooks, *The Zombie Survival Guide*

Doomsday Preppers: What's in Your Bug-Out Bag?

National Geographic has a reality TV show that follows American citizens and documents their preparation for the end of the world...as we know it. The show is called *Doomsday Preppers*. In this show, ordinary people go to many lengths to make sure they are fully prepared in case the unimaginable happens. As each episode documents the efforts of different preppers, it becomes obvious that each person has their own strategy and approach to making sure they have everything they need. They literally leave no stone unturned! Some throw a ton of money at the anticipated problems, while other are more DIY in their solutions. The show is actually a great resource for teachers looking to implement design thinking through making, prob-lem-based learning, and projects rooted in STEM. Survival is always an engaging theme!

Preparing to design and teach a lesson can be very similar to prepping for the end of the world, and it could very well feel like the end of the world if your lesson fizzles. There is so much to consider: *What theorist does your teaching style most align with? What framework will you use? What standards are covered? How can you creatively engage your students to want to learn the content? What technology can you integrate? What materials do you need? If you are teaching a unit, how can you make it transdisciplinary and rooted in a real-world problem? What activities can you facilitate? What will students create? What assessment tools should you incorporate?*

Historically, we have both been in schools where lesson plans are due a week at a time or even more! Sometimes these documents can be ten to twenty pages long and require minute details. There goes the weekend! We have also found ourselves in situations where we haven't been held accountable for lesson planning. Neither situation is ideal. While we believe you should be fully prepared to teach a class and should spend adequate time designing activities for the entire duration of class, writing a ten-page document is ridiculous unless you are writing to share your successes with peers or creating content you hope to be replicable. After a lesson plan is implemented and deemed successful, documenting steps and strategies that worked is a good habit and a contribution to the profession overall. These are also great artifacts to submit in teacher portfolios for future employment opportunities or to include for evaluators on formal walk-through/evaluation days.

Though the curriculum-pacing map and lesson template you use will vary depending on the district or school you are in, we are huge advocates of one-page planners. Considering both of our backgrounds (administrator and teacher and instructional designer), we used these perspectives to collaborate on a one-page lesson plan template to guide your planning process that connects theory to practice for a couple of reasons.

Teacher Zombification via burnout through lesson plan writing is a legit problem we have experienced personally in K–12, and most of the teachers we asked on social media agreed.

Most planning templates are antiquated and teacher centric. If we are truly embracing the instructional paradigm shift, lesson templates should reflect the paradigm shift from teacher-centered classrooms to student-centered classrooms. We believe in this so much with all our essence that we have a tagline for the template: One-Page Sage: Share the Stage! When I (Savannah) taught at The STEM Academy, my principal invited me to the decision-making table, empowering me to share my voice! It should be no different with students! While you can't negotiate red-tape items such as standards, all the blue-tape planning and creativity can be communal.

Whether you turn in paper lesson plans or prefer to use Google Drive, Google Sheets, or a digital planner, our Bug-Out Bag includes all the components necessary (and a few pieces that are unnecessary but super fun!) for success. Now we are going to break it down and explain why we included each element.

Unpacking the Teachingland Bug-Out Lesson: Our One-Page Sage

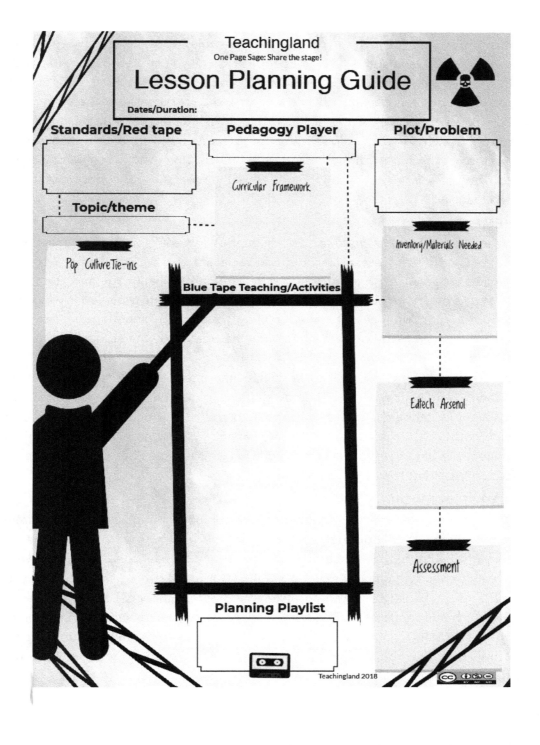

Standards/Red Tape

No matter where you teach, the content that you are responsible for is likely communicated in the form of standards. Remember the rule, "It's a marathon unless it's a sprint; no, It's a sprint as long as a marathon"? Well, when we came up with this rule, this is what we were referring to. When you sit down and look at the vast topics and standards you are responsible for teaching in 170 days, it can feel overwhelming, and the urgency to begin covering all standards as quickly as we can takes over. But this is a marathon, and we need to pace ourselves and give focus to each step that completes the journey around the curricular track! Remember that these standards are the starting line for each lesson, and once the baton is handed to you, the whistle is blown, and your door is closed, how you teach these things is up to you! Don't let the standards become red tape and hold you back from embracing the true art of the profession. The *how* we teach it—with passion and creativity!

TOPIC/THEME

Bundling standards together under a topic or theme can be a great start to covering curricular ground; for example, if you teach sixth-grade social studies, the five themes of geography may be bundled together. In literature, you may teach figurative language and literary devices through the theme of a poetry unit. In most cases, pacing guides are provided in which the year is mapped out for you, but in case it is not, creating your own pacing map that bundles standards under themes can help build thematic units that resonate with students. And provided pacing guides are not always the best plan. If you have a better way to teach the curriculum, it is okay to challenge it and adapt it to best meet the needs of your students. Often these guides are canned and handed down. The best guides are created by you and your colleagues, as they will leverage standards in a way that speak to your strengths and passions as teachers. Planning with colleagues to account for (STEM) transdisciplinary connections and reinforcing the interconnectivity of content areas is more difficult, but research has shown the benefits to this approach of planning topic and themes.

CURRICULAR FRAMEWORK

We covered frameworks earlier in Chapter 4. If the curriculum map is the *what* we are teaching, the framework is not only our perspective or approach to how we communicate content but how students are going to interact, engage, create, and be evaluated. The frameworks you choose will vary depending on your content, goal, and favored strategies; additionally, frameworks aren't pure or absolute and can be mixed for greatest impact. The flipped framework, for example, can be integrated to a PBL framework or blended framework. Within frameworks there are various models to implementation, and how you teach PBL will vary from the teacher in the trench next to you. You can both be right! It is whatever works. Your trench, your rules. Remember?

PEDAGOGY PLAYER

You remember the O.P.P.s? Yeah, these guys are important! They are the Rick Grimeses (*The Walking Dead*) or the Gerry Lanes (*World War Z*). Their theories are still relevant and should guide planning and instruction, so we think it's important to be able to connect their theories to frameworks and activities. You don't have to pick a pedagogy player first, but you should make sure you can identify which theorists your strategies align with and that they are rooted in good pedagogy. There may even be overlap! Our list is not comprehensive, and there are amazing, modern O.P.P.s that are contributing to education all the time!

BLUE-TAPE TEACHING/ACTIVITIES

And now the fun part! Leveraging creative strategies to design engaging activities for students! We call this blue-tape teaching, because as you read in Chapter 3, blue tape is the tape of makers, painters, and creators—and teachers! Combining your knowledge of theories, frameworks, and technologies intersects, and it's time to use this in conjunction with standards (the what) to design student-centered activities for learning to occur. One of the characteristics of blue tape is that it is pulled up after you are done. This tape should be pulled up every year, and lessons and activities should be evaluated and modified to make sure they are still impactful, relevant, and appropriate for your current students—which are different from last year's! Don't find yourself the victim of a different type of red tape...the teacher who uses the same lesson plan without adaptation year after year... .

This is also the part of the lesson plan where students should be invited stakeholders, and our R.E.M.E.D.Y. Model comes into play! Students should have voice and choice in the M.E. part of the model: make and evaluate. When we let students choose how they want to show what they know either through deciding what tech tools they will use or what they make, we are also giving them the power to determine how they will be evaluated. I have also witnessed an increase in student accountability and ownership when letting them design their own rubrics. While certain skills and content should be present in their work and within the rubric, designing diagnostic tools together goes a long way in developing student agency. It leaves them yearning for the next project and dreaming up new ways to show what they know! Learning is way more fun when you have some say in the matter!

DATE/DURATION

How long do you think it will take to teach this lesson? Our R.E.M.E.D.Y. Model was designed with PBL in mind and can last anywhere from a day to nine weeks. It depends on the number activities, research, and artifacts students are expected to produce. Maybe you are a doing a one-day challenge? Maybe you are planning an ongoing project for a longer duration. Estimating realistic timelines is important from the marathon perspective to ensure all content is covered. Allow time and plan opportunities for students to revisit work; for example: A nine-week unit shouldn't have work turned in for grading in the ninth week. Allow time for students to implement feedback and promote the iterative process.

INVENTORY/MATERIALS NEEDED

This component is pretty straightforward. What technology, materials, and items do you need to pull this lesson off? Think of it as a lesson-plan checklist or a shopping list, depending on the activity. Materials can also get expensive, so if completing activities that require a grocery-store run, you can crowdsource these things from parents and the community. For more on crowdsourcing, read the next section.

EDTECH ARSENAL

After you have determined your standards, topic, framework, and model, it's time to evaluate what tech tools you can use to complement and facilitate learning. While new tech tools can be flashy and fun, selecting the right tools should be based on the devices your students are using and how they interact with the tool; for example, you could pick edtech tools that foster collaboration and communication, such as Padlet, Flipgrid, or important  twenty-first-century skills. Choosing tools that also streamline assessment, give immediate feedback, and take the pulse of the class can also add value and save you time in the long run!

Use this checklist to help decide if tech is enhancing your lesson.
Does it...
- Add value?
- Save time?
- Facilitate creativity?
- Contribute to a classroom knowledge base?
- Promote collaboration?
- Provide opportunity for critical thinking?
- Demystify the learning process?

ASSESSMENT

Assessment is a complicated component of instructional design, so there is an entire chapter dedicated to it. To sum up assessment succinctly, you need to have formative and summative assessments embedded throughout a unit. Remember Rule #6, Double Tap? You need to check students' understanding of learning as you go so you don't leave anyone in the backseat (Rule #7). There is a reason these rules are back to back! We have a whole chapter on assessment. Skip ahead to Chapter 7 to learn all about assessment strategies.

PLOT/PROBLEM

When we say plot, we mean storytelling components of the lesson. Plot is included as a disconnected box, because it doesn't necessarily need to be used every time, but storytelling is a powerful way to share information. There is research that shows that the brain retains information longer when told within the context of a story as opposed to relaying facts and information out of context. It can be particularly powerful for problem-based learning, and a great tactic is to launch a problem through carefully crafted scenarios. (Read more about problem-based learning in Chapter 6.)

POP CULTURE TIE-INS

We are big fans of using pop culture, such as movies, music, and trends to reach and engage learners. We added pop culture tie-ins to the instructional design template to make sure you are thinking about ways to relate content back to modern media that students may be into. Whether it is a fad, such as the dab, the Harlem Shake, or a sitcom or movie, this strategy embraces activating prior knowledge, or schemas…John Dewey anyone? Find a pop culture tie-in, you find an in! Our whole book is based on one! Zombies!

PLANNING PLAYLIST

This one is just for you—-though you may choose to share it with your students if it relates directly back to the content. When I write, think, read, or just exist, I have a playlist for it. Lesson planning is no different. It's how I connect things and how I mentally prepare myself for what is to come. What songs can you find that get you pumped about teaching a topic? Maybe you aren't pumped about the topic and just need to get through it! Play a motivational mantra that is going to get you pumped to deliver the best lesson you can when you walk through those doors. Passion and delivery are more contagious than *zombieism*. When you have your morning coffee, instead of sipping in silence, consider playing a daily anthem to get into the zone.

R.E.M.E.D.Y.—The Student-Centered Design Piece

It can be difficult to learn where to begin synthesizing theory, frameworks, and technology in a seamless system that promotes student growth. Revisiting Teachingland Survival Rule #5, Bare Hands, reminds us that worksheets and canned digital curriculum usually fail to engage students, especially if they are the only type of assignment in your trench. Using their bare hands to build, make, and create facilitates deeper learner experiences.

The materials that are far more likely to engage your students the most are built by you (and them). This is a major part of the zombie R.E.M.E.D.Y., our acronym for zombie prevention and transformation in your learning culture. We are going to unpack the acronym and arm you with our strategy to incorporate student needs into your lesson-design process.

After reading Chapter 4, you are up to snuff on learning theory and might even have a few O.P.P.s in your pocket for a quick stat check to remind you of cognitive ideology and the business of brains. We have also just covered our Bug-Out Lesson that provides a snapshot of what is going on. You are now officially going to be let into the secret sauce to classroom apocalypse survival. Welcome to the Teachingland R.E.M.E.D.Y. Model and planning guide!

The R.E.M.E.D.Y. guide embodies the student-centered activities that can be designed by the teacher and what we hope is eventually a shared responsibility between the teacher and students. This way, learning is truly personalized. Let's go into what each letter stands for!

R IS FOR REACH

Every year the students in your classroom leave and are replaced with a new horde. How will you reach them? How will you learn about who they are and where they are academically? Are your students suffering from symptoms of zombieism? Or are they coming to you this year prepared and warm-blooded? Understanding the learning histories and interests of your students goes a long way in relationship building and lesson design.

E IS FOR ENGAGE

When you know who is walking into your classroom every day, you are better equipped to engage them on an academic and personal level. This should really start with open house. The information you learn about your students' personal interests and academic competencies should be used as a guide when designing lessons that will capture their attention. Then do whatever it takes to make sure your students are sucked into the lesson. After all, we wrote an entire book comparing the first years of teaching to a zombie apocalypse to engage you!

M IS FOR MAKE

Not only should you be making your own curriculum and crafting personalized lessons for your students, students should be making things with their bare hands. Whether it is a website, a 3D model, a VR space, or even an essay, it is important that students become creators of content, not just consumers. By the way, if all your students make the same exact thing and you find that you have twenty-seven of the same outcomes, all you created is a recipe. What they make should include pieces of themselves and reflect their uniqueness.

E IS FOR EVALUATE

Evaluation is a necessary component of our R.E.M.E.D.Y. Model. To know if students are thriving, you must evaluate where they are in their learning journey; additionally, students should be equipped with the skills to evaluate themselves. They should also understand that an Innovator's work is never done and should be taught an iterative process through which they learn to improve upon their work. When students create a product that meets and even exceeds expectations, make sure to celebrate and share their successes!

D IS FOR DEMYSTIFY

Your content delivery and curricular structure should be somewhat predictable and tacit to students. Predictability gets a bad rap, but initially you should make the process of designing, making, and problem-solving transparent so you can demystify learning so students can transfer those skills into other aspects of their lives beyond the classroom. This takes students beyond what they should learn and teaches them how to learn, a far more valuable skill that students will put to good use beyond your time with them. To quote Dr. Seuss, "It's better to know how to learn than to know." Spontaneity has its place in the classroom, too, but that should come after students have an understanding of structure and expectations.

The best way to demystify learning is to pick a student-design cycle and post it in your classroom for students to reference. Use the language consistently when referencing where students are in their learning process. A good cycle uses language and wording that is relevant in most learning situations whether the lesson or unit is problem-based, project-based, STEM/STEAM, or whatever nomenclature is the current fad; for example, in my (Columbus) school, the design cycle, which includes the word improve, is deeply embedded in the culture and instruction. One day during standardized testing, I had to remind a teacher to lower her voice when she was talking loudly to another teacher in the hallway. Later that day, I received this text: "Sorry I don't have an indoor voice. #improve." Below is the engineering and design process we use.

Y IS FOR YEARN

By the end of implementing the R.E.M.E.D.Y. Model, your students should be yearning for the next thing you throw at them. There isn't really any magic way to get students to yearn in isolation, and this step is the payoff and culmination of the previous steps at work. If you arrive here and students aren't passionate and ignited by the tasks you assigned them, experiment and try new ways to engage and challenge. In time, you should have students who are autonomous and self-guided with a warm-blooded love of learning.

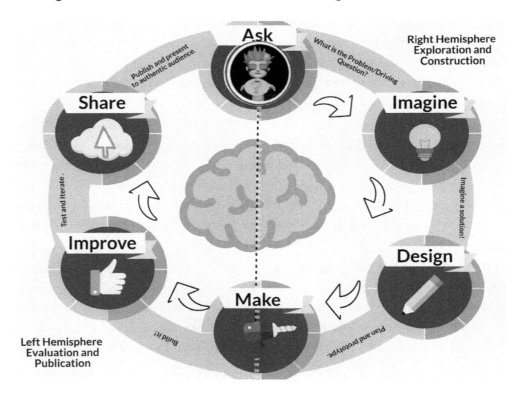

More on R.E.M.E.D.Y.

We consider R.E.M.E.D.Y. to be instrumental to engaging the brains of young learners. As the R.E.M.E.D.Y. Model graphic on the previous page reveals, this is a cyclical process. The journey is not necessarily meant to be a straight progression through the phases. The activities you design to reach and engage students might not reach everyone. In that case, you might need to revisit and revise earlier strategies that were not effective. Similar to evaluation, this phase of the R.E.M.E.D.Y. cycle should be repeated! Learning is continuous, and projects are not finite. A due date should not necessarily mark the end of the project, and students should be encouraged to improve upon their work and apply feedback. Learners should be permitted to go through the iterative process of revision and re-evaluation as many times as needed.

Some schools and districts have their own regimented planning templates they require teachers to strictly adhere to, while others offer flexibility. Both scenarios can leave a teacher feeling overwhelmed. You are either locked into a box with a template that might not fit what you actually do in the classroom, or you are swimming in a sea of options. What do you do? Skip ahead to Tales from the Trenches to read an anecdote from an administrator and a teacher about lesson planning.

While understanding the R.E.M.E.D.Y model is key to designing your overall classroom instruction to reach and engage students (while placing importance on student agency), it is also important to consider what your day-to-day lesson planning should look like. The rest of the chapter will support you in designing the perfect Bug-Out Bag (Lesson), so the possibility of doomsday happening in your classroom is significantly reduced! In order to take the stress out of planning, we include a Bug-Out Lesson template to accompany the R.E.M.E.D.Y. Model. We offer practical advice on how to implement this model in your classroom while scaffolding students to take charge of their learning and shift them into the role of personalizing their learning and empowering them with student agency.

HOW DOES OUR BUG-OUT LESSON: ONE-PAGE SAGE TEMPLATE WORK WITH THE R.E.M.E.D.Y. MODEL?

Reducing the lesson-plan template to one page is possible because we removed what is traditionally the activities and strategies section into a second document: the R.E.M.E.D.Y. Model. The R.E.M.E.D.Y. Model is removed to remind teachers that this part of the planning process should eventually include students. When beginning to implement this model and lesson plan, we recommend completing the R.E.M.E.D.Y. portion in the first few assignments to model expectations to students. As students show interest in personalizing their learning experiences, the R.E.M.E.D.Y. Model provides a design construct that involves students in choosing how to show what they know, which directly corresponds to how they will be evaluated. This scaffolds and supports students in taking ownership of the Make and Evaluate part of the cycle for students and increases student agency. This puts students at the center of learning and empowers them through choice and design!

When using our R.E.M.E.D.Y model you can also use our Chapter 6 Teachingland Monster Tech Table to pair tech tools with strategies that work. This ensures that technology isn't being used for the sake of technology and ask teachers to contemplate why and how they are using it in regard to learning objectives and outcomes. Students can use our Monster Tech Table, too!

For more information on how to use this framework to put students in charge of their learning, read Chapter 6, and check out our website for resources on how to use the R.E.M.E.D.Y. Model effectively.

THE BEST LAID PLANS OF MICE AND MEN OFTEN GET AMBUSHED BY ZOMBIES?

Even though you have included all there is to consider about your lesson, and you've over-planned and accounted for everything, the wild card is always there: the students. The themes and strategies you taught last year may not work for your current group due to collective and individual interests. It's important to be flexible, adaptable, and responsive when implementing

A note on adapting—*Savannah went to teach a lesson on stop-motion animation and had planned on having students design a new product and create an animation pitch. It just happened to be October 21, 2015. Date not ringing a bell? It was "Back to the Future Day"! I ditched my planned pitch and immediately channeled my content through this theme. It was kismet. Sometimes all the planning in the world will go out the window when a better strategy surfaces. The student response was absolutely amazing. They made gifs and animations featuring technology advancements from the movie and even created some of their own!*

A note on modifying—Modifying on an individual basis may work as well. When I taught at the STEM Academy in Savannah, I struggled to get one student to turn in work on time— if at all! After looking to remedy the problem, I decided to utilize the Reach strategy on a personal level and find out more about his

interests. I was teaching sixth-grade social studies, and we were on our Canada unit. Students were exploring Canada's environmental issues and human environmental interaction. I had made a pretty cool student-choice assessment playlist that allowed students to pick projects that appealed to them. Nothing on the menu was speaking to him. Come to find out, the student loved Minecraft! I asked him if he could demonstrate what he learned by building something for me in the sandbox game. His imagination just came to life, and he started rambling off how he could apply content within the construct of the game. I was amazed at this new side I was seeing! Sometimes we must remember that our lessons can box some students in while liberating others. If our strategy and approach is not working for everyone, we need to go back to the beginning of the R.E.M.E.D.Y. Model and reattempt "Reach" in order to better engage them.

lessons. For help with this, refer back to Rule #9: Break it up, and shake it off! If your lesson plan is obviously flopping, it's okay to ditch the plans or adapt them even in the moment! You have probably ditched a book that wasn't all you hoped it would be or homework assignments that didn't seem relevant. You probably have thrown out that lunch that you ordered that wasn't any good, and you wouldn't dare continue to watch the series on Netflix once it jumps the shark, so why continue with lessons that aren't effective? The best strategy to adapt is to break your lesson plan apart. Keep the goals and objectives but reframe your approach or activities. Sometimes this even needs to happen on the fly. Let your students lead you. They will never steer you wrong, and this can diffuse a potential outbreak in your trench.

What about the "shake it off" part? Well... the reality of being a teacher is that sometimes our attempts will fail. We are human. And even the best laid plans of mice and men are often ambushed by...zombies? We just need to make sure that our failures mean something by learning from them, reflecting, and revising our approaches. So the lesson didn't work out. It's not the end of the world. It's just the classroom apocalypse, but if you don't put your skin in the game, you won't have any wins either.

CANADA'S ASSESSMENT PLAYLIST

Check out our resource page for Chapter 6 to see an iTunes themed choice menu for Canada's Environmental Issues.

In my (Columbus) bunker, during a teacher evaluation this year, I saw a very risky (but fantastic) lesson on mindfulness and conflict resolution during morning meeting. The teacher was prepared, and everything was going great. The students practiced meditation and then were role-playing various conflict resolution strategies when a little guy—who just needs to be moving and doing something all the time—stood up and started beating on his chest Tarzan style. She could have let that throw her and derail her lesson; instead, she took a (very quick) moment, processed what was happening, shook it off, and called him over to hold the poster she was using to explain the strategy they were using. He immediately got back on track, and so did her lesson.

Failure has become such a big part of the educational conversation, and rightly so. Talking about failure opens up the opportunity to discuss how we assess student success and what it means to be successful. It's critical for students to see you recover when things don't quite work out the way you planned and that you provide space for them to fail fast, fail forward, and try again armed with what they have learned from their experience.

Tales from the Trenches

Deanna Fanning
Macon
c. 2015

Learning and teaching have always been my passion. I have been teaching for sixteen years. Four years ago, I was hired to teach at a STEM school, and at the time I didn't realize my learning and teaching style would blend so beautifully into that format. But that's exactly what happened. We are now a STEAM school, and with the art component added to the science, technology, engineering, and math curriculum, I feel as if I am the proverbial Brer Rabbit flung into the briar patch! Creativity has always been embedded into my lesson plans, but now it is officially recognized. I am a research teacher, and it is my goal to lead students to their personal learning experiences.

Two of my favorite units cultivate every facet of STEAM pedagogy and allow students the joy of discovery as a learning tool. I have found that learning by doing as well as researching has proved most beneficial for my students.

Imagine you are a forensic scientist called in to work on a super-secret mission. You have heard talk that a life-sustaining planet has been discovered. You did not realize, however, that two renowned scientists had furtively superseded any of the colonization teams. You learn during debriefing that the spacecraft that took this duo to the planet to conduct field work and analyze the living conditions had returned to earth and crash landed on the school's campus. Skeletal remains are found in five distinct locations around the campus. This of course coincides with teaching five research classes.

This is how students are introduced to the lesson. Teams are organized, and students assume the role of forensic scientists and head out into the field to secure the site and create a quadrant grid in order to document where each bone is found. Students carefully dig and brush the area when remains are located. Photographs are taken, and an artist creates a detailed drawing of each bone. The bones are gently removed and returned to the lab where each disarticulated bone is identified and reassembled on a lab table. Once the skeleton has been rearranged properly according to its bodily placement, the forensic scientists determine the gender, race, approximate age, and height of the person to whom the bones once belonged. They explore the remains for any clue to cause of death. At this point, that cause is inconclusive. The next lesson revolves around mysterious diary pages that were found near the wreckage. After consulting with the philanthropist who spearheaded the newly discovered planet's colonization, it is determined that these diary pages do indeed belong to one of the scientists on that mission. The students also learn that the two scientists that were assigned to this mission were a famous husband-and-wife scientific team. The remains on the table have been determined to be male and that of the husband. The forensic scientists take on new roles as epidemiologists in order to determine the cause of death of this renowned scientist. After painstakingly returning the pages to their proper order, the epidemiologists scour the diary pages, seeking clues.

Intensive research ensues, and the epidemiologists must defend their diagnosis with documented research that coincides with the symptoms preceding the scientist's death. Each team of scientists presents their findings to a board (the other teams in the class), and a discussion is held in order to determine correctness of diagnosis and if additional research is needed. Once the correct diagnosis is discovered, the students report their findings to the mission's leader. This is how I chose to teach human anatomy and physiology to a group of seventh-grade students. Every day, students were anxious to learn more and get started with their own discovery of learning! They even wanted to write a sequel to the diary pages to tell about what happened to the female scientist who stayed behind on the distant and uncharted planet.

Teaching the ecological web of life brought me around to the small yet infinitely essential honeybee. Students were given the task of imagining a world in which bees no longer existed. Field research was conducted by having students visit a local beekeeper and supplier of local honey. Students also attended an exhibition at one of our local museums that looked at the importance of pollinators and the chain of life that benefits from and is affected by these tiny creatures. Upon our return, students were allowed freedom of choice to exemplify their position on the necessity of honeybees in our world. Extensive research as well as field notes and interviews were utilized to create documentary or PSA videos, children's books, short stories, games, and artistic representations. The students presented their creations, practicing their voice as an expert in the field to an audience of colleagues. The response and excitement as well as the discovery of the importance of every creature in the web of life led the students to request additional studies in ecology. The students designed their ensuing lesson that led to the production of educational materials and aids about our biological footprints and how humans affect the living world around us. Not every lesson concludes with a clamoring to further their studies; however, engaging every student and allowing for their self-discovery in learning is what inspires me to continue to seek new and exciting ways to instill in my students a love of learning each and every day!

Alexis Buton
@MissButon
Westerville
c. 2017

What they say is true—you don't know what you don't know. This was the case for me during my first year of teaching. I was hired to teach fourth-grade math two days before the school year started. To say it was a whirlwind would be an understatement. I was introduced to my team, who assured me they would help with anything I needed, which was wonderful. The only problem was that I didn't have any clue what I needed.

As the school year started I had so many questions, but as a first-year teacher, I didn't want to be put down for asking about something so intuitive. There are things they don't explicitly teach you in college. How do you actually plan a lesson for more than just one day or one unit? How do you know when and what to teach? How do you know when it's time to move on? These were all questions I had but was too afraid to ask. However, not asking these questions was like standing on a sinking ship. Soon enough, my head was going under and I didn't know what to do. I needed help, starting with lesson planning.

Help was presented in the way of the most incredible district math coach. We talked through all the things I didn't know that I didn't know. We talked about different ways to teach and assess, and how crucial it was to spiral review. I finally got into a routine, and things started to look up. The year ended and my classroom had some kind of structure.

Going into my second year, I knew I couldn't make that mistake again. I changed my grade level and had new teammates. I felt like it was an opportunity to start fresh. I had a new perspective and decided I was going to make more of an effort to talk to my team to make sure we were on the same page. Having the least amount of experience put me in a place to learn from anything and everyone. My team was full of different strengths, and learning from everyone's strengths helped me to piece together my own routines and plans. My new teammates taught me how to meaningfully assess students and how to pace lessons so that my students were effectively engaged and learning.

Once I prioritized my lesson plans so that each of my students' needs were being met, my classroom was a much happier place with more learning and fewer behavior problems!

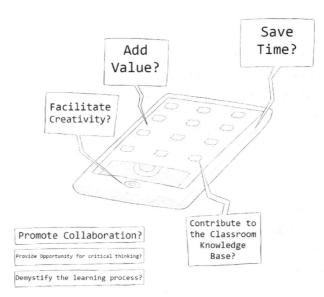

Add Value?

Save Time?

Facilitate Creativity?

Promote Collaboration?

Provide Opportunity for critical thinking?

Demystify the learning process?

Contribute to the Classroom Knowledge Base?

BRAIN STRETCHERS

1. What tools and strategies do you use in your trench to counter the classroom apocalypse?

2. How can you use the R.E.M.E.D.Y cycle in your trench?

3. Can you explain how the R.E.M.E.D.Y cycle works with the Bug-Out Lesson?

4. How do you cope when your best laid plans get ambushed by zombies?

PART 2
Fighting the Plague: Diagnosing and Resurrecting the Dead

CHAPTER 6

iZombie: Zombie Zips and Recipes from the Personalized Pantry

My need to feed on brains is weird, but how many people can say that satisfying their munchies could potentially help solve a murder case? This is my contribution to society. I'm just a fake, psychic zombie trying to do her part.
—Liv Moore, *iZombie*, "Brother, Can You Spare a Brain?"

In the popular CW sitcom *iZombie*, the protagonist, Olivia Moore, is a medical resident-turned-zombie. Eating brains keeps her from going full into zombie mode, so to keep her humanity intact—and ensure a continuous supply of brains—she takes a job at the coroner's office. What Liv finds out—and becomes the basic plot of every episode—is that she can see the memories, inclinations, past experiences, and motivations of the people whose brains she eats. Literally filled with their knowledge, she uses this complex side effect to solve crimes and make amends on behalf of the dead.

As teachers, it is also our responsibility to gain insight into the motivations, interests, and prior experiences of our students to inform our lessons to maximize engagement and learning. Fortunately, we can reach students by probing and stretching—not eating—their brains!

We have broken this chapter section into the following categories:

- Low Tech: Zombie Zips (ZBL)
- Hi-Tech: App-etizers and Bytes.
- Hi-Tech PBL
- Personalized Pantry: Leaving Learning Ajar
- PBJ: Adding Problems to the Jam

Low tech Zombie Zips utilize Teachingland Survival Rules #5 and #11: Bare Hands and Ziploc Bags! While Ziploc bags may not have made the final cut for the movie *Zombieland*, we can't get enough of them in Teachingland! We call them Zombie Zips because in less than an hour's time, students can build and create with items in the bag following our problem-based learning design framework. Using Zombie Zips stimulates the brains of your students and gets their creative juices flowing! We know what it feels like to be in survival mode, so we got creative with our design challenges that are standard aligned. We provide you with ten to get started, as well as a blank template to create your own (check our website for the blank template).

Our hi-tech section includes the Teachingland Monster Tech Table. It unpacks each letter of the R.E.M.E.D.Y. Model and suggests strategies and over eighty edtech tool to use for littles, middles, and bigs. When paired with our R.E.M.E.D.Y. template, you can design hi-tech learning experiences for students that aligned to strategies.

Which brings us to our hi-tech PBL section. Here we give a few examples of how the problem-based learning framework can be used with tech tools, like cospaces for digital projects.

Next, our personalized pantry strategy is all about leaving learning ajar, which you may find an uncanny *(ba-dum-tss)* solution to ensuring students have voice and choice when it comes to project design and planning.

Last, but not least, we discuss problem-based learning in a project-based world, and how to add problem-based elements to your lesson.

We hope you find this chapter useful and can implement its strategies immediately in order to become the Liv Moore of your classroom and solve the case of how to reach, each individual student and make learning personal!

Remember: You can access the examples and resources mentioned in this chapter by scanning the QR code on page 120 or by visiting TeachinglandTheBook.com.

Low Tech: Zombie Zips

Our Zombie Zips are low-tech design challenges that encourage students to create solutions while thinking critically, communicating with peers, and collaborating through problem-solving. They come in sandwich size, quart size, and gallons of goodness depending on the materials in the bags. In addition to low tech, we have tried to keep zip costs close to zilch. We have included ten zombie-based learning (PBL with a zombie/survival theme) challenges and a Teachingland Student Design Process Journal and rubric. These low-cost, low-tech challenges have a making component that can be completed in approximately an hour, or as we like to say, in a zip (for a true STEM lesson you have to consider front loading the content)! A handful of the challenges are rooftop-themed because, frankly, rooftops can be a safe haven from the undead—but eventually what goes up must come down before what is down comes up—and before you run out of supplies. (They are always finite.) When students approach design challenges through empathizing with their hearts, thinking with their brains, and making with their hands, we know the learning is authentic and meaningful, and our ZBL theme makes it fun as well.

Each ZBL challenge is presented in a graphic format made in Piktochart. We also include the digital link to share directly to your students' LMS or even through social media! We aren't typically a big fan of the color green (zombie skin—hello!) but we are all about saving the environment and humanity! You may also choose to print the challenge and include the graphic in the Ziploc bag with the materials. Created pre-made challenge bags is a great option for learning commons, makerspaces, and library spaces with maker areas, so students can grab a bag and make.

You can find bag labels to download and print, as well as simplified student design instruction cards to be placed in each bag. Below are examples of the labels and one design card! Additional digital versions can be found on our website.

Zombie Zip Maker Challenges vs. STEAM Challenges

Like STEAM design challenges, maker challenges are engaging for students and are problem based. Maker challenges can be a lot of fun for students—they encourage collaboration and creative problem-solving, and they most definitely have their place in the classroom. They can last one class period or span an entire unit. In addition to using a design-thinking framework, the focus is on the iterative process and not necessarily the final product. The primary difference between a maker challenge and a STEAM challenge is that STEAM challenges are transdisciplinary instead of approached in silos, so students will have to draw on knowledge from all content areas. Because the problems are relevant to academic content as well as students, STEAM challenges allow students to make direct curricular connections. Maker challenges can also be considered STEAM if they are approached in a transdisciplinary manner.

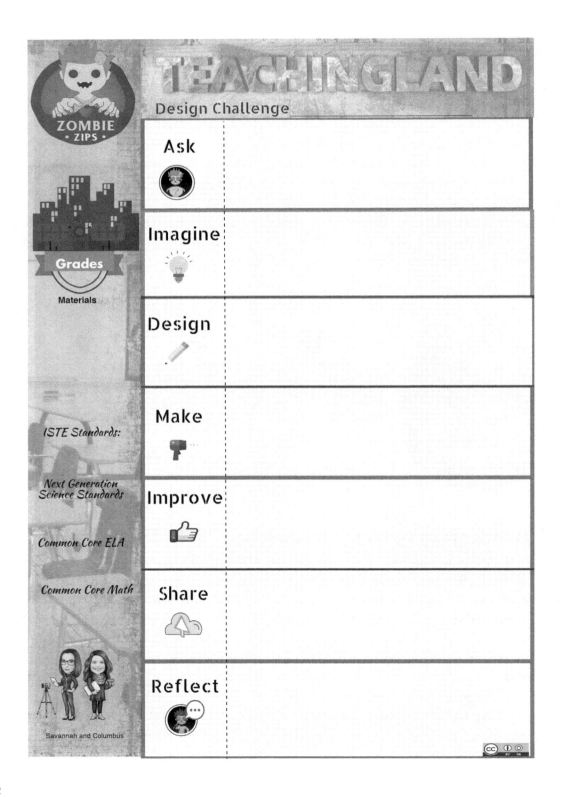

TEACHINGLAND

ZOMBIE ZIPS

Grades

Materials

ISTE Standards:

Next Generation Science Standards

Common Core ELA

Common Core Math

Savannah and Columbus

Design Challenge

Ask

Imagine

Design

Make

Improve

Share

Reflect

Want to make our Zombie Zips STEAMY? Make sure to embed lessons and research opportunities within the design process. Hit on cross-curricular skills and content information that students need to complete the challenge as students identify knowledge gaps. Ultimately, Maker + STEAM affords students more hands-on experiences when approaching content, and integrates technology within the process.

A STEAM rubric that assesses content in addition to the design process can be found on our website.

Hi-Tech: App-etizers and Bytes

Our hi-tech section of this chapter simply lists apps (appetizers) and (bytes) websites that embody our R.E.M.E.D.Y. Model. Each appetizer and byte is categorized by a letter of the R.E.M.E.D.Y. Model. While it is important to use technology in classroom activities, we believe the focus should be on the impact that the tool will have on student learning and why you are using it rather than the tool itself. Model!

The table is not only for teachers to utilize when designing lesson plans, it's also for students. It focuses on leveraging edtech tools as strategies to reach, engage, make, evaluate, demystify, and personalize learning through voice and choice—making students yearn for more! Most of the tools listed are content agnostic and can be adapted to any lesson! Each table of tools is categorized by a pedagogical strategy provided with a description of how that strategy looks with examples in action. We also categorize tools by age group and what we find appropriate for littles, middles, and bigs. Each table is preceded by a series of questions to get you thinking about why you or a student should select an edtech tool for that particular part of the R.E.M.E.D.Y. Model and help keep learning goals at the forefront of the selection process. Check out our list of app-etizers and web bytes to R.E.M.E.D.Y. your trench!

Teachingland Monster Tech Table

We have included sample ingredient cards for the Reach section of our Teachingland Monster Tech Table. Digital cards for all the other sections that can be found on our website under Chapter 6 resources. We have also included the blank template for you to create and add your own ingredients to design successful learning experiences for your students in your bunker!

Zombie Zip Design Challenges

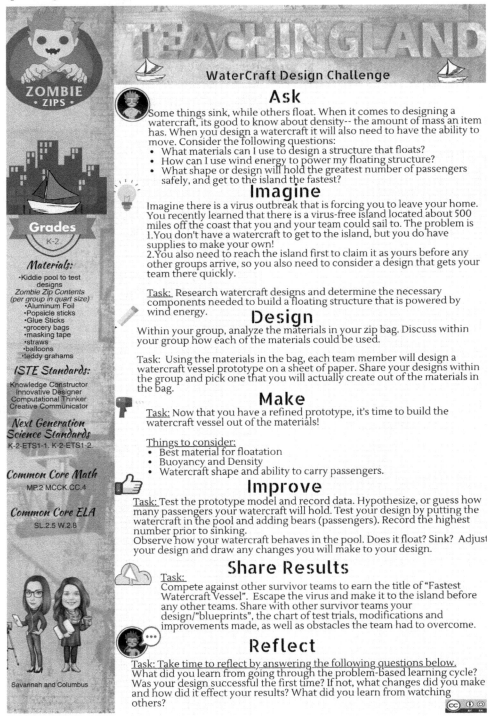

ZOMBIE ZIPS

Grades K-2

Materials:
- Kiddie pool to test designs

Zombie Zip Contents (per group in quart size)
- Aluminum Foil
- Popsicle sticks
- Glue Sticks
- grocery bags
- masking tape
- straws
- balloons
- teddy grahams

ISTE Standards:
Knowledge Constructor
Innovative Designer
Computational Thinker
Creative Communicator

Next Generation Science Standards
K-2-ETS1-1, K-2-ETS1-2.

Common Core Math
MP.2 MCCK.CC.4

Common Core ELA
SL.2.5 W.2.8

Savannah and Columbus

TEACHINGLAND

WaterCraft Design Challenge

Ask

Some things sink, while others float. When it comes to designing a watercraft, its good to know about density-- the amount of mass an item has. When you design a watercraft it will also need to have the ability to move. Consider the following questions:
- What materials can I use to design a structure that floats?
- How can I use wind energy to power my floating structure?
- What shape or design will hold the greatest number of passengers safely, and get to the island the fastest?

Imagine

Imagine there is a virus outbreak that is forcing you to leave your home. You recently learned that there is a virus-free island located about 500 miles off the coast that you and your team could sail to. The problem is
1. You don't have a watercraft to get to the island, but you do have supplies to make your own!
2. You also need to reach the island first to claim it as yours before any other groups arrive, so you also need to consider a design that gets your team there quickly.

Task: Research watercraft designs and determine the necessary components needed to build a floating structure that is powered by wind energy.

Design

Within your group, analyze the materials in your zip bag. Discuss within your group how each of the materials could be used.

Task: Using the materials in the bag, each team member will design a watercraft vessel prototype on a sheet of paper. Share your designs within the group and pick one that you will actually create out of the materials in the bag.

Make

Task: Now that you have a refined prototype, it's time to build the watercraft vessel out of the materials!

Things to consider:
- Best material for floatation
- Buoyancy and Density
- Watercraft shape and ability to carry passengers.

Improve

Task: Test the prototype model and record data. Hypothesize, or guess how many passengers your watercraft will hold. Test your design by putting the watercraft in the pool and adding bears (passengers). Record the highest number prior to sinking.
Observe how your watercraft behaves in the pool. Does it float? Sink? Adjust your design and draw any changes you will make to your design.

Share Results

Task:
Compete against other survivor teams to earn the title of "Fastest Watercraft Vessel". Escape the virus and make it to the island before any other teams. Share with other survivor teams your design/"blueprints", the chart of test trials, modifications and improvements made, as well as obstacles the team had to overcome.

Reflect

Task: Take time to reflect by answering the following questions below.
What did you learn from going through the problem-based learning cycle? Was your design successful the first time? If not, what changes did you make and how did it effect your results? What did you learn from watching others?

Zombie Zip Design Challenges

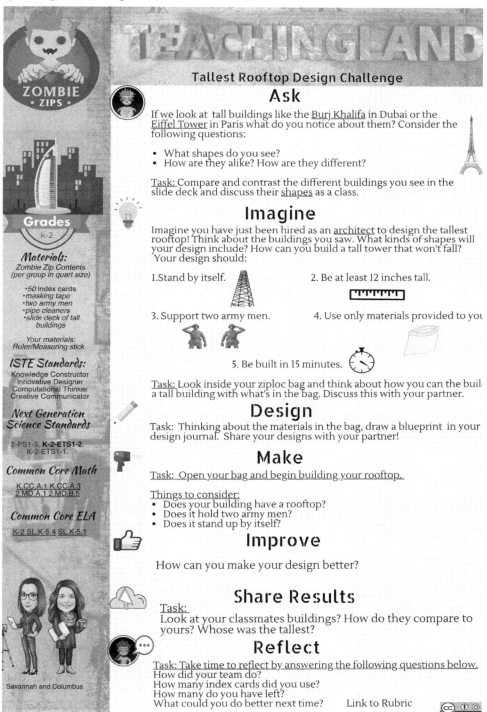

TEACHINGLAND

Tallest Rooftop Design Challenge

Ask

If we look at tall buildings like the Burj Khalifa in Dubai or the Eiffel Tower in Paris what do you notice about them? Consider the following questions:

- What shapes do you see?
- How are they alike? How are they different?

Task: Compare and contrast the different buildings you see in the slide deck and discuss their shapes as a class.

Imagine

Imagine you have just been hired as an architect to design the tallest rooftop! Think about the buildings you saw. What kinds of shapes will your design include? How can you build a tall tower that won't fall? Your design should:

1. Stand by itself.

2. Be at least 12 inches tall.

3. Support two army men.

4. Use only materials provided to you

5. Be built in 15 minutes.

Task: Look inside your ziploc bag and think about how you can the buil a tall building with what's in the bag. Discuss this with your partner.

Design

Task: Thinking about the materials in the bag, draw a blueprint in your design journal. Share your designs with your partner!

Make

Task: Open your bag and begin building your rooftop.

Things to consider:
- Does your building have a rooftop?
- Does it hold two army men?
- Does it stand up by itself?

Improve

How can you make your design better?

Share Results

Task:
Look at your classmates buildings? How do they compare to yours? Whose was the tallest?

Reflect

Task: Take time to reflect by answering the following questions below.
How did your team do?
How many index cards did you use?
How many do you have left?
What could you do better next time?   Link to Rubric

Sidebar

ZOMBIE ZIPS

Grades K-2

Materials:
Zombie Zip Contents
(per group in quart size)

- 50 index cards
- masking tape
- two army men
- pipe cleaners
- slide deck of tall buildings

Your materials:
Ruler/Measuring stick

ISTE Standards:
Knowledge Constructor
Innovative Designer
Computational Thinker
Creative Communicator

Next Generation Science Standards
2-PS1-3, K-2-ETS1-2.
K-2-ETS1-1.

Common Core Math
K.CC.A.1 K.CC.A.3
2.MD.A.1 2.MD.B.5

Common Core ELA
K-2 SL.K-5.4 SL.K-5.1

Savannah and Columbus

Zombie Zip Design Challenges

Portable Parachute Escape Pouch

Ask

Rooftops are a continuing problem in the zombie apocalypse. When you find yourself high and dry without an escape plan, having a portable parachute increases your odds of survival. How can you design and build a portable parachute that will glide Savannah and Columbus to safety? What are the good characteristics of a parachute? What materials would work best in your design and why?

Imagine

Imagine you have been hired by ZomBiz, a company that specializes in apocalyptic safety, and it's your job to design a Portable Parachute that will help glide Savannah and Columbus to safety. The design needs to fit into a portable pouch and be able to be assembled quickly to ensure escape, and provide a gentle landing! Now for the challenge!
<u>Task:</u> Research parachutes and how they work.

Design

Think about how to design a parachute that is aerodynamic and will support
 • What is the purpose of a parachute?
 •What kind of materials are the best to create a parachute out of?
 • How does air resistance and drag apply to my design?

<u>Task:</u> Given the materials draw a paper prototype of your parachute.

Make

<u>Task:</u> Now that you designed your parachute escape pouch let's make it out of the materials in our zombie zip bag!

Things to consider:
 • Best material for air resistance
 • Newton's Second Law of Motion
 • Portability and quick assembly

Improve

Ready to test? Assemble your parachute and test your design by dropping it from a height of one foot (12 inches).
If the "parachuters" do not make a gentle landing, collaborate with peers to improve your design. Study any problems and redesign your parachute!
 •What problems do you have?
 • Does the material you used first provide a safe, gentle landing?
<u>Task:</u> Log your observations, and take on notes on any tweaks, or improvements you make.

Share Results

Now that you have designed a prototype, built your Parachute Escape pouch, tested your design, and redesigned based on data, it's time to share with other groups!
<u>Task:</u> Discuss your design, and present your findings!

Reflect

<u>Task: Take time to reflect by answering the following questions below.</u>
What did you learn from going through the problem based learning cycle? Was your design successful the first time? If not, what changes did you make and how did it effect your results? What did you learn from watching others?

ZOMBIE • ZIPS •

Grades
3-5

Materials (per bag)
 • tissue paper
 • string
 • Savannah and Columbus paper cut out
 • Plastic army guy
 • paper towels
 • construction paper
 • newspaper
 • plastic table cloth cut into a square foot
 • scissors
 • tape
 • ziploc snack bag
 • metal washer

ISTE Standards:
Knowledge Constructor
Innovative Designer
Computational Thinker
Creative Communicator

Next Generation Science Standards
MS-ETS1-1
3-5-ETS1-2

Common Core ELA
SL.31 SL.3.1.b SL.3.2
SL.4.1 SL.4.1.b SL.4.2
SL.5.1 SL.5.1.b SL.5.2

Savannah and Columbus

Zombie Zip Design Challenges

Bird Beak Tweets Design Challenge

Ask

Charles Darwin was a scientist who studied bird beaks in the Galapagos, and is widely known as the father of evolution. Through observation he discovered birds have different types of beaks depending on the type of food habitat they live in, and in some cases they evolve, or adapt to their environment in order to survive. Consider the following questions:

- What do you notice about the shape of birds' beaks?
- What do they eat?
- What do you think would happen if they were forced to change habitats or their food supply became scarce?

Task: Compare and contrast the different bird beaks you see in the slide deck and discuss their shapes and types of food you think they eat as a class.

Imagine

In the zombie apocalypse, communication is key. It is vital that messages get transmitted, but how? With the power grid down and cellular towers no longer working (no Twitter), the only viable option is to train birds to pick up messages and deliver them to rooftops occupied by the living. But which beaks make the best carriers? You and your team of survivors will investigate through designing your own with the materials at hand! Your design should:

1. Be able to open and close.

2. Use only materials in bag.

3. Be completed in 15 mins.

4. Be able to pick up/drop paper scrolls and deliver the most from one rooftop to another within 30 seconds.

Task: Look inside your Ziploc bag and think about how you create a bird beak with the given supplies. Discuss this with your elbow partner.

Design

Task: Thinking about the materials in the bag, draw a blueprint in your design journal. Share your designs with your peers!

Make

Task: Open your bag and begin building your bird beak.

Things to consider:
- Can it open and close?
- Can it pick up a rolled scroll?
- Can it drop a rolled scroll?

Improve

What are the strenghts/weaknesses of your design? How can you make your design better? Record your thoughts in your journal.

Share Results

Task:
Look at the bird beaks your classmates designed? How do they compare to yours? Compete against their designs in the 30 second scroll delivery challenge!

Reflect

Task: Take time to reflect by answering the following questions below. How did your team do? Which beak shape was the best? What could you do better next time?

Grades
3-5

Materials:
Zombie Zip Contents
(per group in quart size)

Popsicle sticks
Rubber bands
Tape
Plastic spoons
Paper clips
Post-It Notes rolled
into a thin scroll
(Rooftops can be
desktops)

ISTE Standards:
Knowledge Constructor
Innovative Designer
Computational Thinker
Creative Communicator

Next Generation Science Standards
3-LS4-3.

Common Core Math
4.MD.A.1

Common Core ELA
SL.4.1 SL.4.4

Savannah and Columbus

Zombie Zip Design Challenges

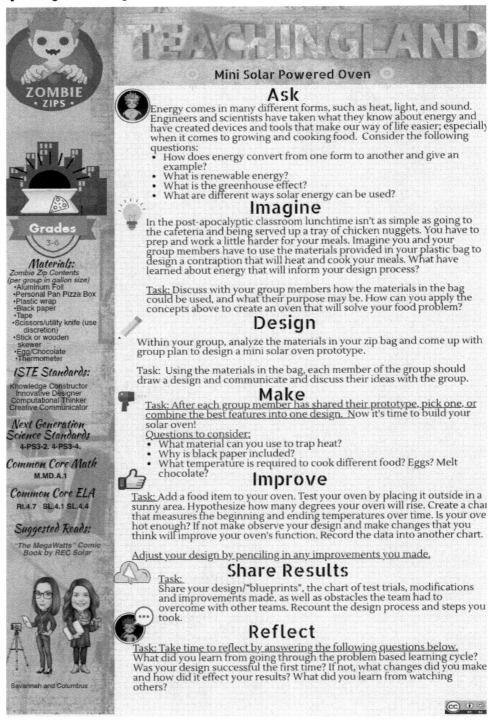

Mini Solar Powered Oven

Ask

Energy comes in many different forms, such as heat, light, and sound. Engineers and scientists have taken what they know about energy and have created devices and tools that make our way of life easier; especially when it comes to growing and cooking food. Consider the following questions:

- How does energy convert from one form to another and give an example?
- What is renewable energy?
- What is the greenhouse effect?
- What are different ways solar energy can be used?

Imagine

In the post-apocalyptic classroom lunchtime isn't as simple as going to the cafeteria and being served up a tray of chicken nuggets. You have to prep and work a little harder for your meals. Imagine you and your group members have to use the materials provided in your plastic bag to design a contraption that will heat and cook your meals. What have learned about energy that will inform your design process?

Task: Discuss with your group members how the materials in the bag could be used, and what their purpose may be. How can you apply the concepts above to create an oven that will solve your food problem?

Design

Within your group, analyze the materials in your zip bag and come up with group plan to design a mini solar oven prototype.

Task: Using the materials in the bag, each member of the group should draw a design and communicate and discuss their ideas with the group.

Make

Task: After each group member has shared their prototype, pick one, or combine the best features into one design. Now it's time to build your solar oven!
Questions to consider:
- What material can you use to trap heat?
- Why is black paper included?
- What temperature is required to cook different food? Eggs? Melt chocolate?

Improve

Task: Add a food item to your oven. Test your oven by placing it outside in a sunny area. Hypothesize how many degrees your oven will rise. Create a chart that measures the beginning and ending temperatures over time. Is your oven hot enough? If not make observe your design and make changes that you think will improve your oven's function. Record the data into another chart.

Adjust your design by penciling in any improvements you made.

Share Results

Task:
Share your design/"blueprints", the chart of test trials, modifications and improvements made, as well as obstacles the team had to overcome with other teams. Recount the design process and steps you took.

Reflect

Task: Take time to reflect by answering the following questions below.
What did you learn from going through the problem based learning cycle? Was your design successful the first time? If not, what changes did you make and how did it effect your results? What did you learn from watching others?

ZOMBIE ZIPS

Grades
3-6

Materials:
Zombie Zip Contents
(per group in gallon size)
- Aluminum Foil
- Personal Pan Pizza Box
- Plastic wrap
- Black paper
- Tape
- Scissors/utility knife (use discretion)
- Stick or wooden skewer
- Egg/Chocolate
- Thermometer

ISTE Standards:
Knowledge Constructor
Innovative Designer
Computational Thinker
Creative Communicator

Next Generation Science Standards
4-PS3-2. 4-PS3-4.

Common Core Math
M.MD.A.1

Common Core ELA
RI.4.7 SL.4.1 SL.4.4

Suggested Reads:
"The MegaWatts" Comic Book by REC Solar

Savannah and Columbus

Zombie Zip Design Challenges

Rooftop Disembarkation Craft

Ask

In the zombie apocalypse sometimes we find ourselves stranded on rooftops of buildings. That's why we need a Rooftop Disembarkation Craft: to safely escape demise without meeting our demise! How can you design and build a shock-absorbing Rooftop Disembarkation Craft that will protect Savannah and Columbus when they land? What does shock-absorbing mean? How does kinetic and potential energy come into play?

Imagine

Imagine you have been hired by ZomBiz, a company that specializes in apocalyptic safety, and it's your job to design a Rooftop Embarkation Craft that will keep Savannah and Columbus and other survivors safe as they make their way to the ground! These crafts will be placed on top of buildings all over Zombieland to provide an escape plan if necessary. Now for the challenge!

Design

Think about how to build a craft that can absorb the shock of an asphalt landing.
• What kind of shock absorber can you make from the materials that can help soften a landing?
• How will you make sure the craft doesn't tip over as it falls through the air?
• How can you keep the survivors safely inside the cabin?

Make

Given the materials draw a paper prototype of how the materials will work together to create a Rooftop Disembarkation Craft.
Things to consider:

• Shock-absorbing features included
• Platform to attach the landing craft
• Cabin for Team Members

Improve

Ready to test? Drop your Rooftop Craft from a height of one foot (12 inches). If the "survivors"fall from the lander, collaborate with peers to improve your design. Study any problems and redesign your craft!

What problems do you have?
• Does the craft tip over as it falls through the air?
• Do the survivors fall out of the cabin?

Log your observations, and take on notes on any tweaks, or improvements you make.

Share Results

Now that you have designed a prototype, built your rooftop craft, tested your design, and redesigned based on data, it's time to share with other groups! Discuss your design, and present your findings!

Reflect

What did you learn from going through the problem based learning cycle? Was your design successful the first time? If not, what changes did you make and how did it effect your results? What did you learn from watching others?

ZOMBIE · ZIPS ·

Grades 3-8

Materials (per group)
• 1 piece of cardboard (approximately 4 x 5 in/10 x 13 cm)
• 1 plastic 5oz cup
• 3-5 index cards (3 x 5 in/8 x 13 cm)
• 2 regular marshmallows
• 10 miniature marshmallows
• 3 rubber bands
• 8 plastic straws
• scissors
• tape

ISTE Standards:

Knowledge Constructor
Innovative Designer
Computational Thinker
Creative Communicator

Next Generation Science Standards
MS-ETS1-1
3-5-ETS1-2

Common Core ELA
SL.6.1 SL.6.1.b SL.6.2
SL.7.1 SL.7.1.b SL.7.2
SL.8.1 SL.8.1.b SL.8.2

Savannah and Columbus

Zombie Zip Design Challenges

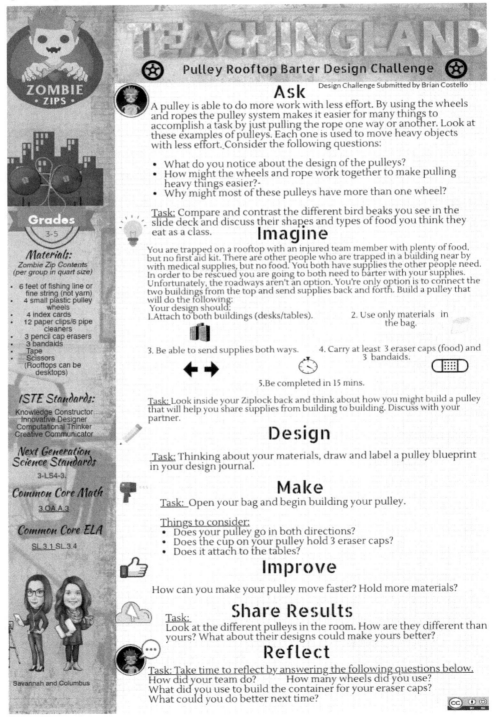

ZOMBIE ZIPS

Grades 3-5

Materials:
Zombie Zip Contents
(per group in quart size)

- 6 feet of fishing line or fine string (not yarn)
- 4 small plastic pulley wheels
- 4 index cards
- 12 paper clips/6 pipe cleaners
- 3 pencil cap erasers
- 3 bandaids
- Tape
- Scissors
- (Rooftops can be desktops)

ISTE Standards:
Knowledge Constructor
Innovative Designer
Computational Thinker
Creative Communicator

Next Generation Science Standards
3-LS4-3.

Common Core Math
3.OA.A.3

Common Core ELA
SL.3.1 SL.3.4

Savannah and Columbus

TEACHINGLAND
Pulley Rooftop Barter Design Challenge

Design Challenge Submitted by Brian Costello

Ask

A pulley is able to do more work with less effort. By using the wheels and ropes the pulley system makes it easier for many things to accomplish a task by just pulling the rope one way or another. Look at these examples of pulleys. Each one is used to move heavy objects with less effort. Consider the following questions:

- What do you notice about the design of the pulleys?
- How might the wheels and rope work together to make pulling heavy things easier?
- Why might most of these pulleys have more than one wheel?

Task: Compare and contrast the different bird beaks you see in the slide deck and discuss their shapes and types of food you think they eat as a class.

Imagine

You are trapped on a rooftop with an injured team member with plenty of food, but no first aid kit. There are other people who are trapped in a building near by with medical supplies, but no food. You both have supplies the other people need. In order to be rescued you are going to both need to barter with your supplies. Unfortunately, the roadways aren't an option. You're only option is to connect the two buildings from the top and send supplies back and forth. Build a pulley that will do the following:
Your design should:
1. Attach to both buildings (desks/tables).   2. Use only materials in the bag.

3. Be able to send supplies both ways.   4. Carry at least 3 eraser caps (food) and 3 bandaids.

5. Be completed in 15 mins.

Task: Look inside your Ziplock back and think about how you might build a pulley that will help you share supplies from building to building. Discuss with your partner.

Design

Task: Thinking about your materials, draw and label a pulley blueprint in your design journal.

Make

Task: Open your bag and begin building your pulley.

Things to consider:
- Does your pulley go in both directions?
- Does the cup on your pulley hold 3 eraser caps?
- Does it attach to the tables?

Improve

How can you make your pulley move faster? Hold more materials?

Share Results

Task: Look at the different pulleys in the room. How are they different than yours? What about their designs could make yours better?

Reflect

Task: Take time to reflect by answering the following questions below.
How did your team do?   How many wheels did you use?
What did you use to build the container for your eraser caps?
What could you do better next time?

Zombie Zip Design Challenges

TEACHINGLAND

Water Filtration Design Challenge

ZOMBIE ZIPS

Grades 3-5

Materials:
Zombie Zip Contents
(per group in 2 gallon size)
• 2 .5 liter bottles (one with cut bottom and one with cut top)
• masking tape
• coffee filter
• cotton balls
• snack bag of sand
• snack bag of aquarium gravel
• paper towels
• 20 oz sample of contaminated water
• 3 5 oz sample cups
Dirty water:
Water, sand, pet hair, oil, or food coloring

ISTE Standards:
Knowledge Constructor
Innovative Designer
Computational Thinker
Creative Communicator

Next Generation Science Standards
3-5-ETS1-1, 3-5-ETS1-2,

Common Core Math
MP.2 MCCK.CC 4

Common Core ELA
3-5 SL 3-5.4 SL 3-5.1

Savannah and Columbus

Ask

Having access to clean drinking water is important for our survival. Water from lakes often contain dirt, minerals, and bacteria that make it unsafe to drink, while rain water picks up contaminants from the atmoshphere and toxins from surfaces it runs off of. Consider the following questions:
• Where does our drinking water come from?
• What is water pollutants and why are they harmful?
• How do we filter them out of our water supply?

Task: Research water filtration plants, and where our drinking water comes from.

Imagine

Imagine you are in a zombie apocalypse and you have lost access to running, filtered water. You are limited to the materials in the bag to design a filtration system to filter water from a nearby lake. Your water filtration device should:
1.Try three combinations of materials to filter water.
2. Provide three four ounce filtered samples from each test (118ml).
3.Have the clearest water sample of all groups.
4. Use only materials provided to you.

Task: After researching water filtration practices and studying the contents provided in your bag, begin to brainstorm which materials may be best for the challenge, and discuss how you could use them in a filtration prototype.

Design

Task: Using the materials in the bag, each team member will design and draw a water filtration prototype in the design journal. Share your designs within the group and pick one that you will create and test first using the materials in the bag.

Make

Task: Apply masking tape to your sample cups and label your them 1, 2, and 3 with your group letter. Now that you have a refined prototype, it's time to engineer a water filtration device as a group using the materials in the bag!
Things to consider:
• Best material for filtration
• Pollutants
• Testing your design and recording data.

Improve

Now that you have tested your design consider the following:
• How can you make it better?
• Can you use different materials, or arrange them in a different ways to achieve better results?

Task: Make improvements and observe your results.

Share Results

Task:
Compare your water samples with your peers.Who had the cleanest, clearest sample? Share with the other teams your design/"blueprints", the chart of test trials, modifications and improvements made, as well as obstacles the team had to overcome. Which material filtered water the best?

Reflect

Task: Take time to reflect by answering the following questions below.
What did you learn from going through the problem based learning cycle? Was your design successful the first time? If not, what changes did you make and how did it effect your results? What did you learn from watching others?

Zombie Zip Design Challenges

TEACHINGLAND

Hydroponic Rooftop Gardening and pH

ZOMBIE ZIPS

Grades 6-8

Materials (per group)
- 1 wide mouth quart mason jar
- hydroton pellets or perlite
- 3 in net pot
- Nutrients for water
- Painters tape
- Trash bag
- Black spray paint
- Plant seeds (lettuce)
- rockwool cube
- pH meter
- pH control kit

ISTE Standards:

Knowledge Constructor
Innovative Designer
Computational Thinker
Creative Communicator

Next Generation Science Standards

MS-ETS1-1
3-5-ETS1-2

Common Core ELA

SL.3.1 SL.3.1.b SL.3.2
SL.4.1 SL.4.1.b SL.4.2
SL.5.1 SL.5.1.b SL.5.2

Savannah and Columbus

Ask

As a member of a rooftop bunker, food is scarce and you are investigating starting a rooftop garden. What is the best way to grow food to sustain your small group? What is pH and how does it impact how plants grow? How can we get soil to the rooftop safely, and is there a safer alternative that doesn't require soil, like hydroponic gardening? Which will yield better results?

Imagine

In the postapocalyptic world food is needed to survive, but with mainstream grocery stores and farms we are back to feudal times, and even open farming can be dangerous. A scout team recently collected soil samples to determine if the local region can viably grow crops to support a small bunker. You are the scientist that has to analyze the samples and determine if their pH levels will support a garden. If not, how can we produce enough food for a small rooftop bunker? Is it sustainable and could it support a flourishing population?

Design

Think about what goes into growing a food source such as lettuce. Looking at the materials provided design a system to grow food. If growing food in soil is not an option, you can use water. This is called hydroponics. Latin root: Hydro=water ponos=labor "Working Water"
- What pH level does lettuce need to thrive?
- What is circulating vs. non circulating hydroponics?
- Can you use the materials given to create a hydroponic system to grow lettuce?

Task: Given the materials draw a paper prototype of your gardening system.

Make

Task: Now that you designed your gardening system escape let's make it out of the materials in our zombie zip bag!
Things to consider:
- Plant needs for survival
- pH levels and nutrients
- Optimal growth environment for lettuce

Improve

Ready to observe your hydroponic system for functionality? Lettuce seeds take 7-10 days to germinate. Do you see a sprout or growth? Are any roots forming? What is your water level? Record your observations and discuss your results. What could you do differently to get better results? What would you repeat?
Task: Log your observations, and take on notes on any tweaks, or improvements you make.

Share Results

Now that you have tested pH levels, researched hydroponics (non circulating and circulating) it is time to share your findings, and the results of the system you made. Choose a way to visualize your data and share with the class.
Task: Discuss your design, and present your findings!

Reflect

Task: Take time to reflect by answering the following questions below.
What did you learn from going through the problem based learning cycle? Was your design successful the first time? If not, what changes did you make and how did it effect your results? What did you learn from watching others?

Zombie Zip Design Challenges

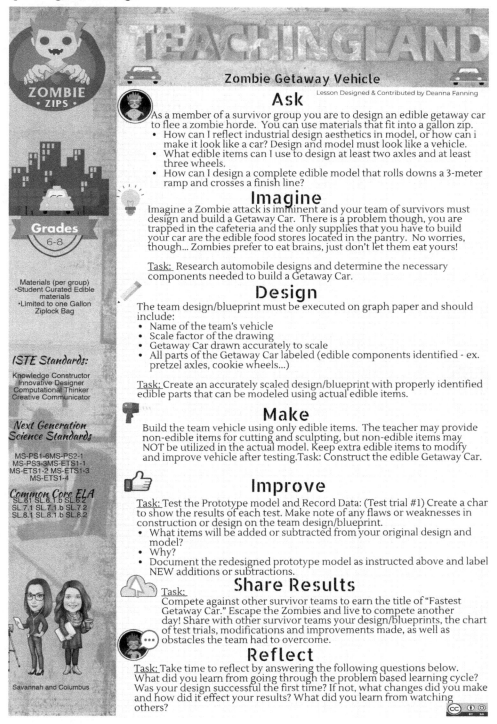

TEACHINGLAND

ZOMBIE ZIPS

Grades 6-8

Materials (per group)
• Student Curated Edible materials
• Limited to one Gallon Ziplock Bag

ISTE Standards:
Knowledge Constructor
Innovative Designer
Computational Thinker
Creative Communicator

Next Generation Science Standards
MS-PS1-6 MS-PS2-1
MS-PS3-3 MS-ETS1-1
MS-ETS1-2 MS-ETS1-3
MS-ETS1-4

Common Core ELA
SL.6.1 SL.6.1.b SL.6.2
SL.7.1 SL.7.1.b SL.7.2
SL.8.1 SL.8.1.b SL.8.2

Savannah and Columbus

Zombie Getaway Vehicle
Lesson Designed & Contributed by Deanna Fanning

Ask

As a member of a survivor group you are to design an edible getaway car to flee a zombie horde. You can use materials that fit into a gallon zip.
- How can I reflect industrial design aesthetics in model, or how can i make it look like a car? Design and model must look like a vehicle.
- What edible items can I use to design at least two axles and at least three wheels.
- How can I design a complete edible model that rolls downs a 3-meter ramp and crosses a finish line?

Imagine

Imagine a Zombie attack is imminent and your team of survivors must design and build a Getaway Car. There is a problem though, you are trapped in the cafeteria and the only supplies that you have to build your car are the edible food stores located in the pantry. No worries, though... Zombies prefer to eat brains, just don't let them eat yours!

Task: Research automobile designs and determine the necessary components needed to build a Getaway Car.

Design

The team design/blueprint must be executed on graph paper and should include:
- Name of the team's vehicle
- Scale factor of the drawing
- Getaway Car drawn accurately to scale
- All parts of the Getaway Car labeled (edible components identified - ex. pretzel axles, cookie wheels...)

Task: Create an accurately scaled design/blueprint with properly identified edible parts that can be modeled using actual edible items.

Make

Build the team vehicle using only edible items. The teacher may provide non-edible items for cutting and sculpting, but non-edible items may NOT be utilized in the actual model. Keep extra edible items to modify and improve vehicle after testing. Task: Construct the edible Getaway Car.

Improve

Task: Test the Prototype model and Record Data: (Test trial #1) Create a char to show the results of each test. Make note of any flaws or weaknesses in construction or design on the team design/blueprint.
- What items will be added or subtracted from your original design and model?
- Why?
- Document the redesigned prototype model as instructed above and label NEW additions or subtractions.

Share Results

Task:
Compete against other survivor teams to earn the title of "Fastest Getaway Car." Escape the Zombies and live to compete another day! Share with other survivor teams your design/blueprints, the chart of test trials, modifications and improvements made, as well as obstacles the team had to overcome.

Reflect

Task: Take time to reflect by answering the following questions below. What did you learn from going through the problem based learning cycle? Was your design successful the first time? If not, what changes did you make and how did it effect your results? What did you learn from watching others?

We also have included a Teachingland Student Design Process Journal template, which can be found on our website under Edtech Arsenal Chapter 6 resources.

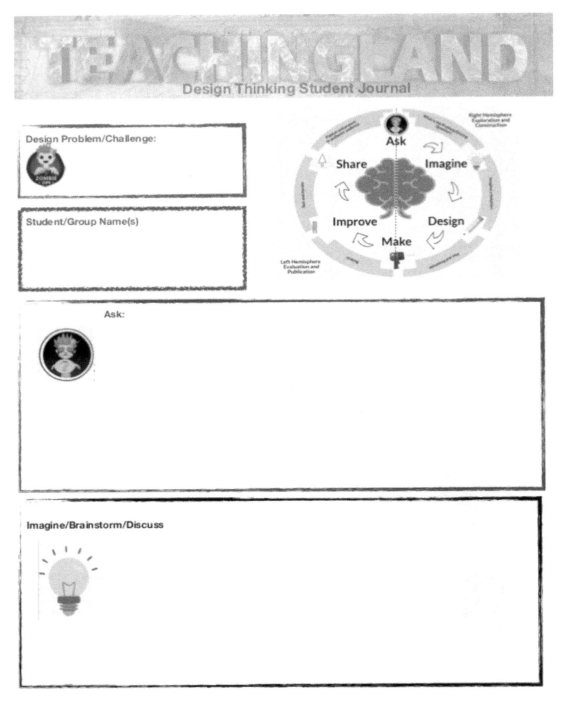

Plan/Design

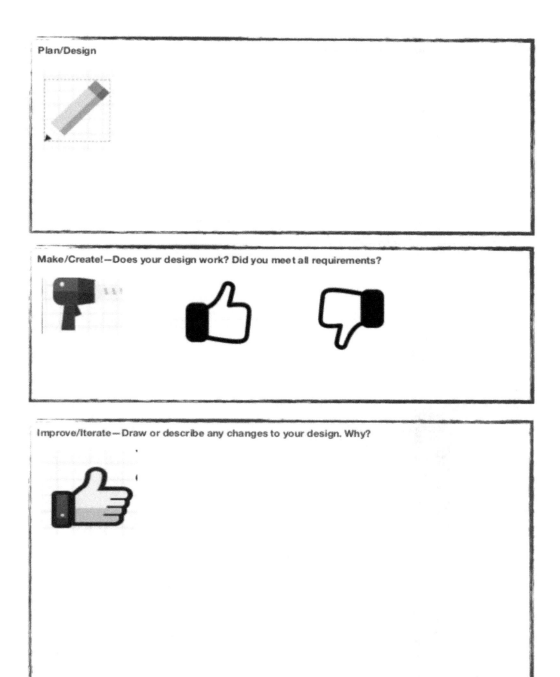

Make/Create!—Does your design work? Did you meet all requirements?

Improve/Iterate—Draw or describe any changes to your design. Why?

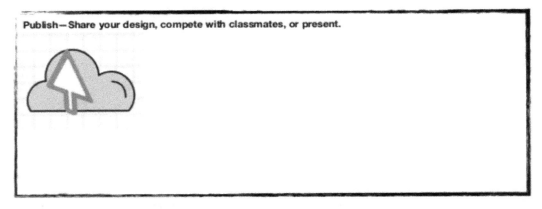

Publish—Share your design, compete with classmates, or present.

Reflection: Design Exit Ticket.

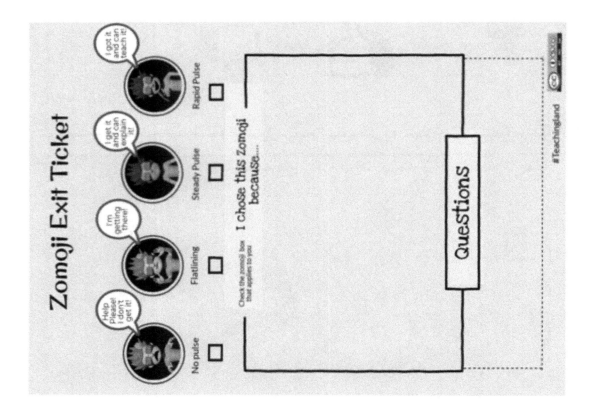

Additionally, here are two rubrics. One for littles and one for middles and bigs.

Rubric for the Zombie Zip Maker Design Challenges here (editable by saving to your drive). Check our website for Chapter 6 resources for a downloadable copy.

Name(s):_____Date:_____

Design Challenge:_____

Teachingland Zombie Zip Design Challenge Rubric

Does the student meet the criteria?	+	-	Evidence
Students can understand and explain/define the problem.			
Students brainstormed and collaborated together.			
There is evidence of students' plans/prototypes.			
Students' have clear connection between design challenge and product.			
Students made revisions/improvements.			
Students shared their solutions with the teacher and their peers.			

Additional Comments:

Name: _____   Date _____

Teachingland Zombie Zip Design Challenge Rubric

	Emerging-1	Developing-2	Proficient-3	Exemplary-4
Prototype	Prototype is not a functional solution to the problem and/or ignores design constraints.	Designed a prototype design that provides a partial functional solution based on the problem and constraints.	Used research to design a prototype that is functional based on the problem and constraints.	Brainstormed and discussed solutions with peers and/or experts. Applied research to design a prototype that is functional based on the problem and constraints.
Iteration	Final product has not changed from prototype design.	Changes and iterations on made but only to the appearance and not function.	Changes and iterations lead to improvements in the appearance and function of the design.	The final product underwent multiple iterations and was aesthetically pleasing and functional.
Presentation	Presentation makes no connections to how the student or group worked through the design cycle to prototype a functional solution to the	Presentation makes some connections to how the student or group worked through the design cycle to prototype a functional solution to the	Presentation clearly demonstrates how the student or group worked through the design cycle to prototype a functional solution	Presentation clearly demonstrates how the student or group leveraged empathy and the design cycle to prototype a functional solution to the problem..

Teachingland © 2018 by Amanda Fox and Mary Ellen Weeks

Creativity	to the problem.	problem	to the problem.
	The solution to the problem is not functional or original. OR the student did not remain within the constraints of the assignment.	The solution to the problem is functional but not original. The student remained within the constraints of the assignment.	The solution to the problem is original, and functional, and is within constraints of the assignment.	The solution to the problem is original, useful, and unique, and is within the constraints of the assignment.
Collaboration/Teamwork	Team did not work well together. While some team members participated, the team did not come together to design a solution to the problem.	Worked collaboratively as a team with most members contributing at some point during the design process.	Worked collaboratively as a team with all members making contributions during the design process.	Worked collaboratively as a team with all members making meaningful contributions at all steps of the design process.
Reflection	Self Assessment: 1.What role did you do within the design process? 2.What did you do well? 3.What would you do differently next time? Group Assessment: What did your group do well together? Were there any struggles? Do you have any suggestions on how you could work together better next time?			

Total Points/Brainpower	___ /24

If the rubric doesn't quite fit what you are looking for, or you adapt our challenge, be sure to create your own design challenge rubric or have students develop one using our rubric creation tools mentioned in the hi-tech section of this chapter!

Teachingland
Reach

Every year the students in your classroom leave and are replaced with a new horde. How will you reach them? How will you learn about who they are and where they are academically? Are your students suffering from symptoms of zombiism? Or are they coming to you this year prepared and warm blooded? Understanding the learning histories and interests of your students goes a long way in relationship building and lesson design.

- How can I reach my students?
- What EdTech tool can I use to reach my students?
- Am I trying to reach them in class or beyond the trench?
- Do I want to find out about their hobbies?

- Am I looking for a tool to access prior knowledge?
- Do I want students to individually construct answers?
- Do I want to build a community knowledge base of answers?

R.E.M.E.D.Y

R(each)EMEDY

How Can I Reach My Students?

- What edtech tool can I use to reach my students?

- Am I trying to reach them in class or beyond the trench?

- What is the best way to reach my students?

- What can I learn about their hobbies, likes, and dislikes?

- What prior knowledge do I want to access?

- Do I want students to individually construct answers?

- Do I want to build a community knowledge base of answers?

The questions above will help you determine which tool is appropriate when trying to reach your students. Each strategy lists tech tools that act as vehicles to help the teacher reach students in various ways. Whether it's staying in touch with them and their family members beyond the classroom walls, assessing prior knowledge, or finding out their hobbies and interests to guide your lessons, these tools are perfect for getting to know your students individually!

"Reach Them" Apps and Bytes!

REACH THEM: Beyond the Trench

LEVEL: Elementary—Homeroom/Seesaw
Middle—Remind/Bloomz
High—Twitter/Facebook

DESCRIPTION: It is important not only to reach students in your trenches but also to establish a line of communication after they have gone home. With the Homeroom app you can safely post photos of littles and leave comments for parents. They may also join the group and post photos from the bunker, holiday parties, events, etc. Seesaw has a feed that feels like a social media feed. It allows teachers to engage students in high-impact learning experiences in the classroom and then sends parents a message through an app that allows them view and even comment on their child's work. It provides both parents and students with the opportunity to be active participants in the classroom experience. Remind and Bloomz are also great ways to communicate with students and parents and are great for littles through high school. You can send whole-group reminders, messages, or individual notifications and keep numbers private and safe. For high school students, you may even choose to use your professional Twitter to keep communication going outside the walls of the trench. We are huge fans of learning on the run!

EXAMPLE: For this book, we have created the hashtag #Teachingland. As you read, share your thoughts on Twitter and social media so we can learn as a community! We also have a Facebook page and will be sharing updates, resources, and learning opportunities as they arise! Make sure you are creating these types of opportunities in your classroom and beyond.

REACH THEM: By Crowdsourcing Info!

LEVEL: Elementary
Middle } Padlet/Wakelet/Symbaloo/Jamboard App Google
High

DESCRIPTION: Sometimes when you design activities to reach students, you want to reach them collectively and create a community-knowledge-based artifact! By curating individual answers from students into a shareable resource, students inspire and learn from each other. With Padlet, students can post notes, videos, links, and other content to a digital pin board. We have used Padlet with K–12. For littles, curate resources as a class, and share the link with parents. You can even have parents help students add videos of site word practice or read pages of a book from home.

Wakelet is a web-based tool and app similar to Padlet that is free but currently lacks some of the collaborative features. You could curate resources as a class or curate them for your class and embed the Wakelet in a website. You can also curate the old-fashioned, low-tech way and use a bulletin board or giant post-it notes with markers! Either way, group brainstorming is great! You can also use this tool in other parts of the R.E.M.E.D.Y. Model. How can you use it to engage students or for evaluation? Check our more ways to reach students using Padlet/ Wakelet on our website!

EXAMPLE: Check out this example of using Padlet to crowdsource topics for STEMtalks students were interested in!
padlet.com/amandafoxflip/stemtalk

REACH THEM: With Personal Timelines

LEVEL: Elementary—Timeline Maker
Middle—Popplet
High—Sutori/Story Maps by ArcGis

DESCRIPTION: Prompting students to create personal timelines is a great way to get to know them. Whether they are creating a reading timeline or their own personal histories, it gives you insight into their interests and backgrounds while teaching sequence and chronological order. When introducing this strategy, let them tackle a personal or fun topic before transferring it to a formative evaluation tool to assess their content knowledge! Timeline Maker and Popplet are both great apps for creating timelines. ArcGis is web-based and made by Esri.

EXAMPLE: Using ArcGis, students can combine storytelling and maps to create a geographic timeline. Check out their website to find great examples!
storymaps.arcgis.com/en

REACH THEM: Using Short Video

LEVEL: Elementary—Seesaw/Shadow Puppet Edu
Middle—Flipgrid/iMovie
High—Snapchat (Look at Chapter 9.)

DESCRIPTION: Finding out information about what your students are interested in or how they might like to be assessed has never been easier than using quick video prompts. Seesaw or Shadow Puppet Edu are great free apps for littles, while #flipgridfever has taken over the world and is appropriate for all age groups. For high school students, you can use Snapchat, and students even customize their videos with fun filters and Bitmojis! Flipgrid has a freemium, and videos are posted to a grid that can be private or shared, and each video has a link or QR code. #GridPals is a cool way to connect with classrooms all over the world! Recap is completely free and has a daily mix feature where you can choose to highlight exemplary work.

You can also use iMovie to update and reach parents about what is going on in your classroom!

EXAMPLE: Here is a Flipgrid of students reading "The Hangman" poem from a Holocaust unit: https://flipgrid.com/68d021d9; grid password: stem

Gridpals: http://blog.flipgrid.com/news/gridpals

iMovie Robotics class update: youtube.com/watch?v=Dei8zsflgz0

Check out Snapchat for our educational snaps on Teachingland! When we combine Twitter and Snapchat, we use the hashtag #brainsnaps.

REACH THEM: With Presentations

LEVEL: Elementary—Google Slides/Buncee
Middle—Screencastify
High—Emaze/visualize.me

DESCRIPTION: Using Google Slides or Buncee can be a fun way to reach students and find out more about who they are! You can have them create biographies, interest slides, favorite subjects…literally anything you want to know about them. In addition to using Google Slides individually, you can create a collaborative class version and have students add their own slide to the same presentation. If you are feeling even more adventurous, you can have them record their presentation using tools like Screencastify to add narration. Emaze is another great online presentation tool that brings a wow factor that makes creation fun! For high-school students, you can have them begin the year creating a presentation in VIsualize.me that is a visual way to showcase résumés, interests, and personal histories.

EXAMPLE: See the Chapter 6 Resource section at TeachinglandTheBook.com for an example of students working on a Google Slide presentation.

REACH THEM: With Gif Creation!

LEVEL: Elementary
Middle   } Giphy, GifGab, Giffer, FaceFilm, Emoji Me Gifs
High

DESCRIPTION: Who doesn't love gifs? If a picture says a thousand words, an animated gif says a million! We love using gifs to communicate in their pure form in our presentations and on social media. It is a fun way to express learning, share interests, and hook students. Allowing them to make their own to showcase their thoughts is a great way to leverage this tool in the classroom. You can even make augmented gifs with Gabsee or personalize them with GifGab. These two apps allow students to augment their work with cool gifs with their face! You can download the gifs to your camera roll and share them in an LMS, Facebook, or Instagram. We like to add our gifs to our Giphy channel to keep them all curated in one spot! Explore all the apps we listed and check our examples!

EXAMPLE: Here is a gif Savannah made to get teachers excited about PBL! gph.is/2JVXs1e
Check out Amanda's Giphy channel here: giphy.com/channel/amandafoxstem

Made with GifGab: gph.is/2KH4yYl

Find more examples at TeachinglandTheBook.com!

Remind

remind

Remind is a private mobile-messaging platform that allows teachers to send real-time messages and attachments to students or parents. You can download the app or use the website.

Ways to use remind to REACH your students/parents:

- ❏ Send due date reminders
- ❏ Post schedule changes
- ❏ Ask for donations/volunteers
- ❏ Send permission slips
- ❏ Schedule F2F meetings/conferences
- ❏ Study reminders
- ❏ Any announcements

Teachingland

Bloomz

bloomz

Reach

Bloomz is a single app and website that is used to communicate with parents and students. It works on any internet-capable device.

Ways to use Bloomz to REACH your students/parents:

- ❏ Ask parents about students' interests
- ❏ Send homework reminders
- ❏ Schedule conferences
- ❏ Use the calendar feature to send notifications and reminders of events
- ❏ Send digital flyers through attachments

Teachingland

Twitter

Reach

Twitter is an online social media app and website where people communicate in short messages or microblogs. It is a great way to get bite-size news and catch up with what is going on in the world.

Ways to use Twitter to REACH your students:

- ❏ Create a class/school hashtag (ex. #stemsav, #teachingland)
- ❏ Tweet assignments/due dates
- ❏ Use Twitter as an icebreaker
- ❏ Tweet out content questions
- ❏ Create a twitter poll
- ❏ Survey your students' interests
- ❏ Have students tweet Gifs that relate back to content

Teachingland

Padlet

Reach

Padlet is a real-time, collaborative, digital pin board that allows you to organize and post ideas, notes, videos, and links. You can share the link to the padlet with anyone!

Ways to use Padlet to REACH your students:

- ❏ Brainstorming new topics
- ❏ Curating research topics
- ❏ Curating links and information
- ❏ Assessing students prior knowledge of a topic
- ❏ As a beginning-of-the-year icebreaker
- ❏ To find out students' interests and hobbies
- ❏ Create classroom rules with students

Teachingland

Popplet

popplet

Popplet is an app and online brain-mapping tool that allows students to capture and map their ideas.

Ways to use Popplet to REACH your students:

- ❏ Create content and topic brainstorms
- ❏ Comparing and contrasting
- ❏ Character analysis
- ❏ Student interest mindmaps
- ❏ Timelines and historical information

Teachingland

Sutori

Sutori

Reach

Sutori is known as a timeline tool but with the option to embed digital media such as videos and sound files and also create quizzes and discussions, it has become valuable to teachers. It is web-enabled but no app.

Ways to use Sutori to REACH your students:

- ❏ Create interactive timelines of themselves
- ❏ Create drag-and-drop matching questions to assess prior knowledge
- ❏ Create a question forum for class
- ❏ Make multiple-choice surveys on a content topic
- ❏ Build collaborative stories together

Teachingland

Flipgrid

FLIPGRID

Reach

Flipgrid is a video-response platform that presents students video in a presentation grid. It is available as a byte and an app-etizer.

Ways to use Flipgrid to REACH your students:

- ❏ Ask them about their hobbies-this allows you to match names and faces!
- ❏ Icebreaker: Two Truths and a Lie
- ❏ Show what you know! Assess prior knowledge
- ❏ Video discussion
- ❏ Flipgrid debate

Teachingland

Emaze

emaze

Reach

Emaze is a web-based tool that prompts students to create and share presentations online. It is available as a byte only. Sorry, Apple peeps.

Ways to use Emaze to REACH your students:

- ❏ Create an "All About Me" presentation
- ❏ Share hobbies and interests
- ❏ Present on their learner profile and how they like to learn
- ❏ Favorite books presentation
- ❏ Technology tips/tool presentation

Teachingland

Giphy  **GIPHY**

Reach

Giphy is gif platform that allows you and
students to share, create, embed, and search
gifs. It is available as a byte and an
app-etizer.

Ways to use Giphy to REACH your students:

- ❏ Icebreaker in a Giphy
- ❏ Create a collaborative, gif Google
  Slides introduction
- ❏ Writing prompt in a Giphy!
- ❏ Use Giphy to create classroom rules
  gifs
- ❏ Use gifs to compliment students and
  build rapport!

Teachingland

Apps and Bytes to Engage Students

- How can I engage my students?

- What interests and hobbies do my students have that I can leverage in my lessons?

- How can I use edtech tools to take the pulse of my students' learning?

- What devices do my students have access to?

- How can I enhance my lectures/presentations with edtech tools?

- How can I use edtech to make my lesson student centered?

ENGAGE THEM: With Teacher-Made Instructional Videos

LEVEL: Elementary—ScreenChomp; Powtoon
Middle—Educreations; Go Animate
High—VideoScribe; AdobeSpark

DESCRIPTION: Using the tools listed above to make instructional videos to relay content, instructions, or expectations is a great way to engage students. While you can use any of the resources listed above, we tried to categorize by what we thought was age-group appropriate. When you model the use of these tools, students often like to take a crack at creation as well! These resources are also perfect in the Make section, when students take control of their learning. Listed below are examples of how to use some of the apps/websites above to engage students!

EXAMPLE: Check the Chapter 6 resources at TeachinglandTheBook.com for a Powtoon Video to teach about stock market and a student-created video on STEM.

ENGAGE THEM: With Gamifying Your Class

LEVEL: Elementary—Class Dojo
Middle—Classcraft
High—Classcraft

DESCRIPTION: Using an LMS such as Class Dojo or Classcraft can engage even the least motivated student! Class Dojo is the perfect tool to gamify/badge learning and provide students with the opportunity to earn points through positive behavior. Using these tools provides motivation and helps to make classroom management fun! Classcraft is more than a gamified classroom manage-ment tool. You can use it as an LMS and assign points for completion.

It has a fun social component that fosters collaboration among students and has other features built in, such as random events. It really transforms your curriculum into an epic adventure and integrates with Microsoft and Google Classroom.

EXAMPLE: When Savannah used Classcraft in her classroom, she started every day with a random event! You can customize your random events to be content related and build in tasks that tie back to curriculum. The native events listed, such as Chant of the Master and Crazy DJ, are also fun. One particular event allowed a student to play a song and make Savannah sing it in front of the class. This tool was good for laughs, increased student engagement, and built a great rapport!

ENGAGE THEM: With Inspiring Them!

LEVEL: Elementary—Wonderopolis
Middle—TED-Ed
High—TED-Ed

DESCRIPTION: What better way to engage students than content-based wonder! Using Wonderopolis to generate discussions and start lessons is perfect for hooking littles and middles into topics and wanting to explore more. They also have an educator section. So find a wonder topic that ties into your standards or have students deconstruct the standard and find a wonder topic themselves! TED-Ed also is a great resource for students and can technically be used across all age groups! Using TED Talks in the classroom can spark conversations around curricular topics and launch lessons by piquing curiosity to delve deeper into topic through research and inquiry. You can search talks by topic and share links in your LMS or play for the entire class.

EXAMPLE: Savannah used TED Talks as a springboard in her classroom to get students thinking about STEM topics they wanted to explore when drafting their own topics.

ENGAGE THEM: With Augmenting Your Lesson!

LEVEL: Elementary—Merge Cube Apps/Storyfab/Kouji
Middle—Metaverse
High—HP Reveal, Layer, DAQRI, Zappar

DESCRIPTION: Students can hold and manipulate interactive learning experiences in their hands with Merge Cube! With a growing catalogue of experiences, Merge Cube uses augmented reality technology to allow students to interact in ways that are not possible through mere text alone. The experiences can be triggered by app or Chromebook. Cubes can be purchased or printed and assembled for classroom use. Students can also use Storyfab or Kouji to create their own augmented stories. While this is great for student making, you can also use these tools to make exemplars to model the technology and tools for students. You can also engage students by making augmented scavenger hunts an experience with Metaverse. HP Reveal and Zappar are another excellent starting point for adding augmented dimension to your classroom walls!

EXAMPLE: At St. John's Episcopal School in Dallas, Savannah worked with science teacher Mrs. Torrey to have students create element superheroes. Students made comic book panels and then created videos that added to the story line. Check out the one-page challenge and an HP Reveal Tutorial Video on the resource page for this chapter at TeachinglandTheBook.com.

ENGAGE THEM: With Flipping Your Classroom!

LEVEL: Elementary—Khan Academy
Middle—Swivl/Edpuzzle (interactive options)
High—SchoolTube/YouTube/Find/Upload

DESCRIPTION: Flipping your classroom or changing the structure by having students cover new content outside of your classroom walls or doing it independently through the In-Flip can be achieved with premade video on YouTube and Khan Academy. For the ultimate flipped experience, make your own videos using Swivl, a platform that allows you to turn PowerPoint presentations into interactive learning experiences that can be watched collectively or individually. You can also create one-take whiteboard videos (Lodge McCammon style) or app smash and create engaging flipped videos and upload them to YouTube or SchoolTube for students to access from anywhere. If you do upload them to YouTube, import them into Edpuzzle and add interactive elements to embed formatives on the fly!

EXAMPLE: Here are a few things you'll find our resource page for this chapter:

- Swivl Flipped Lecture

- Flipped Parent's Night

- YouTube Flipped Playlist on Government

- Flipped Lesson about the Russian Revolution

ENGAGE THEM: With Breakouts

LEVEL: Elementary
Middle } Breakout Edu/Google Sites
High

DESCRIPTION: Breakouts are an educational spin on the escape room and prompt students to work together to solve riddles or clues designed by a teacher. You can purchase physical breakout kits from BreakoutEdu.com or you can make your own puzzles and riddles. They can be physical, digital, or hybrid breakouts, and the main focus is the students' collaboration and reviewing and analyzing of clues multiple times to find key details to solving the puzzle. You can also create your own using Google Sites and Google Forms!

EXAMPLE: Brian Costello is a teacher from New Jersey who has mastered breakouts! Check out his web page of breakouts and learn how to design your own! Want to introduce your teachers to Teachingland rules? Invite Savannah to do Outbreaks2breakoutsPD.

ENGAGE THEM: With A Scavenger Hunt

LEVEL: Elementary—QR codes (QRstuff.com, Qrafter app)
Middle—GooseChase
High—Waypoint Edu

DESCRIPTION: Using scavenger hunts to engage students can be great way to get students moving around and engaged in new topic exploration! You can create QR codes that give students digital clues or link to Google Forms to collect observations, answers, and evidence of learning. You can make them using an app or website; you can use the ones we listed or find one that suits your trench. GooseChase is also a unique app/website that sends student off on an adventure! You can use premade scavenger hunts, search by topics, or make your own! It is an excellent way to engage families in open house, school events, or change up your learning. Similarly, Waypoint Edu uses the scavenger hunt concept but combines augmented reality to add another layer of engagement. Check them out for yourselves and share how you envision using them in your bunker.

EXAMPLE: Download the GooseChase app and check our book scavenger hunt! Create a book scavenger hunt.

ENGAGE THEM: With Outside Experts

LEVEL: Elementary—Double Robot)
Middle—Google Hangouts/Skype for the Classroom
High—rumii

DESCRIPTION: We are beyond being the single sage or deliverer of knowledge in our classrooms as we shift to global learning communities and social knowledge construction. Bringing in outside experts is another way to expand the walls and expose students to multiple perspectives and connect to other classrooms. With Skype, you can do mystery skypes with classrooms around the world, connect with content experts via Google Hangouts, and even speak with them avatar to avatar. Video and VR conferencing really brings the world to your classroom when geographic constraints get in the way.

EXAMPLE: Columbus's school uses Double Robots to send students on virtual field trips. Someone takes the robot to the location, and then the students can drive it around and engage with experts and ask questions. It's almost as good as actually being there!

When Savannah's students were exploring game design, the CEO and developer from OhHeckYeah, a game design company out of Denver, did a GHO with students to explore the career connections and asked questions about the process of game design.

http://ohheckyeah.com

Savannah is working on a PD cohort using the VR platform rumii to bring educators together to brainstorm how to integrate it into the K–12 classrooms. There aren't any examples at the time of writing, but they are coming soon! Be an EdTech Hipster and be an early adopter!

Check the resource page for this chapter to watch a video of Savannah's students working in rumii.

Apps and Bytes to Make things!

- How can my students show what they know?
- What are my students' interests?
- What edtech tools do my students have access to?
- What edtech tools can my students use to make and create?
- Which edtech tools would be appropriate for the content and learning objectives I need to cover?

MAKE A...: Movie

LEVEL: Elementary—Do Ink/iMovie
Middle—TouchCast/WeVideo
High—TouchCast/Camtasia

DESCRIPTION: Using video to make movies on content, PSAs, documentaries, movie trailers, and process videos can be a powerful way to create a knowledge artifact that also teaches communication and writing skills. #PowerofVideo is a hashtag worthy of following on Twitter, with a ton of great research and examples constantly being shared. Do Ink, iMovie, and TouchCast are great iPad apps, while WeVideo is accessible from a browser or from an app and does a great job of fostering collaboration and group projects. Starting a broadcasting or journalism club at your school is a great way to provide opportunities for students to learn how to use this media. You can also app smash and use other apps like Animoto, VideoScribe, and Super Power FX to make your videos more dynamic.

EXAMPLE: Savannah is a former English, history, and film teacher. Visit the resource page for Chapter 6 on TeachinglandTheBook.com to see a variety of videos from her students.

MAKE A…: 3D Design

LEVEL: Elementary—Morphi
Middle—TinkerCad
High—AutoCad/Blender/Maya

DESCRIPTION: Using CAD apps or programs for 3D model creation is a great way to design prototypes that can be manipulated 360° or printed and held in our hands. Morphi is a great website or iPad app where students can create 3D models that export as .stl files and can be 3D printed. TinkerCad and AutoCad are other great options to use with students, while our grade-level recommendations are mere suggestions, as Morphi and TinkerCad can certainly be used K–12.

EXAMPLE: In a STEM unit at the STEM Academy, students used their knowledge of species to design and print a new insect. They used 3D modeling software, TinkerCad to create their insects, then printed them and made videos for the Nevermore Species database. They used stop-motion animation videos to showcase their new bugs!

MAKE A…: Sound Project!

LEVEL: Elementary—ChatterPix/Blabberize/Voki
Middle—Vocaroo/DropVox
High—Soundtrap/GarageBand

DESCRIPTION: Adding sounds to images to showcase learning can be done in so many ways, but the apps curated above have a special place in our heart. ChatterPix (app) or Blabberize (byte) are great ways to bring images to life and get them to talk. Voki, on the other hand, allows students to create their own avatar, and they record their voice or use voice to type to have it share information. Vocaroo and DropVox are also voice apps that create

QR codes for sound files that can be added to site words, stories, or images on your website or in your physical classroom. Soundtrap or GarageBand is a great tool to work on collaborative projects such as podcasts, but traditional video-editing platforms work as well!

EXAMPLE: Check out our Voki examples at TeachinglandTheBook.com.

MAKE A...: Stop-Motion Animation

LEVEL: Elementary—LEGO Stop Motion
  Middle—Stop Motion Studio
  High—WeVideo (stop-motion animator); Chrome Extension

DESCRIPTION: Stop-motion animation is another great option students can choose as a creation format. Stringing together images to create the illusion of movement is super fun, and there are so many ways to accomplish this! You can do drawing, LEGO or brick animation, combine green screen, use clay, or 2D construction paper and markers. It has been a favorite in Savannah's classes. There are different tools you can use, including Google Slides, but our absolute favorite is Stop Motion Studio app on the iPad. There are web-based options as well, such as WeVideo or the Chrome extension, Stop Motion Animator.

EXAMPLE: See a few examples online, including . . .

- Sixth-Grade Stop-Motion Animated Geography

- NOAA Ocean PSA

- Group-Made Stop Motion Video

MAKE AN...: Animation

LEVEL: Elementary—Shadow Puppet Edu/Puppet Pals Pocket/Tellagami/Buncee (app & byte)
  Middle—Powtoon/Animaker/GoAnimate (bytes)
  High—Plotagon (app & byte)

DESCRIPTION: The animation game is when it comes to multiple options and various ways to have students animate their learning. Shadow Puppet, Puppet Pals, and Tellagami are great for littles, and all have freemium and paid Edu versions. While the freemiums are sufficient, we highly recommend spending the extra money to get all the features and animation characters even if you only do it on a few iPads and make them part of a station.

We recommend Powtoon, Animaker, and GoAnimate for middles. These apps have more mature characters compared to their littles counterparts. Buncee, though listed in littles, can also be used by middles. Really, most of the apps can span K–12 if it is just a matter of where your students are with technology. We listed them according to entry level. Plotagon has some more sophisticated characters that would appeal to middles and to high-school students.

EXAMPLE: See a few examples online, including...

- "7 Deadly Camera Sins" Powtoon Video
- Thanksgiving Mayflower Design Challenge Plotagon

MAKE A...: Story!

LEVEL: Elementary—Writer Reader App
Middle—Storybird/Book Creator
High—Google Docs/OneNote

DESCRIPTION: Having students use platforms like the Writer Reader app helps littles to learn how to read by writing their own books! Storybird is also a great app that provides students artwork for their book and prompts them to sequence the art and unlock the story within. Book Creator is another platform that works both on iPads and web browsers. Students can create their own textbooks and document the learning process and in Chrome and can collaborate with other students. And of course, Google Docs, OneNote, or Pages are excellent for older students to write and solicit peer feedback using the cloud or share options.

EXAMPLE: You can see student examples of Storybird projects as well as a book Savannah created with Book Creator on the Chapter 6 resource page online.

MAKE A...: Programming

LEVEL: Elementary—Kodable/ScratchJr/Code.org
Middle—Scratch/Code.org
High—Swift/Grok Learning/Udemy

DESCRIPTION: There are so many coding apps out there that allow students to gain computational-thinking skills while also showcasing content knowledge. ScratchJr and Scratch are excellent examples of how students can use coding platforms to create digital stories. The beautiful thing that is they can use content from pretty much any class to include in their project. Whether kindergarteners are summarizing a story they read or second graders are creating a story on biomes using science, it's a vehicle to drive content. Scratch is a more advanced version of ScratchJr and is appropriate for the middle-school level. Kodable, Code.org, and Grok Learning also offer fantastic opportunities for students to learn code. All three provide scaffolded lessons that teach students coding foundations all the way to advanced languages such as Python and JavaScript.

EXAMPLE: At the STEM Academy, students used Scratch to create video games on marine conservation using the Savannah coastline and maps as the background. At Herbert Mills STEM Elementary, students begin learning to code in kindergarten through Code.org and various other computer science apps and programmable robots, and by the time they leave in fourth grade, many are prepared to take on more advanced languages in middle school.

MAKE A...: Virtual Reality Space

LEVEL: Elementary—CoSpaces Edu
Middle—Roomful/rumii
High—Unity/Google Tour Creator

DESCRIPTION: Virtual Reality is not just for engaging students with VR field trips using Google Expeditions. With platforms like CoSpaces (app and byte), students can create their own VR spaces and exercise their coding skills as well. CoSpaces is one of those evergreen options that can carry students through their VR journey K–12. Roomful is another cool VR creation gallery app that allows users to customize a room or their images and media. Students could utilize this as a portfolio option for student work and have teachers, or anyone in the world, really, walk around their space. Rumii (byte) is also a great VR conference space where students could meet virtually with other classrooms to collaborate or present ideas. Meetings can be recorded and posted later as a learning artifact. Finally, Unity is the chosen industry platform that most VR platforms or apps are built in.

EXAMPLE: Here are a few things you'll find our resource page for this chapter:

- CSI Student-Designed Example Space in CoSpaces
- A CSI Lesson Plan
- CSI Video Hook
- And more!

MAKE A...: Video Game Design

LEVEL: Elementary—Bloxels/Gamestar Mechanic Jr
Middle—Gamestar Mechanic/Minecraft/Hopscotch/Roblox
High—Unity

DESCRIPTION: Video game design, when leveraged correctly, can be a powerful and fun platform for students to convey content knowledge and a great opportunity to develop twenty-first-century skills. Bloxels (app) and Gamestar Mechanic Jr are great entry points for littles, and there is a ton of curricular resources already created, though as you probably know, we recommend making your own! Gamestar Mechanic, Minecraft, Hopscotch, and Roblox are also great ways for students to showcase what they know. Gamestar focuses more on game mechanics and rules, but the objectives and content of the game can be within the context of one or multiple subject areas, and they often have annual STEM design challenges students can participate in. High school students with some experience can be started with Unity, an industry-standard design platform.

EXAMPLE: Bloxels: With Bloxels, students used this platform to turn their favorite stories—or stories they wrote—into games. Check out some samples on our resource page.

MAKE A...: Podcast

LEVEL: Elementary—Synth
Middle—Anchor
High—Soundtrap

DESCRIPTION: Podcasting is a great way for students to do no-frills research while also using technology! When students are just producing audio bytes that reflect their learning, they must learn to be good story tellers and use descriptive language and learn how to present research in an engaging, auditory way. Synth is a fairly new tool and is great for littles. It is available as an app.

Anchor is multi-platform and allows you to produce an entire podcast from audio to audio FX and editing. It's the most comprehensive and easy-to-use platform we have found and even hosts the podcast! SoundCloud is a great audio hosting platform for older students and probably is better known by this demographic. For age crossover power and ease of use, we award Anchor the Pulse Award (a Teachingland award approval for getting little hearts racing for learning).

EXAMPLE: Savannah used Anchor to have students record, edit, and produce podcasts on topics of their choice. The *Teachingland* podcast is also hosted through Anchor!

MAKE A...: Student Choice

LEVEL: Elementary
Middle } What app-etizer or Byte will they pick? 'Nuff said.
High

DESCRIPTION: Even with all the choices, a few students may come up with a novel way they want to show what they know! Let them pick how to demonstrate mastery—or put it in their yearn jar for a later assignment! Also, you may find all the choices may overwhelm. You will have to determine whether you open up choices to infinite possibilities or limit them on a case-by-case basis.

EXAMPLE: Ask your students for examples on how they may want to show what they know! Many teachers in Columbus's bunker leverage choice boards and menus for students to choose assessments that make sense for them and their learning preferences.

How can I evaluate students? Apps and Bytes!

- What kind of assessment is this, and what edtech tool can I use to evaluate students?

- How can I use technology to help me grade?

- How can I get a quick pulse on student knowledge?

- What kind of tools are best for summative assessments or portfolios?

- How can I use technology to provide timely real-time feedback to students?

EVALUATE THEM USING…: A Learning Management System

LEVEL: Elementary—Edmodo/Seesaw
Middle—Google Classroom
High—iTunes U/Canvas

DESCRIPTION: A learning management system is a great way to curate all your assignments, lessons, and materials in one spot for students. It is also a great place to facilitate conversations, share student work, and solicit feedback and peer reviews. Edmodo, Google Classroom, and iTunes U are all great platforms to communicate expectations and design learning experiences. You can post quizzes, Google Forms, and pretty much anything with a link in an LMS.

EXAMPLE: The STEM Academy used iTunes U for grand challenge projects where a capstone was required. All content area teachers posted their assignments in iTunes U along with rubrics.
Herbert Mills STEM Elementary uses Seesaw to create meaningful learning experiences for kids every day, and it has a fantastic parent involvement component as well!

EVALUATE THEM USING…: Response Systems

LEVEL: Elementary
Middle } The Answer Pad, Socrative, Go Formative, Plickers, Poll Everywhere
High

DESCRIPTION: All the platforms listed above are there to help evaluate students digitally and provide real-time feedback to the students and the teachers. The Answer Pad has an awesome Go Interactive feature where students join the class with a code, and they can quickly complete a formative multiple choice, thumbs up/thumbs down, graph, or drawing without logging in. It is great to see data for the entire class in one spot to adjust instruction for a small or whole group. Socrative and Go Formative are very similar tools. If you are not 1:1 and want to get in on the formative feedback action and collect whole class data, we highly recommend Plickers. Plickers are cards you give students, and they turn them a certain way to signify their answer. The teacher uses one device to scan the room and can do an instant read on student pulse.

EXAMPLE: When Savannah taught film, she used the Go Interactive feature in the Answer

Pad to have students draw examples of camera shots. This gave a whole-class snapshot of content understanding.

EVALUATE THEM USING...: Websites and Blogs

LEVEL: Elementary—Kidblog/Edublog
Middle—Weebly/Google Sites
High—Wix

DESCRIPTION: Websites can be a great tool to evaluate students on a formative or summative basis. If students are responsible for curating work into a culminating portfolio, a website can be a great way to organize this information. You can also use a forum feature on a class website to have students respond to prompts and to each other. Enabling comments and sharing all student websites in a bookmarking site like Symbaloo makes it easy for students to browse the work of their peers and engage in peer reviews.

EXAMPLE: Savannah used Weebly to create her STEMFilmClass website and had students create websites to host their writing, photography, and film. Columbus had students use Kidblog to blog about what they were reading and respond to one another. This experience was highly engaging for students and allowed her to see how they were comprehending their texts.

EVALUATE THEM USING...: Voiceover Feedback

LEVEL: Elementary—Seesaw
Middle—Kaizena
High—Kaizena

DESCRIPTION: Traditional assignments called for traditional grading, but in the time of the classroom apocalypse, voiceover feedback is as edgy as it gets! Not only does it allow you to provide feedback on the fly and save time, it also prompts students to actually listen to suggestions and hear the logic behind assessment. Work that receives a flat, two-dimensional grade without proper feedback doesn't get a proper second go or iteration by the student. Recording your thoughts on a paper written in Google Docs using Kaizena, a voice feedback tool integrated with Google. You can also use Seesaw to drop littles feedback, and encouragement makes assessment more meaningful and has greater impact.

EXAMPLE: Savannah's students wrote scripts for their documentaries, and Kaizena was a great way to offer voiceover feedback! Columbus also used Kaizena as a teacher to provide her students feedback on writing assignments. At Herbert Mills STEM, her teachers can use Seesaw to provide voiceover feedback for all sorts of assignments.

EVALUATE THEM USING...: Gamified Quizzes

LEVEL: Elementary—Kahoot
Middle—FlipQuiz
High—Quizlet

DESCRIPTION: A fun way to get a quick pulse on the learning going on your classroom is to use gamified assessment tools like Kahoot or FlipQuiz. Kahoot quickly turns a formative assessment into a fun multiplayer clicker game complete with a leader board. FlipQuiz is a customizable *Jeopardy!* equivalent, where students can complete individually or in teams. Quizlet, popular for its flashcard-like quiz features, offers a variety of ways to study or brush up on content and has a classroom feature to collect data. Remember to use the results to inform your instruction and provide additional scaffolding and support to students who may need it.

EXAMPLE: Savannah used Kahoot! to get the pulse on students' knowledge. Check out sample quizzes on this chapter's resource page at TeachinglandTheBook.com.

EVALUATE THEM USING...: Interactive Learning Apps

LEVEL: Elementary
Middle } LearningApps/BookWidgets
High learningapps.org/createApp.php and bookwidgets.com

DESCRIPTION: LearningApps is an amazing byte that offers teachers the power to customize learning games and provides an interactive alternative to boring drill-and-practice strategies. Teachers have the option to save time and use pre-existing apps made by other teachers, but we recommend making your own to best suit your students. You can browse by category and grade level. Using this tool for reinforcement of a concept or enrichment is an excellent application of LearningApps. BookWidgets are awesome opportunities to create interactive practice for students that can be embedded into books, HyperDocs, a website, or shared via a link anywhere you can post it! Options include flashcards, sequencing, puzzles, exit slips, quizzes, timelines, games, and much more. It also automatically grades them!

EXAMPLE: Savannah created flashcards for multiple angles for her class using BookWidgets.com.

EVALUATE THEM USING…: Artificial Intelligence

LEVEL: Elementary—Alexa with Echo Buttons/ABCmouse
Middle—Hubert.ai
High—Plagiarism Checkers/Turnitin

DESCRIPTION: Artificial intelligence is becoming more present in education as the technology becomes more sophisticated and accessible. Alexa is great for pre-readers with voice activation, but it also offers echo buttons and the option where users can create their own content—think *Jeopardy!* Also, Hubert.ai is the first AI chat bot of its kind to talk with students and ask for feedback on content, projects, or whatever else. And then plagiarism checkers like Turnitin.com are fantastic ways to have papers scanned using algorithms. Adaptive learning is becoming a common phrase in education, which usually is a tip-off that there is some sort of AI at work.

EXAMPLE: We plan on using Hubert.ai to get feedback on this table and their tech suggestions along with additional apps that could be added in different sections.

Demystification of Apps and Bytes!

- What tool can I use to demystify the learning process?
- How can I curate my resources for easy navigation?
- How can I communicate expectations and deadlines?
- In what ways can I organize learning?
- How can I make the learning process interactive?

Your Demystification part of the R.E.M.E.D.Y. cycle should bring all the other parts of the cycle together in a way that makes sense, either through organization, task mastering, or setting expectations. Consider these:

DEMYSTIFY LEARNING WITH…: Digital Organizers

LEVEL: Elementary—Wunderlist
Middle—Tes.com/lessons/(Blendspace)
High—LiveBinders

DESCRIPTION: Organizing learning experiences and labeling the phases learners go through can help students understand what to expect in the classroom. When we are consistent with how we design learning experiences and use organizers such as Wunderlist, Blendspace, or LiveBinders, it helps students mentally understand the learning process, transfer it to other content areas, and develops good learning habits.

EXAMPLE: Savannah created entire projects from start to finish in Blendspace. This allowed students to see the rubric, expectations, and all assignments associated with the project so they could understand the time obligation and scope and sequence.

DEMYSTIFY LEARNING WITH…: Games and Simulations

LEVEL: Elementary—Legends of Learning
Middle—PHET Interactive Simulations
High—PHET Interactive Simulations

DESCRIPTION: Simulations have a proven success rate at helping students gain a deeper understanding of how something works. Legends of Learning, and PHET Simulations both offer students the opportunity to explore difficult concepts through simulations. While Legends of Learning is gasified and allows students to experience science concepts through gamification, PHET interactive is a free website that provides STEM content area simulations and is more suited for middles and bigs. We classify this as a demystification tool because it helps students better understand hard-to-grasp concepts. Legends of learning is multi-platform and is expanding to more grade levels and content areas in the coming years.

EXAMPLE: In a camp on circuits, Savannah had students complete the virtual circuit lab: phet.colorado.edu/en/simulation/circuit-construction-kit-dc-virtual-lab

DEMYSTIFY LEARNING WITH...: Rubrics

LEVEL: Elementary—RubiStar

Middle—Rubric-Maker.com/Peergrade

High—Google Form/Doctopus and Goobric

DESCRIPTION: Rubrics are super important in the demystification process, as they let students know what content they will be responsible for and the time frame and due dates of the project. They also set expectations. When approaching a project, Buck Institute suggests providing the rubric ahead of time to give students the opportunity to identify any knowledge gaps they need to fill.

EXAMPLE: At the beginning of the year, Savannah completes rubrics and gives them to students at the beginning of a project. As the year progresses, she unpacks standards by having students pose questions they think they need to answer and then designs the rubric with the class. This gives students ownership of how they will be assessed and on what criteria. Rubrics are important for littles too. Columbus's teachers spend a ton of time creating and revisiting rubrics that are already in place to make sure that they are a true measure of student learning.

DEMYSTIFY LEARNING WITH...: Backchannel

LEVEL: Elementary—ClassroomScreen.com

Middle—Weebly or Classroom website forum

High—Backchannel chat.com/Padlet

DESCRIPTION: A backchannel is a quiet inquiry communication system that you can run in the background of your classroom to provide an opportunity for students to ask questions about content, activities, and expectations. This is a fantastic opportunity to address questions as they arise without disrupting class while catering to individual student needs. ClassroomScreen.com and Padlet can serve this purpose for littles, while a Weebly or website forum has worked for middles. Providing a forum also gives students the opportunity to crowdsource answers from peers. Backchannel Chat is good for high school classrooms and professional learning sessions. And we mentioned Padlet earlier, but it's applicable as here as well!

EXAMPLE: Whenever Savannah is teaching a class or workshop, she uses Padlet as a backchannel where students or attendees can post their questions as they think of them without interrupting the session or forgetting them. When Columbus was in the classroom, she had students record their questions, write comments about the lesson, and record their aha moments when something clicked.

DEMYSTIFY LEARNING WITH…: HyperDocs

LEVEL: Elementary—Buncee
Middle—Google Docs/Google Slides
High—Google Docs/Google Slides

DESCRIPTION: A HyperDoc is a digital document that curates all elements needed for learning in one place. Providing hyperlinks to digital resources can condense the learning process down into one neatly packaged page that is easy for the brain to digest. The beautiful part about a HyperDoc is all phases of the learning cycle are present, and students can see how all the elements and task work together to demystify learning. You can literally use any edtech tool mentioned in the R.E.M.E.D.Y. Model as long as you can link out! This is perfect to app smash and bring all your favorite tools together to facilitate learning. When you create a one-stop shop for a unit, project, or topic, you are also helping students visualize learning.

EXAMPLE: Check out the book *The HyperDoc Handbook: Digital Lesson Design Using Google Apps.*
For more great examples, check out their webpage!
hyperdocs.co/index.php/about_us

Apps and Bytes to leave them Yearning for more!

- What do you want to know more about in terms of content?
- Are there any questions you still have about this unit?
- What technology would you want to use in the future?
- How would you do this differently next time?

LEAVE THEM YEARNING FOR MORE...: By Surveying Your Students

LEVEL: Elementary
      Middle   } Google Forms, Padlet, Backchannels
      High

DESCRIPTION: For the Yearning part of our R.E.M.E.D.Y. process, we suggest you create a survey, have a suggestion jar, or a post-it note wall for students to reflect on not only what they want to learn more about, but also what tech tools they may want to use in the future. While these aren't all high-tech solutions, the whole point is to field questions and interests from your students during a project and for future ideas they may have.

EXAMPLE: Using chalkboard paint, Savannah painted a wall in her classroom and always allowed students to write down new apps they had discovered and wanted to be considered for classroom projects. This is one way to keep in touch with tools and technology students are using. Another great option is using the whiteboard post-its by mcSquares as a parking lot by the door to the classroom. They are reusable, and students can write down suggestions or questions they have about content or ideas for future projects!

High-Tech PBL

While our Zombie Zips were low-tech maker challenges, our hi-tech PBLs are heavy on technology and STEM components. Using tools from the monster table, we have created a few hi-tech examples and included them below. Check out this STEM Design Challenge involving periodic elements, comic books, and augmented reality using the HP Reveal app! Combining science and math with periodic table elements and atomic properties, English language arts with storyboarding and scripting, artistic design with comic book paneling, film and media with the production process, and technology with the augmented reality component using HP Reveal, students get a true transdisciplinary STEAM experience. Being driven by researching individual elements and understanding their composition led to fantastic super hero stories of origin.

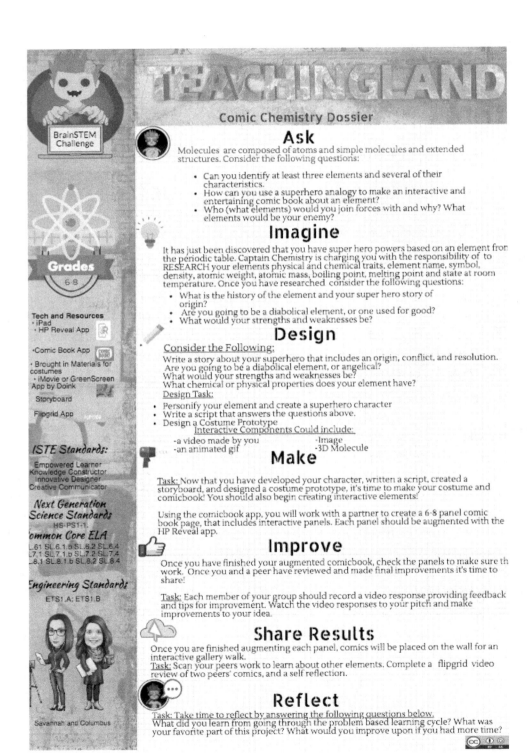

TEACHINGLAND

Comic Chemistry Dossier

BrainSTEM Challenge

Grades 6-8

Tech and Resources
- iPad
- HP Reveal App
- Comic Book App
- Brought in Materials for costumes
- iMovie or GreenScreen App by Doink
- Storyboard
- Flipgrid App

ISTE Standards:
Empowered Learner
Knowledge Constructor
Innovative Designer
Creative Communicator

Next Generation Science Standards
HS-PS1-1

Common Core ELA
L.6.1 SL.6.1.b SL.6.2 SL.6.4
L.7.1 SL.7.1.b SL.7.2 SL.7.4
L.8.1 SL.8.1.b SL.8.2 SL.8.4

Engineering Standards
ETS1.A; ETS1.B

Savannah and Columbus

Ask
Molecules are composed of atoms and simple molecules and extended structures. Consider the following questions:
- Can you identify at least three elements and several of their characteristics.
- How can you use a superhero analogy to make an interactive and entertaining comic book about an element?
- Who (what elements) would you join forces with and why? What elements would be your enemy?

Imagine
It has just been discovered that you have super hero powers based on an element from the periodic table. Captain Chemistry is charging you with the responsibility of to RESEARCH your elements physical and chemical traits, element name, symbol, density, atomic weight, atomic mass, boiling point, melting point and state at room temperature. Once you have researched consider the following questions:
- What is the history of the element and your super hero story of origin?
- Are you going to be a diabolical element, or one used for good?
- What would your strengths and weaknesses be?

Design
Consider the Following:
Write a story about your superhero that includes an origin, conflict, and resolution.
Are you going to be a diabolical element, or angelical?
What would your strengths and weaknesses be?
What chemical or physical properties does your element have?
Design Task:
- Personify your element and create a superhero character
- Write a script that answers the questions above.
- Design a Costume Prototype

Interactive Components Could include:
-a video made by you   -Image
-an animated gif   -3D Molecule

Make
Task: Now that you have developed your character, written a script, created a storyboard, and designed a costume prototype, it's time to make your costume and comicbook! You should also begin creating interactive elements!

Using the comicbook app, you will work with a partner to create a 6-8 panel comic book page, that includes interactive panels. Each panel should be augmented with the HP Reveal app.

Improve
Once you have finished your augmented comicbook, check the panels to make sure th work. Once you and a peer have reviewed and made final improvements it's time to share!

Task: Each member of your group should record a video response providing feedback and tips for improvement. Watch the video responses to your pitch and make improvements to your idea.

Share Results
Once you are finished augmenting each panel, comics will be placed on the wall for an interactive gallery walk.
Task: Scan your peers work to learn about other elements. Complete a flipgrid video review of two peers' comics, and a self reflection.

Reflect
Task: Take time to reflect by answering the following questions below.
What did you learn from going through the problem based learning cycle? What was your favorite part of this project? What would you improve upon if you had more time?

Personalized Pantry: Leaving Learning Ajar

Now that we have provided you various Zombie Zip maker challenges and a monster table of hi-tech goodness, let's talk about personalized learning and choice. In order to incorporate voice and choice in your classroom, we have developed the concept of the personalized pantry: a take on choice boards, as it takes all the ingredients (edtech tools from the high-tech table) from our R.E.M.E.D.Y. Model and puts them in physical jars (can be done digitally as well for our EdTech Hipsters—maybe Padlet?). You can get actual mason jars and curate tools and resources throughout the year for each part of the R.E.M.E.D.Y. design cycle, or you can print out large jars and write the tools on them so they appear inside the jar. Sticking with our Doomsday chapter theme with canning ideas and tools—not curriculum—we used jars in order to save and preserve tools and features in one place as a constant resource. Remember Rule #5? The most effective curriculum and lessons are ones created by you and your students!

We find this effective because sometimes putting abstract concepts like the learning process into tangible forms (in this case printing out options for students to complete each learning phase) can help students get a better grasp on the process of learning. It is important to leave lesson design open (or ajar—hardy har har) to your students and invite them to the prepping party so they can co-create personalized learning pathways that focus on voice and choice. It also helps create students that have agency, are self-efficacious, and in charge of their learning. This helps these skills transfer to other content areas and sets students up for success in future learning endeavors. The edtech tools and strategies you decide to place in your jars may be different from the ones in our monster table, but it is a great place to start! It is good to personalize your jars with the resources your trench has access to. Not all bunkers are equipped the same. Your students may also have suggestions on tools they may want to add to the jar. Go to our website and watch the video about the Personalized Pantry: Leaving Learning Ajar.

Using the Jars to Design Learning Experiences

As you begin a new lesson, create a rubric that assesses the content students will be responsible for, but leave the way they will research, design solutions or projects, and showcase their learning up to the students. Invite them to explore various tools and include both high-tech and low-tech vehicles that will get them on the path to learning. Once students have designed how they are going to achieve their goals, have them create a rubric that considers their presentation using any of the rubric makers included in our table. This puts ownership on the students!

Check out our jars! If you go to our website we have more in-depth resources on how we use these!

PBJ: Adding Problems to the Jar

So far we have mostly covered project-based learning in this chapter. There is often confusion when it comes to differentiating *problem*-based learning from project-based learning, so in this section we are going to try to do that for you. While problem-based learning almost always has projects involved, project-based learning doesn't always start out with a problem. Our R.E.M.E.D.Y. Model has all the ingredients necessary for project-based learning to occur, but if you are looking to incorporate problem-based learning into your classroom, it's as easy as starting with a problem scenario or scientific misconception and having students use the R.E.M.E.D.Y. Model to select tools to guide them through the inquiry process.

The easiest way to transform your project-based learning unit to a problem-based unit is to start with the standards that guide your instruction and ask how they can be presented as a problem. When first introducing problem-based learning, we recommend defining the problem for students and letting students focus on a solution. To do this, we have added a Problem-Based Jar to the front of the R.E.M.E.D.Y. Model. Either you or your students can ask questions and define the problem scenario. After students have completed a problem-based unit, instead of providing them with the problem, try giving them a contextualized scenario and let them identify and define the problem for themselves. The goal is to equip students with the skills to identify problems in new situations and provide them with explicit understanding of the problem-solving process so they can do all of this on their own. These are skills that will transfer to other domains and will also be useful later in life.

Want a cool hook to introduce students to problem-based learning? Savannah wrote a *Hamilton* parody song to teach the steps of PBL. Check it out here: bit.ly/10PBLCommandments

Innovative Ways to Stock Your Survival Kit: Hoarding for the Horde

Not every classroom comes equipped with the tools and resources that we hope for; for example, Savannah got a raiseless promotion to teach film—what she considered a dream job! The catch: there were neither computers nor editing software in the room. While two classes were 1:1, the eighth-grade class only had access to five flip cams. So what do you do when you have high-tech dreams on a low-tech budget? You get just as innovative with your strategies to stock your classroom as you do with your pedagogical approach! Below are several ways you can supplement the technology you have and start building the classroom your students deserve.

Donor's Choose is a great website that allows teachers to write up classroom project dreams. It's complete with edtech equipment needed to make those dreams a reality. The platform verifies your eligibility (confirms teacher status) and then your project goes live. There are a lot of companies that match individual donations, and a lot of times in the first five days of the project, you can get double bang for your buck. Sending flyers home with students and sharing projects on social media is a great way to get the word out about your project so that it gets funded within the set timeframe.

Once a project is funded, your students write thank-you notes to be delivered to the donors. Funded materials usually show up within thirty days!

Another great way to make your budget stretch is to purchase second-life hardware. Buying gently loved devices can help stock your bunker and provide a lower ratio of tech to students. There are two different companies we recommend: Tech to School and STS Education.

Tech to School provides iPads and iMacs at an affordable rate without sacrificing your vision. They often provide bulk discounts and have even recently partnered with LocknCharge to provide charging and storage solutions as well. Savannah bought thirty iPads and five MacBook Airs for her STEAMPunk program, and the devices included a warranty and cases.

STS education is also another great company that offers a Second-Life Hardware program where you can purchase technology at 40–70 percent off the normal price.

Check out these two options before spending a fortune outfitting your classroom. Reducing the cost of purchasing technology frees up money in your budget to spend on other accessories!

Tales from the Trenches

Renee Coley
@renee_coley
Pataskala
c. 2016

I may have been the one who decided to become a teacher, but it's my students who have acted as my navigators, picking the path I have followed throughout my career. My decision to dive into teaching computer science is a perfect example of the influence of my students on my choices. I did not grow up with computers, and the extent of their impact on my own education was trying in vain to learn DOS in college. As a result, I often viewed computers as a means to create and complete more traditional projects and assignments, such as essays and presentations. Students could have accomplished these same tasks with pens, paper, poster boards, books, and worksheets. The reality was that using computers in my classroom was doing nothing to advance student learning.

Then my district sent us an email about Hour of Code from Code.org. Three years ago, there was a push to have all the buildings in my district do an hour of code during computer science in Education Week. As a teacher in a low-income minority-majority school, I saw the value in exposing the students to coding and computer science even if it was only for an hour. That hour turned into hours as students asked to "get on code" any time there was free time, an incentive, or indoor recess. They were completing levels at home and showing me their progress each Monday. They started using other tools from Code.org to create art and animated scenes of books and stories we were reading. They were talking out loud as they worked, collaborating and learning from each other, sharing their ideas, problem-solving, failing, trying again, and persisting until they got it right. They were engaged, excited, and passionate, and I followed their lead.

Their excitement and engagement encouraged me to fill out an application to pilot a new middle-school curriculum from Code.org aimed at sixth through tenth grades. Through the pilot, my students were exposed to a curriculum that not only taught them JavaScript, which is what Hour of Code activities teach, but also HTML, CSS, digital citizenship, the design cycle, prototyping, and app development. The result has been that in my school, computer science has moved from a fun activity that students do in their free time to classes that are being taught for the same reasons that math, science, social studies, and reading are taught. What remains the same is the interest and excitement that comes along with the skills and accomplishments found in the lessons of the curriculum. As one female student said to me recently, "I can see myself doing this for the rest of my life."

Brian Costello
@btcostello05
Jersey
c. 2017

"YES!" A seventh-grade girl shouts from the back of the room. "I can't believe I actually got it." There she was, near tears at how she had managed to solve several math problems on her own.

"Will you come to my birthday party?" A popular seventh-grade boy requests after spending the previous forty-five minutes working on fractions.

What prompted such engagement? These are some of the many excited, dedicated responses that came from various homemade editions of BreakOut Edu in my classroom. It started out simple. I had a few questions, a series of resources, and my classes would dig through those resources in hopes of solving some relatively simple puzzles. Together, as the year went on, my classes ventured down the rabbit hole with me. They were learning to collaborate, problem-solve, think critically, and connect information at an incredible rate; meanwhile, I was developing an aptitude for creating more complex challenges, in-depth ideas, and different ways for them to decipher information through the content their classroom teachers were providing. As I grew to an almost maniacal level of complexity worthy of a Panem Game Maker, they, too, grew in analyzing not only the information but also its source.

One of the things I always want for my classes is to learn to think critically, work together, and identify problems and solutions. I had created in those various groups of students an aptitude for all those things. It didn't matter what the content was, they digested that by default in order to solve the various puzzles laid before them.

Over the past few years I have gone through this cycle with classes. Sometimes I reuse games, but other times I create new experiences. By tailoring them to the needs of the kids with whom I work, I can ensure the experiences mesh the various practical skills I want them to develop with the content they are learning.

Breakouts have served as a great review activity in many cases. Other times they have been the hook for an exciting new topic.

"Today you will get to test out and code these tiny robots," I told my students recently. "There are thirty in the box; just come get one." I put down a box containing thirty Ozobots sealed with three separate locks. Instead of a groan, there was a buzz of excitement.

These days, every time kids walk into my room, there is the possibility of the unexpected. Breakouts are one of the many ways we build a sense of community as well as collaboration and critical problem-solving skills that will benefit my students in everything they do.

Chris Aviles
@TechUpTeacher
Jersey Shore
c. 2013

I decided to make student voice part of my life's work in 2013, at the start of my sixth year teaching sophomore English. I started that school year with one goal: Take what students love and incorporate it into the classroom. I made this my mission because I had been teaching the lowest track of English since I had started my career. My students hated school and made it clear on a daily basis that they didn't want to be there, let alone do any work. I was tired of it. Especially because there was nothing wrong with them; they had simply been let down by the education system. I wanted to win them back, and I knew student voice could help me do it.

I first embraced student voice by asking them, "How do you want to show me what you learned?" as the end of every unit. I gave them a week to answer that question and create something amazing. Students came up with all kinds of great projects that married their class-work with their passions. I had so many engineering, art, and computer science projects in my class that administration actually asked me if I was even teaching English. Students' grades, and more importantly their attitudes, improved drastically.

Fast-forward three and a half years. It is 2016, and I'm just starting my current job at Fair Haven. The Innovation Lab, the class I made to cultivate growth mindset as I exposed students to design thinking, computer science, engineering, and the digital arts, is in its first year. Student voice was still the driving force in my pedagogy, as the class was designed around students creating their own STEAM projects.

Deconstructing donated electronics and then trying to put them back together was a favorite project back then, and it still is today. Often students couldn't get the electronics back together, so we were left with a lot of junk for the recycling center. Some students had a problem with this. "Can we make something out of the parts?" students asked. "Absolutely," I said. The Parts to Arts project was born.

Students made all kinds of neat pieces of jewelry and sculptures out of disassembled electronics, but students quickly realized that now we just had a bunch of upcycled art sitting around. "Can we try to sell it?" students asked. "Absolutely," I said, and I built them an online store to sell their upcycled goodies. They named the store FH Gizmos. FH Gizmos launched in May of 2016. We made $8 that school year. The next school year, 2016–2017, we made about a $100, but FH Gizmos also got an amazing email.

Slack, the massive communication company, had seen pictures of the stuff students were creating on Twitter. They asked if we could make them something for their welcome bags. It took us the rest of that school year (up to October of this school year), but we did it. While some schools banned fidget spinners, we sold fifty professional-quality fidget spinners to Slack.

From upcycled jewelry to a manufacturing contract with Slack, my kids were hooked on entrepreneurship because it came from them. I didn't realize entrepreneurship was the missing piece of the Innovation Lab; they did. The class became so popular that it evolved into a program, FH Innovates, and FH Gizmos became its own class in a lineup of four student-driven classes that I now teach to every kid in our school.

Reaching my kids by caring about what they care about and walking them through the creation process helped them to see their learning in an entirely different way. What they care about matters. What they want to learn and how they want to learn it matters. They matter. Student voice became the R.E.M.E.D.Y. to my high school students' apathy, drives my middle school students' learning, and very likely kept me from quitting the profession. What could it do for you?

BRAIN STRETCHERS

1. What high-tech tools in the monster table do you have access to in your bunker?

2. How can you use Zombie Zips with your students?

3. Have you done similar design challenges in your trench?

4. How can you use the personal pantry concept and jar printouts to help students take ownership of their learning?

5. What high-tech tools would you add that aren't listed?

CHAPTER 7
28 Days Later: Surviving Assessment

We all hope we would be the person who would not leave anyone behind, but we really don't know. In times of catastrophes, some people find their humanity while others lose theirs.
—Glenn Stutzky, professor, Michigan State University

Believe it or not, *28 Days Later* isn't about zombies at all. When protesters break into a science lab and release a test monkey infected with a rage-inducing virus, a female protester is infected. As you might guess, things go downhill pretty quickly from there, and it's not long before Great Britain is plunged into violent chaos. Those who manage to survive are left to navigate a treacherous landscape where man's inhumanity to man seems to reign supreme. People begin questioning why they should keep fighting to live only to be greeted with carnage and terror day after day. For many, life becomes a series of fruitless motions, devoid of joy or hope. Twenty-eight days later, those infected by the rage virus start to die from starvation while scores of survivors bunker down to face the uncertain future ahead.

In the bunkers across Teachingland, twenty-eight days after the first day of school, teachers have typically administered their first formative assessments and might be reaching the time for a summative of some sort. But before we dive right into old-school testing, we must ask ourselves why we are testing in the first place. What are we trying to learn? What is the purpose of collecting this data? How will it be used? How do students want to demonstrate their knowledge? Similar to the survivors in *28 Days Later*, we have to consider the big picture and explore assessment through the lens of purposefulness, authenticity, and creation.

Let's face it, a packet of worksheets or a one hundred-question, multiple-choice test sucks the joy right out of your classroom or even the entire bunker, much like survival mode sucks the joy out of living. Testing can often have this effect on students and teachers—especially if the focused outcome of assessment is making a certain grade or surviving until the next year. A swarming, disengaged mob of students might be an inadvertent outcome. If students aren't truly invested in not only the components of your lesson but also how their learning is measured, they might become resigned to merely going through the motions and not giving learning their best shot.

A disconnect between assessment and learning can be massaged when you pick the correct assessment tool for the job. In the quote above, catastrophe can help one person find their humanity and one person lose theirs. Similarly, our assessment choices can motivate and inspire a love for learning in one student while causing another frustration and resignation. Engaging students in authentic ways, providing variety, choice, and opportunities for creation is the answer. Whether strategically checking the pulse of students every day to get a read on whether they are warm or cold blooded on topics or assigning a capstone project twenty-six weeks later (roughly 180 days), assessment is necessary to Teachingland survival.

Moving Beyond the Grading and Groaning

All over Teachingland, the moans of teachers and students chained to the grade-and-groan assembly line can be heard emanating through the hallways. Teachers are constantly assessing their students to make sure they have a firm grasp on the standards and are ready to perform on district and statewide assessments so that they can prove their worth. Unfortunately, state and district assessments are often traditional and summative in nature, and in an effort to properly prepare students, teachers often feel forced to make sure classroom assessments match what they will see on the high-stakes tests. This vicious cycle leaves everyone susceptible to infection.

Fortunately, there is another way. We believe that when students are given opportunities to engage with content in a meaningful way and design solutions to authentic problems that are rooted in the standards, they will learn. And when they are truly engaged in their learning, they retain the knowledge and skills they have learned and still perform well on any high-stakes assessment that comes their way.

Being mindful of *how* you are assessing students is just as important as *why* you are assessing them. Remember, no one is immune to infection. It can strike anyone at any moment—especially when students lose sight of the real purpose of learning, which can be blurred by multiple-choice summatives that result only in a letter grade. Read on to demystify assessment!

> BEING MINDFUL OF *HOW* YOU ARE ASSESSING STUDENTS IS JUST AS IMPORTANT AS *WHY* YOU ARE ASSESSING THEM.

Checking the Pulse of Your Students

Checking the pulse of your students—assessing where they are in their learning—is vital to maintaining the health of your trench, but it can be tricky business. The zombie infection can manifest in different ways among your students, and drill-and-practice and other monotonous practices can be the root cause for zombie-like groans. To prevent a grade-and-groan assembly line, you will need to use a variety of assessment strategies. This will keep tabs on everyone's health while also ensuring your assessment tactics are appropriate and aligned with the kind of data you need to get an accurate picture of how students are progressing. Some of the assessments you might use include the following:

Bite Size: Formative Assessments

Formative assessments are bite-sized strategies that provide the teacher with ongoing and sometimes even real-time feedback on how students are understanding concepts. In Chapter 6 we listed a few edtech evaluation tools that can be used to capture a snapshot of individual learning. These are low-stakes opportunities for students to show what they know so that the teacher has a pulse on who needs what.

PRE-ASSESSMENT (REACH STRATEGY)

WHAT IS IT?: It's determining what students know about a specific topic before teaching it.

PURPOSE: To tailor our instruction to meet individual needs of students

EXAMPLE: KWL charts, clustering, text preview, quiz

HIGH-TECH TOOL SUGGESTION: Padlet, LearningApps.com, Go Formative, Kahoot

SKILL/CONTENT-BASED ASSESSMENT (EVALUATION STRATEGY)

WHAT IS IT?: It's determining how well students are grasping and retaining new content in the classroom.

PURPOSE: To know if we need to provide additional instruction to address remaining knowledge gaps

EXAMPLE: Quizzes, labeling, timelines, and other activities or classwork that require application of new knowledge

HIGH-TECH TOOL SUGGESTION: The Answer Pad, Edpuzzle, Popplet

SELF-ASSESSMENT (DEMYSTIFICATION STRATEGY)

WHAT IS IT?: It's having students monitor their learning and evaluate their work.

PURPOSE: To lead to better understanding of performance tasks and expectations—to lead to self-improvement

EXAMPLE: Journal reflections, exit tickets, rubrics, reflection vlogs, blogs

HIGH-TECH TOOL SUGGESTION: Weebly, Flipgrid, Google Forms, Recap, Zomoji Exit Ticket (on the following page)

PEER ASSESSMENT (DEMYSTIFICATION/ENGAGE STRATEGY)

WHAT IS IT?: It's having students evaluate and discuss work done by peers.

PURPOSE: To provide multiple perspectives and valuable feedback to improve

EXAMPLE: Paper rubrics, online rubrics, commenting

HIGH-TECH TOOL SUGGESTION: Comment feature in Google Docs, Google Forms, Peergrade.io

Bite-Sized Assessments as a Diagnostic Tools

The four types of formative assessments referred to in the table above serve different diagnostic purposes throughout the R.E.M.E.D.Y. Model, and the data from each type is used a different way. For a preassessment, the data collected is used to inform the teacher's instruction. If the majority of your students have a strong grasp of a skill or topic, you may choose to spend less time than you originally planned to go over it and move on to the next topic or skill. Pacing guides and plans should be flexible and reflective of student needs. For content/skills assessments, data can be used to change your instructional strategies to meet student needs, pull small groups for targeted instruction, group students according to ability level, and identify students for extension or remediation. It is vital that you formatively assess your students often to make sure you set them up for success when they do a summative or performance-based assessment; additionally, self-assessment and peer review can help students monitor and manage their own progress, demystifying the learning process. Check out our Zomoji Exit Ticket! You can find additional digital formatives on our webpage.

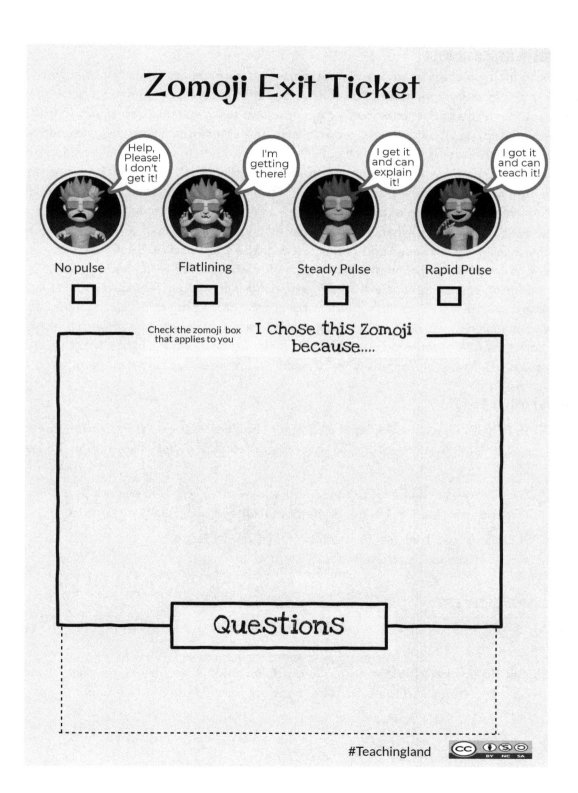

Summative Assessments

In choosing the type of assessment you want to use, it is important to figure out what you want to learn from the assessment and how you will use this information. Do you need a quick snapshot of which students are understanding the content as you teach so you know whom to pull into a small group? If so, you probably need a quick, formative assessment like one we covered above.

Unlike formative assessments, which collect short-term data to drive instruction and personalize learning, summative assessments are culminating diagnostic tools that measure learning over a length of time. There are different types of summative assessments just as there are various formatives, and the type of performance task is the key differentiator.

If you want to figure out what students have retained at the end of a chapter, a traditional summative assessment such as an end-of-unit test might be your best bet. If you want to know if students have truly internalized content and can generalize what they have learned and use it to solve a real-world problem, a performance-based assessment is the ticket. To showcase what students have learned over the course of the semester or year, a capstone project is ideal. As is the case with most everything in education, there are a variety of high-tech, low-tech, and no-tech tools you can use to check the pulse of your students. Several of these can be found in Chapter 6. Let's take a look at the table below to explore various types of summative assessments and their purpose.

END-OF-UNIT TEST

WHAT IS IT?: It's typically traditional assessment (multiple-choice, short answer, true/false, etc.) that covers content over the duration of a unit of study (unit, midterm, semester).

PURPOSE: To measure learning progress and achievement on a unit of study. It often provides an academic letter grade or percentage of accuracy on content.

EXAMPLE: Perimeter Unit Test, 5 Themes of Geography Exam, Dystopian Literature 9 Weeks Exam

STANDARDIZED TEST

WHAT IS IT?: It's a formal test, often state or government issued, that is scored in a predetermined, standardized way.

PURPOSE: To compare performance of individual students, groups of students, districts, and states and to derive data that determines student placement

EXAMPLE: SATS, State Standardized Tests, PSAT, STAR, ACT, MAP Testing

PERFORMANCE-BASED ASSESSMENT

WHAT IS IT?: It's process oriented and focuses on creation, design, and solutions. It can be completed in one class period or over the course of a semester or year.

PURPOSE: To apply knowledge in an authentic way to demonstrate learning

EXAMPLE: STEM Challenges, Design Challenges, Problem-Based Learning Solutions, Music Recital, Art Showcase, Debate, Skit, Film Festival

CAPSTONE PROJECTS

WHAT IS IT?: It's a type of performance-based assessment that produces a cumulative artifact(s)/portfolio that captures student growth. Topics can be assigned but are generally passion driven and student choice.

PURPOSE: To showcase learning that has taken place over the course of the semester or year or even multiple years and to provide a meaningful venue and authentic audience

EXAMPLE: The STEM Academy Grand Challenges, High-Tech High-Exhibition, Multi-genre Research Projects, Portfolio Projects

End-of-Unit Testing

End-of-unit tests are what many people who are outside the field of education think of when they talk or hear about summative assessment. They can entail traditional multiple choice, true/false, and short- and extended-response questions as well as the snazzy "next-generation" drag-and-drop and multi-select type of questions. While these assessments have their place, they typically provide only a snapshot of what a student knows and can do and are very narrow in terms of appealing to various learning styles and preferences. They should be used in conjunction with performance-based assessments to give better insight into student learning. Some teachers offer end-of-unit tests to students who want to opt out of a presentation or a performance piece. Other teachers require both.

Standardized Testing

Standardized testing refers to state or government-mandated, predetermined assessments that measure performance of students and have recently been used to determine school performance, state rankings, and as of late, teacher accountability. They are part of the trickle-down zombienomics variables that have led to the classroom apocalypse.

Performance-Based Assessments (PBAs)

Performance-based assessments are more process oriented than other types of assessments and provide students with opportunities to demonstrate their understanding of content through the creation of authentic products. These types of assessments can be transdisciplinary (involving more than one subject area), and/or project based (focused on designing some variation of an end product) or problem based (focused on designing a solution to a real-world problem). PBAs that are transdisciplinary, open ended (meaning all students will not have the same end products), and require students to design solutions to authentic, real-world problems are also known as design challenges.

When choosing a PBA, it's important to give students constraints so they know your expectations, their project doesn't go off the rails, and you can measure what you need to measure. That said, the constraints shouldn't be so limiting that all the end products look exactly the same. If the latter is the case, then you have given a cake box recipe, my friend. Anyone can make box cakes where they come out looking the same, but when you assign a PBA, there should be enough flexibility for student agency, empowerment, and personalization.

Giving students access to a design cycle helps them imagine, plan, design, and make their product. Their understanding of the learning process also goes from tacit to explicit, and demystification helps with transference into new contexts. You can use our design cycle and design process journal from Chapter 5, or you can adapt it to fit your needs. Regardless of the design cycle or verbiage you choose, it's important to embed its language into your everyday teaching practice and allow students to use their creativity to design their own solutions to whatever project or problem they are working with. It will then become a part of your curricular culture; additionally, performance-based assessments are often graded using a rubric or checklist, which allows you to give them a wide berth in terms of creativity. When students are given choice, they should also take part in creating their rubric and addressing content in their project. Some edtech tools and hands-on approaches will require various skill sets depending on the students' choices. They will need to demonstrate competence with their choice of assessment medium and show a strong understanding of the content using the assessment tool (rubric or checklist).

We mention rubric creation tools in Chapter 6 under our R.E.M.E.D.Y. evaluation hi-tech arsenal. Be sure to browse our R.E.M.E.D.Y. Model for planning and be sure to include students in the Make and Evaluation phases of project planning. In completing these types of tasks, students should be given multiple opportunities to improve their designs.

There is also a lot to be said for allowing students to have voice and choice in selecting an assessment that matches their interests and learning styles. In addition to introducing you to our R.E.M.E.D.Y. hi-tech table in Chapter 6, we also talked a great deal about personalized learning. Using our hi-tech table, you can create choice boards and menus or allow students to decide what problem they want to solve based on the content that has been covered in the classroom by adding a Problem-Based Jar (PBJ). Of course, you decide what constraints will be in place, but when students are passionate about a project and get to choose how they show what they know, they are more likely to give it everything they've got. At the same time, you are more likely to get a better read on what they have learned.

Capstone Projects

A form of performance-based assessment, capstone projects typically mirror all the characteristics of PBAs and are differentiated by their cumulative nature. While PBAs can be an hour-long design challenge, a week-long STEM unit, or any other duration, a capstone project is a culminating showcase or cumulative portfolio that curates knowledge artifacts into one space or presentation. They are usually evaluated by rubric and can be a body of work across the duration of a class or a school year. Capstone projects are an opportunity to showcase student work before an authentic audience and allow students to get expert feedback.

EXAMPLE

The STEM Academy in Savannah, Georgia, had sixth- through eighth-grade students complete a semester-long capstone project on restoring and improving urban infrastructure. During an end-of-the-semester presentation day, professionals from the community came in to listen to the students make presentations on their solutions to a variety of problems.

Refer to our Edtech Arsenal Chapter 7 Online Resource page for examples of Grand Rubrics for presentations and projects, along with work samples to go with it.

Breaking the Grade-and-Groan Assembly Line through Badging

Another way to demonstrate true learning is through badging students for mastery of content. Badging is a way to recognize learning visually, award learning achievements, and motivate students to push for better results. You can even create a badging system for soft skills such as showing empathy and personal responsibility. After designing the age-appropriate criteria for each badge, share it with your students and parents and provide students with multiple opportunities to earn them. Creating an active list of available badges will continue to push students all year long.

There are several badge creators out there to simplify the process. The teachers in my (Columbus) school use openbadges.me/ to make theirs. In addition to a tangible classroom display for badges, you can create a virtual display online using a bulletin board. One of our teachers has created a virtual corkboard for each student—using Google Slides—where they can place their badges as they earn them.

In my school (Savannah), I created digital badges for our Computer Science Pathways. Within our computer science program, we have four coding pathways: video game design, app design, robotics, and immersive technologies. Leveraging a Harry Potter theme, students self-sort into various computer science pathways. They are expected to complete three different courses between grades six through eight. Using Mozilla's open badge program to digitally track student progress and creating custom badges within Canva, student's work and mastery can follow them as they go to high school. Below are the badges created for our school, themed after the housing colors from Harry Potter, along with the program's statement about badging.

Wizards of Computer Science

Wizard badges are a combination of physical and digital badges that are portable and data rich. They also represent course completions and pathway distinction. Students can earn micro-badges that represent performance-based skills that have been observed and are stackable. Once students earn all the micro badges that are aligned with ISTE Standards in specific modules, the micro badges stack up to earn an uber badge: an end-of-course completion badge. As students make their way through the computer science program, they will continue to stack up not only digital badges but will also be awarded physical uber badges that can be fixed to their lab coats as an outward representation of mastery. The metadata included with digital badges includes learning objectives, performance tasks, and skills demonstrated in the modules they have completed. For the purpose of tracking student success, we utilize Mozilla's Open Badge Infrastructure: openbadges.org.

We have also created digital badges for this book! You can earn badges by completing our Metaverse trivia. If you subscribe to our website you can learn how to earn badges for our book, as well as awesome prizes. We highly recommend joining one of our book studies and enlisting colleagues for accountability, communication, and collaboration. Interested in starting a book study in your school or district? Contact us for more information on getting one on the schedule!

Twenty-Eight Weeks Later: A Year of Summative Choices

Regardless of the type of assessment you choose and whether you are offering choice to your students, assessment should never be a one-shot deal or a gotcha. It should also not be a one-size-fits-all tool; rather, during the twenty-eight weeks (more like twenty-six) you have students, they should be given multiple chances to demonstrate mastery at their level. The ultimate goal of assessment is to consistently check the pulse of your students so you can uncover and fill gaps in their understanding and help them improve. If you simply assess and move on, or if students cannot access what the assessment is asking them to do, regardless of the reason, they don't have that chance. With every assessment, like a sequel, you will hone your craft at designing meaningful diagnostic tools. That authenticity will guide students to becoming forever learners.

When you get down to it, all assessments are formative if you are using the data to target student strengths and needs and differentiating instruction accordingly; for example, while benchmark tests at the district and building levels are designed to be summative in nature, if you look for trends, you can figure out which students are grasping the content and which students still have gaps. These trends can also tell you which instructional strategies are working and which ones aren't, allowing you to adjust your approach in areas where understanding is lacking for most. Examining trends in the data and making instructional decisions based on what the trends are telling you allows you to keep close tabs on the health of your trench.

Tales from the Trenches

Angela Forino
@MrsForino
Toledo
c. 2010

I walked into my classroom for the first time at the end of September. School had already been in session for three weeks. I was hired because my new class's previous teacher had taken over a new section in a different grade. I observed her on a Friday, and I had to start teaching on a Monday. I took over a classroom that had already been established and joined a team that already had its plan for the year—all while learning the ins and outs of being a teacher. That first year I barely held on, and I lived by every file folder that was given to me of what everyone else did. When we covered something in class, I gave the same assessment that everyone else gave and had given for years and years. When my students completed assessments, I graded them, put them into my gradebook, and tried to get a vague idea of what to do next. My students were compliant, but they trudged through the curriculum. They did what they were expected to do but did not seem connected to their learning in a meaningful way.

Going into my second year, I knew something had to change. It was the first year of Common Core in Ohio, so we had to redesign the way we did everything. I also knew that my current model of teaching—copy machine meets assembly line of students, had to end. I felt like I was constantly dangling a carrot in front of my students to try and get them to achieve arbitrary milestones whether they were appropriate for them or not. While my district started to create teams that were exploring problem-based learning and performance assessments, my own classroom started to transform. I was emerging from the zombie apocalypse and entering the land of the living.

The transformation did not happen overnight. My school transitioned from a traditional school to a STEM school with a global focus. We started to integrate design thinking and worked to engage our students in design challenges. These design challenges were initially very contrived. My students took on a pretend role to solve a pretend problem, and there were few possible solutions. Although this was a step in the right direction, it was not enough. The results were expected, and our students knew that this was not how it worked in the real world. We clung to traditional assessments to bolster our early design challenges, and it looked more like Pinterest than real-world, problem-based learning.

One of the biggest lessons I have learned during my transformation is to always look for new ways to engage and involve my students. You find what they are passionate about and leverage it in your room. I use tools like Breakout EDU to gamify learning and make even mundane things like test review exciting. After they learn a tool, my students design their own tasks to engage their peers. I use badging so that my students truly understand their progress and achievement in my class. My students must find the evidence and reflect on their learning to support them getting that badge. They must understand what mastery looks like and know that true learning is a process and not just a grade on their report card.

When you walk into my classroom today, it bears little resemblance to my first-year classroom. The teaching is not always coming from me, because I am not always the expert. Authentic teaching and learning happen when our students engage in real-world problem-solving. They are teaching each other. My school started the journey of engaging our students in transdisciplinary problem-based learning, which has students look at real-world problems and engage in design thinking to find solutions. When the YMCA decided to open a new center in our neighborhood, my students researched, designed, and presented on what they felt our community needed. The YMCA, the local press, the city planner, and the mayor were all there when they presented and took my students' plans into consideration. When the YMCA is finished, my students will go there and know they were a part of the process and the product. They are not only students but citizens of our community and the world.

BRAIN STRETCHERS

1. How do you monitor your students' data?

2. How to you know when students are learning?

3. What is the difference between formative and summative assessment?

4. How do you use formative, summative, and performance-based assessments to check the pulse of your students?

PART 3
~~Don't~~ Be a Hero

CHAPTER 8
Be a Legend: Leave Camp to Explore and Share

He had this idea. It was kind of a virologist idea. He believed that you could cure racism and hate... literally cure it, by injecting music and love into people's lives. When he was scheduled to perform at a peace rally, a gunman came to his house and shot him down. Two days later he walked out on that stage and sang. When they asked him why— He said, "The people who were trying to make this world worse... are not taking a day off. How can I? Light up the darkness."
—Robert Neville (talking to Anna about Bob Marley) in *I Am Legend*

When we think of a zombie apocalypse, thanks to Hollywood, we envision society plunged into chaos, the loss of telecommunications, the violent breakdown of basic civilization, and the terrifying thrust into survival mode. A prime example is *I Am Legend*, the 2007 film based on Richard Matheson's 1954 graphic novel. In the movie, protagonist and brilliant scientist Robert Neville, portrayed by Will Smith, is the sole survivor in a postapocalyptic world, hunkered down in a fortified New York City apartment with his dog. And though the creatures in the movie are called "dark seekers" and based more on vampires than zombies, *I Am Legend* parallels many modern zombie films with its premise that a cure-for-cancer-turned-virus is what caused the global pandemic that sends the world into its deadly spiral.

Neville is alone and isolated as he embarks on a mission to develop a cure, believing the answer to reversing the plague is locked inside his own immune blood.

The conceit we draw between this movie and education is that we all feel like Robert Neville at some point in our careers. Once we close our doors, teaching becomes a one-person show, not in the sense of being the sage on the stage but in a more literal sense of closing everyone else out. Teaching special subjects like music, film, art, or coding can further exacerbate the feeling of being an island unto yourself (John Donne, the master of conceit, anyone?) and Neville literally had the aisle of Manhattan to himself. Isolation can drive us to self-doubt and leave us starved for feedback and validation. In Neville's case, he resorts to talking to mannequins for socialization.

So how can we, as teachers, make ourselves immune to infection like Neville was? While his immunity was genetic, his hope is something we can learn from and kindle within ourselves. We hope to be a positive influence on our students. We hope to change education for the better. We hope for a better world.

There are also many external actions we can take to make ourselves less susceptible to burnout, desperation, self-doubt, and all the symptoms of the classroom apocalypse virus that we all feel from time to time. Neville also embodied perseverance. When he was not relentlessly working on finding a cure, he was broadcasting messages to connect with other survivors.

My name is Robert Neville. I am a survivor living in New York City. I am broadcasting on all AM frequencies. I will be at the South Street Seaport every day at midday, when the sun is highest in the sky. If you are out there, if anyone is out there, I can provide food, I can provide shelter, I can provide security. If there's anybody out there, anybody, please. You are not alone.

Connecting with other teachers is just as important to our sanity (you don't want to find yourself holding conversations about pedagogy with your stapler) as it is to our practice. Finding camaraderie and a place to share similar passions and woes can be the food, shelter, and security we need to get to the next dawn, and may we remind you there are approximately 180 of them. It is also how legendary lessons are created—through collaboration, shared passions, and crowdsourced resources. Read on to learn about some of our favorite online tools and forums:

#BeABetta

You have made it this far, and things are looking like you might actually survive this classroom apocalypse. You have #Teachingland rules to govern your actions, you have mastered navigating the quagmire of relationships with colleagues, parents, and students, and you have some O.P.P.s in your pocket. You have tricked your trench and learned to manage the horde. Your R.E.M.E.D.Y. is bringing children's dreams and creativity back to life, and your assessments are on fleek and authentic. What comes next? Getting out of the bunkers! Venturing out into the world and sharing all of the strategies you have learned. First, however, let's talk about online professional learning.

You might be asking why you should go beyond your bunker? The answer is simple: If you limit yourself to the professional learning communities in your bunker, you will eventually become a goldfish. Aside from the short attention span, a goldfish living in a small bowl stops learning, stops seeking out opportunities, and eventually stops growing. Don't be a goldfish.

In a world of Goldfish,

#BeaBetta!

To keep from falling into this school of thought, (no pun intended) answer these questions:

- What do you define as your bowl?
- The look and feel of your bowl will have a lot to do with where you go to learn about new tools and resources. Is it the colleagues in your building?
- District trainings?
- Social media?

We preach all the time about giving our students authentic audiences and sharing their work with the world in order to grow. We should practice what we preach by sharing our best practices as well as our successes and failures with a global audience. Break out of the day-to-day grind, break down the walls of your bunker, and bring all that you learn into your bowl.

Instead of being a goldfish, we encourage you to be a BETTA fish! BETTA fish fight to be the best they can be for their students and for themselves. They are colorful and one of a kind. They try new things, have a global PLN and are constantly learning and reinventing themselves as teachers. They live life in beta, realizing that they are the best version of themselves in that moment but that tomorrow will bring another day to learn as well as a newer, better version of themselves. (Listen to the "Live Life in Permanent Beta" talk by Reid Hoffman on Standford's Podcast: ecorner.stanford.edu/podcast/live-life-in-permanent-beta.) Bettas model this behavior for their students, and they are never complacent. They push the envelope, leveraging technology and high-impact strategies to open the universe of possibilities. Given the choice, which would you choose?

Become a Wi-Fi Warrior

To be the best bunker warrior for your students you must be adaptive and learn to become a Blue-Tape Thinker (see Chapter 4). Your willingness to grow and refine your craft should evolve as new strategies, technologies, and societal changes inevitably occur; furthermore, it's important to find a kick-ass partner (Rule #10) inside or outside your bunker who will commiserate over daily struggles, celebrate the successes, and challenge your thinking.

By being proactive you can create or join valuable communities of practice or affinity spaces that cover broad topics such as rationing your supplies or more specialized topics like teaching Latin or Mandarin within the context of a STEM program. When you create social media accounts for educational use, your focus shifts from what is happening in your bunker to having access to a global brain bank you can tap for information at any time! Using social media to share strategies, tools, and passions can be more infectious than zombieism and lead to a globalized R.E.M.E.D.Y., ultimately yielding the greatest impact.

Gather and Share Intelligence

Using social media to grow as a professional is respectable, but when it comes to survival, you want to make sure your bunker buds are faring well in the apocalyptic landscape as well. You should be willing to break down the silo walls by sharing your tools, strategies, and successes with others. Hoarding ideas, equipment, and best practices not only stifles a culture of creativity and openness, it also inhibits the potential for widespread change. When you find a new strategy that is truly innovative or a tool that transforms your craft, make sure you share it with your professional learning networks, wherever they may be. Sharing is caring, and we need more caring in the trenches if we are all to survive the apocalypse!

Using social networks to build online communities will help ensure the long-term survival of everyone involved. Finding like-minded educators online and banding together can keep you from the brink of a breakdown on days when it feels like we might not make it out of the bunker in one piece. It can be an oasis to discuss problems, re-energize us with new ideas, and equip us with new strategies.

Use a Variety of Communication Strategies to Strengthen Relationships

Don't limit yourself to face-to-face interactions with students, parents, and colleagues. The Internet provides a variety of platforms you can use to facilitate conversations and build stronger relationships with all stakeholders. Opening up communication pathways beyond brick and mortar and email can be a fantastic way to engage all stakeholders. It provides a digital window for others to see into your learning environment. The walls of your classroom become transparent, which helps build trust and strengthen relationships—and makes you better able to survive.

Common Sense Social Media: Use Your Brain!

In addition to using social media for professional development and relationship building, it is our job to help students navigate the online world and become globally connected "digitizens."

The digital terrain can be mottled with Internet zombies that have ill intentions, and it is important to equip students with the right tools before taking off on a digital adventure. We want edventures online to be both safe and positive experiences. Choosing to use social media raises critical questions that must be answered. Here are just a few:

- Can I use graphics to make the flow chart?

- Which tools will I use?

- How will I use them? For professional learning or in my classroom?

- If in the classroom, what age group are these tools appropriate for?

- Will I manage a class account, or will students post from their accounts?

- What is our social media policy—if we have one?

- How do I protect the privacy of my students?

- How can I prepare my students to become digital citizens?

Before getting started, we highly recommend exploring Common Sense Media, a website dedicated to providing edtech and media reviews and ratings by teachers and parents. This resource is a fantastic evaluation tool for all apps and is especially useful for social media and online tools. It can act as a guide when you're trying to figure out what is appropriate and what is not. Practical application strategies are also included with some of the edtech tool reviews, and in some cases, lesson plans and supplemental resources are available as well.

When it comes to digital citizenship, Common Sense Media also has a program that encourages students not only to model good behavior online but to connect and collaborate in ways that empower them as learners. Google has a similar digital citizenship curriculum, Be Internet Awesome, that combats fake news, discusses cybersecurity, prompts students to think critically about sharing information, and encourages students to be kind online. Introducing these tools and having important conversations about where students are hanging out online can help facilitate safe interactions.

COPPA and FERPA: Check Yourself Before You Wreck Yourself

If you are engaging your students in digital experiences online, there are some key pieces of legislation you should be aware of:

THE CHILDREN'S ONLINE PRIVACY PROTECTION ACT (COPPA)

This law requires commercial websites, social media platforms, and apps that are accessed by children under the age of thirteen to obtain parental consent before collecting any personal data on young children. The FTC allows schools and districts to stand in for parents in providing this consent, but they must notify parents that this is happening. Whether or not the notification districts are providing to parents is sufficient, it can be a challenge if the district is not aware of all of the edtech tools you are using in your classroom. Many companies know that teachers get excited about implementing new tools in their classroom and don't always read the fine print. If you teach littles and middles, we recommend you do not assume this responsibility. Start with checking out your responsible usage policies and any documents that go home with students to make sure you are covered. As a backup, you can send home classroom parental permission slips with students prior to using a new tool. Also, as a general rule, always loop in your administrator when you have a new tool you want to try out.

THE FAMILY EDUCATIONAL RIGHTS AND PRIVACY ACT (FERPA)

This law places restrictions on who has access to student records. It maintains that you must receive parental or guardian consent before releasing any information about students to a third party. This includes student images. Most schools and districts have a standard issue photo/video release. If yours does not, make sure you check with parents and guardians or gain consent from students if they are older than eighteen before posting photos of students online. Additionally, you need to make sure you remove any identifying information like student names from the photo before you post.

Tips to Avoid Savage Social Media Failure

- Make sure you are in line with FERPA.
- Keep your professional social media accounts separate from your personal ones.
- Pay attention to the personal information about students that is posted in your classroom and could accidentally be photographed and posted.
- Brush up on your photo-editing skills and use them to ensure that every photo you post is free of personally identifying information.
- Explain to students and parents how you will use social media in your classroom.

Social Media Tools for Learning on the Run

We have compiled a list of tools and educational applications to use for professional learning, and with your students. Remember the age-old adage: Don't post anything you wouldn't want your grandmother to see! Make sure you connect with us online to keep the #teachingland conversation going. Here are our favorite tools and applications:

TWITTER: HASHTAG, YOU'RE IT!

Twitter is an online social media and networking platform that allows users to communicate through 280-character posts, which are called Tweets. Users can post from any Internet enabled device and can share photos and videos, post polls, and use hashtags to track content by topic. If a topic is "trending," the hashtag is being used by many people at once and creating some buzz. Twitter is a great tool for learning about new edtech tools, understanding twenty-first-century pedagogy, and connecting with educators around the world. Some popular hashtags are #edutech, #tlap, #leadlap, #arvrinedu, #ditchbook, #booksnaps, #makered.

Another valuable Twitter source is Jerry Blumengarten—most commonly known as Cybraryman—who has curated a close-to-comprehensive list of education hashtags and Twitter chat times. He has some great resources and information, and you can find him here: cybraryman.com/twitterpages.html

Here are a few of our favorite ways to use Twitter for your professional growth or with students:

1. Twitter Chats

- Conversations centered around a unique hashtag designed to connect people with similar interests

- Typically take place on a specific day of the week at the same time

- Can be hosted as frequently as the facilitator wishes—weekly, biweekly, or monthly

- Can be a fast-paced one- to sixty-minute discussion or a slower one that unfolds over the span of a day or a week, with tweeters using the hashtag to contribute to the conversation hourly or daily.

Note: Check out #Teachingland to find out when we host our Twitter chats! You may even want to launch your own Twitter conversations using a custom hashtag! Refer back to Chapter 6 for ideas on how to integrate Twitter into the classroom!

2. Hashtag Learning

- A hashtag is a word or phrase that organizes information and conversations about a specific topic (e.g., our hashtag is #Teachingland). All posts centered around the message of our book will be tagged with that hashtag.

- Hashtags can be used to search content that has been posted around specific ideas.
- Hashtags can be used for entire schools, individual classrooms, and specific events or to rally students, parents, and other educators around a particular idea or project.

Note: Some of our favorite hashtags to follow: #tlap, #leadlap, #ditchbook, #arvrinedu, #vrinedu, #iste, #fetc, #edtechbridge, #steampunksedu, #booksnaps, #CSK8, #vrpodcast, #pblchat #edutech

PERISCOPE: AN EXTENSION OF TWITTER

Periscope is a live-broadcast app for Twitter. Users download the Periscope app, sync it to their Twitter account, and make their broadcasts private, available to Twitter followers, or completely public. Broadcasts can be saved to your camera roll to post to other places or social media platforms. Viewers can interact with the stream by commenting and liking the video. This is a great tool for professional development and providing an authentic audience for students in the following ways:

- Stream events, like graduations or assemblies
- Involve parents in the classroom or school experience
- Showcase student work to an authentic audience

FACEBOOK

If you don't know what Facebook is, you must have been living under a rock for the last decade. Facebook was responsible for turning Myspace into a digital apocalyptic wasteland. Facebook is a popular social-media platform where members create a profile, and post videos, pictures, text, polls, and more. Users can set their page to public or private and must be at least thirteen years old to join. You can like, comment, and follow users' content. Here are a few ways to use Facebook:

1. Groups and Pages

You can create a Facebook page for your class or school as a way to post calendar invites and information; however, creating a Facebook group can even be more beneficial than creating a page, because it gives members a sense of community and ownership. We have both built pages and participated in groups, and the groups always seem to be more dynamic with engaged members leading conversations. It is a great way get like-minded individuals in one place and provide value to them by posting content. We recommend creating a group for your parents to keep them in the loop about school happening and events for discussion. Being a member of groups started by edtech companies can also be beneficial, as members are often given the opportunity to beta test new features and receive updates ahead of others. They are the perfect spot for EdTech Hipsters!

Some Facebook Groups we love are The STEM Teacher Tribe, Seesaw Teachers, Merge Educator Group, Tech with Us Community, CoSpaces Edu Community and ISTE Young Educator Group, and Common Sense Educators.

2. Facebook Live

Using Facebook Live has a lot of the same benefits that Periscope does for Twitter. You can post live videos of your classroom in action and stream directly to those who like your page or group. This is an excellent way to get information to parents, as we have found most parents have Facebook profiles but may not have Twitter accounts.

3. Facebook Spaces (VR)

Facebook is pretty good about staying current and modern with technological advances. Facebook spaces is beta VR streaming that allows you to go live from virtual reality, and you can even call reality from VR and invite participants without headsets in while live streaming. You

can connect with friends or stream to a group and showcase creative tools such as 360° orbs where you can change your background or draw in 3D. While currently only available on the Rift, Vive, and Oculus Go, we believe it will prove useful in the hands (or headsets) of educators as it comes to more devices. Being able to pull from a 360° video library allows the broadcaster to take viewers anywhere in the world, and the educational opportunities that exist are ripe for exploration and implementation. Savannah once broadcasted from VR and took viewers around the world (Sydney, Paris, and Dubai) and used her own 360° photos to showcase her travels. The cool part is you can have up to four people in one space! Imagine inviting educators and coteachers from around the world into your space! As viewers comment, the broadcaster can even pick them up! We can't wait for this technology to take off! The picture to the left was a promotion for #thevrpodcast.

INSTAGRAM

Instagram is a social media platform that is based on sharing photos and images, and there is a plethora of educational uses for it. Common Sense Media suggests creating a class account and inviting students to post from this account. Below are a few educational uses for Instagram:

- Create an InstaGallery of student work
- Share photos from the day
- InstaStar: Showcase a star student

SNAPCHAT

Snapchat is a messaging app that allows users to send videos and photos with time limits. Users can edit and modify a picture, text, or video and then send it to a friend. Once sent, the recipient can see the image for the time limit the sender set, and then it disappears. There is a double-tap feature for a replay of the media. Users can also create Stories that last for twenty-four hours and are visible to all of a user's friends. You can also do a video chat with up to thirty-two friends! We highly recommend using Snapchat with students and in your professional learning communities. We outline a few ways to do that below.

1. #BookSnaps

#BookSnaps were created by Tara Martin (@TaraMartinEdu). They are a creative application of Snapchat and Bitmoji (an app that makes cartoon avatars in your likeness) to engage readers. You simply take a photo of a page in the book with a quote that inspired you, mark it up, and add emojis or a Bitmoji. You then save the marked-up image to your camera roll and share it on Twitter using the hashtag #BookSnaps. I have seen variations of this as well (e.g., #mathsnaps, #poetrysnaps, and even #robotsnaps)! The uses are endless! Check out Tara's website (tarammartin.com/resources/booksnaps-how-to-videos/) for step-by-step videos on how to create BookSnaps with Buncee, Google Slides, Seesaw, PicCollage, and more!

2. App Smashing with Snapchat

App smashing with Snapchat involves creating snaps and saving them to your phone, then opening them in another application or platform. We have listed three examples below, but feel free to create your own #edusnapsmash variations.

Snapchat with ChatterPix
Snapchat and Giffer
Snapchat and WeVideo

3. #SnapPat

A #SnapPat is when you see someone doing something awesome in your building and online, and you use Snapchat to share it with them and with your online community. Whether on Twitter, in your Facebook groups, or even your school social media accounts and blogs, let's start a movement of teachers who lift each other up and give virtual pats on the back. All you need to do is take a picture or screenshot, mark it up, give a compliment in Snapchat, then post it online and tag it with the hashtag #SnapPat! If they aren't online, you might also want to print it out and post it on their door. #SnapPats are meant to build a positive digital culture by elevating others.

LINKEDIN

LinkedIn is a professional social networking platform that allows you to build a digital resume and look for and apply to jobs in one spot. You can connect with educational professionals, employers, and colleagues and receive 'endorsements' for skills they have observed in action. LinkedIn is a great way for preservice and current educators to build a professional online presence for the purpose of job searching. Not a fan of working for Fiddler's Green in the land of the dead? Then apply for your dream position in the Sanctuary under the lead of Rick Grimes. Here are some educational uses for LinkedIn:

- Great for those wanting to change bunkers
- Build professional expertise by getting endorsements and posting blogs.
- Create professional communities on hot topics in education.
- Follow edtech developers and companies.
- Have high-school students begin building a digital résumé for future jobs.

VOXER

Voxer is a "walkie-talkie" messaging app that gained popularity for its voiced-based messaging system. It also supports videos, images, and text. You can create groups, join groups, or leave yourself voice notes. This platform has been used in several creative ways:

- Twitter chat backchannel
- Bus duty group
- Professional learning groups

- Team conversations
- Book club Voxer groups

Here are some Voxer groups we recommend or are members of: Teachingland, Aspiring Authors and Writers, EduMatch, Librarians Group, #arvrinedu group, and VR Podcast Group.

PINTEREST

Pinterest is an online idea pinboard that allows you to curate information by topic, interest, hobby, or whatever organization system you want. Users can upload media and pin content for later review. Content is curated into public or private boards, and each item is said to be pinned or saved in the collection.

During the classroom apocalypse, it can be handy to find cool ways to trick your trench, but exercise caution when looking for lessons in the digital terrain. Here are a few ways to use Pinterest for education:

1. Organization

For the Pinterest queens and kings, it's a great place to find organizational nuggets for your classroom; for example, you can transform your trench into a flexible seating area on a budget with all the great pins on DIY seating.

2. Curate Student Work

In the times of the classroom apocalypse, we need to pack light and go green. Whether you teach art, math, or writing, making boards of student work is an easy way to make an online gallery to share with the rest of the world.

3. Lesson Plans and Design Challenges

This is trickier territory. While Pinterest is a great resource for inspiration, be careful selecting fully developed resources without evaluating them for value and tweaking them to fit the needs of students in your trench. Rule #5, "Bare Hands," applies to the curriculum we create as well as what students are creating. There are great STEM and Maker activities out there, but you need to know how to differentiate the nuggets from the negatives. Edison said, "Genius is 1 percent inspiration and 99 percent perspiration." If you see something that inspires you, use it—but put in the perspiration to tailor it for your students! So when using Pinterest, make sure to pin these rules somewhere close:

Mind your Pinterest Ps by asking these Qs:

Purpose

- ❏ Does it have Purpose?
- ❏ Is it content based?
- ❏ Does it lead to growth?
- ❏ Does it empower the Learner?

Personalization

- ❏ Can the outcome be Personalized?
- ❏ Does it create a similar product across the board?
- ❏ Does it appeal to multiple interests?
- ❏ Can it be approached in several ways?

Perspiration

If it doesn't meet the above qualifications, can it with Perspiration?
If you were truly inspired by it, do the following:

- ❏ Run with the inspiration.
- ❏ Alter the lesson to make it personalized and applicable to your students.
- ❏ Make sure it has purpose and that the outcomes vary (no cake-box curriculum).

SKYPE IN THE CLASSROOM

Skype is software that enables teachers to engage in free video and voice calls, send instant messages, and share media with other users on Skype. It works from a mobile device or a computer. It is more important than ever to invite global experts into your classroom, and Skype is a solution to distance and monetary barriers. Check out some awesome ways to use Skype below!

Educational Application

1. Mystery Skype

Mystery Skype is an educational game that brings two classrooms together to solve mysteries, usually through a series of questions to solve where the other classroom is located. To get involved, all you need to do is join Skype in the Classroom and scroll down to Mystery Skype to find participating classrooms you can connect with by time zone or location.

2. Expert Interviews

Whether bringing in experts on topics for students or for faculty members, Skype has a way of bridging distance and providing access to global experts affording you the option to learn from the best. When Savannah's class went to a local museum to view installation art on pollinators, she had the artist, Katha Loher, originally from Zurich, Switzerland, Skype with students about the process of creation and the message behind the work.

3. Book Club

Starting a book club is a great use of Skype. For professional learning, educators can Skype directly with authors and discuss book content and strategies. This makes the experiences more personal and provides a new layer of connection and communication. In the classroom, teachers can connect with other trenches who are reading similar titles and allow students to dig into meaningful discussions on theme, language, and characters.

Similar tools for global connections: Zoom, Google Hangouts

RUMII BY DOGHEAD SIMULATIONS

Rumii is a virtual reality meeting software that really connects the world and makes it feel a bit smaller. You can with anyone from anywhere in the world in a virtual reality classroom equipped with presentation features such as a whiteboard wall, YouTube video viewer, 3D model importer, and slide deck capabilities. It is available on desktop, tablets, mobile devices, and also VR headsets, like the Oculus Go, HTC Vive, and Oculus Rift. If you like Skype, rumii takes the idea of connecting a step further and makes it more immersive and intimate.

Educational Applications

1. Virtual Meetings

You can meet virtual with members from your PLN and bridge thousands of miles with one click. Snow days a problem and you are 1:1? Channel Ready Player One and transport into Rumii. Your avatar can deliver instruction and facilitate conversations in VR!

2. Connect with other Classrooms

Mystery Skype is awesome, but what if your students could connect with another classroom around the world, and pair off to discuss content? This is possible in Rumii! Now to get around those pesky time zones!

3. Virtual Conference

Lethbridge College in Alberta, Canada held an entire conference in virtual reality in April of 2018. I expect to see a lot of professional learning in a virtual format in the future. It allows for anyone in the world to attend, as well as experts from anywhere to present.

Cloud Control to Major Tom

Managing all these social media accounts can get overwhelming and become tiresome work to keep all fronts updated. That is why we recommend a social media management platform you can use to schedule posts to all your social media accounts ahead of time. You can control when and where to post what and buy back some time you would spend posting to each individual site. You can spend all that bought-back time on your hands doing meaningful things, like tricking your trench and making awesome learning experiences for students. Below we have listed three platforms that we recommend and which social accounts they post to. So put your helmet on, because the digital terrain can be just as bumpy during the apocalypse!

HOOTSUITE

Hootsuite is a social media management platform that allows you to connect and schedule up to thirty posts to three different social sites for free. You can post to…

- Facebook
- Twitter
- WordPress
- Instagram
- LinkedIn

Check out this awesome zombie apocalypse post by Hootsuite! It is a hoot! blog.hootsuite.com/social-media-zombies/

TWEETDECK

TweetDeck is a free tool that helps you manage and organize activity in Twitter. It can be hard to navigate, post, and keep up in Twitter chats, and TweetDeck simplifies that with a dashboard that displays separate columns of activity that you customize. You can create columns for specific things like hashtags, trending topics, scheduled tweets, and more.

BUFFER

Buffer is similar to Hootsuite but limits scheduled posts to ten, and the free account does not support posting to Pinterest. The social media accounts it posts to are…

- Facebook
- Twitter
- Pinterest
- Instagram
- LinkedIn

Tales from the Trenches

@DTranthamSTEAM
Villa Rica
c. 2012

Sometimes in Teachingland, you can find yourself sitting on an island. The island isn't too far offshore; you can see others interacting and collaborating, but there doesn't seem to be anyone around with whom to collaborate in your grade level or your content area. This happened to me just a few years into teaching. I was moved from Pre-K to fifth grade math and science. You read that right. The Pre-K teacher was now supposed to teach math and science to fifth graders. The change was a welcome one although the learning curve was steep, and the kicker was that I was the *only* math and science teacher of fifth grade in our school. The intimidation was real. I wasn't sure how I was going be the change maker I wanted to be, but I was determined to find a way.

Thankfully, I was given the advice to create a professional learning network on Twitter. I wasn't familiar with Twitter and when I learned I had to limit my word count, that added an extra challenge. Spoiler: I like to talk. A lot. However, I dove into Twitter. I started following all kinds of people and at first I generally just read a lot. Some of the people I chose to follow at that time are still some of my go-to resources even now as a more experienced teacher. Some of these superstars are Dave Burgess, Paul Solarz, Robert Kaplinski, Graham Fletcher, The STEM Academy, Peter Ulrich, and Amanda Fox. There are others, but these were my main wifi warriors I followed. They were the ones being the ball in education. (*Caddyshack* reference: take a look on YouTube. Timeless advice) These were the movers, the shakers, and the ones who could definitely show me the way of the math and science world. They would help me turn two subjects into pure awesome with a STEM emphasis.

I made Twitter my daily professional learning resource. I tuned in every morning before school over my cup of morning coffee. I soon began to join in on Twitter chats. The things I learned were amazing! I never once felt like I was alone. I never felt that I couldn't ask any of these amazing educators how to better my craft. And I asked a lot of questions! They answered every. Single. One. My mornings were richer and my classes were way better because I had a group of amazing educators, who I had never met, behind me each day.

The day came when I got to meet two of the educators who, to me, were everything I aspired to be one day. Peter Ulrich, the principal of The STEM Academy (at the time) and Amanda Fox, one of The STEM Academy teachers. It was during a conference that our region held and invited them to be presenters. They were genuine, kind, transparent, and sharing. They shared every resource they had ever used and any resource they had created. Not only did they share what they had, but a few months after that, agreed to visit our small town to share with the teachers in our small district. I reached out to Paul Solarz (author of *Learn Like a Pirate*) who agreed to join a Google Hangouts with our teachers!

So what?, you might think. *What difference does this make to me?* Well, here's what I hope you take from this little story. First, I hope you realize that even if you are the only grade-level teacher, the only teacher of your content, or even the only teacher with your educational philosophy, there is a world of support open to you on social media. Even if Twitter isn't your thing, Instagram and Facebook have a ton of resources that you can follow. Second, I hope you know the importance of transparency. So many times as educators we feel as though we need to be perfect all the time. The perfect Pinterest room, the perfect RTI plan, the perfect lesson plans, etc. The fact is that none of us are perfect, but together we can help each other improve and grow. We're in a profession where if we keep everything to ourselves, hoarding our lessons and great ideas, not only does that struggling teacher suffer and eventually leave the profession, but the kids don't get the best of us and at the end of the day, hopefully, we're in it for the kids. Share. It makes a world of difference for everyone. The third thing I hope you take from this is to be brave and have agency. Try new things. Embrace taking risks. Social media gives us access to the best of the best. We get to enter chats with them, we can attend conferences where they share their talent, and if you're brave enough you can reach out to them through direct messages and get their help one on one.

So, while we may be sitting on an island all alone in Teachingland, we don't have to shout to others hoping to be heard in order to collaborate. We are sitting on an island but we are plugged into a world of amazing resources if we have the courage to be transparent enough to know we need help and ask for it, be willing to share as well as receive help and resources, and be brave enough to try new things. I know it made a world of difference for me!

Nicholas Clayton
@crikeypotter
Southern California Desert
c. 2013

Being a special education teacher has its perks. I can utilize different, specialized curriculum, I get to differentiate everything to differing learning styles, and my students get to loop with me for multiple years. This seems to translate to me making a bigger impact in their lives and getting to work on some cool learning projects.

At least, that is how I process it.

When I first walked into my new position as self-contained special education walker…I mean teacher…I found a group of students was eager to break out of the constant reading group, math group, boring tier-three routine and out of their reality of living in an area of high crime and poverty (Yeah, I know there are a lot of us who teach in those conditions; my school was burglarized three times in my first year and a half). So I started putting my techy brain and Twitter/Google+ PLN to work, utilizing Google Maps to measure real-life outdoor structures, building a life-sized Minecraft block, and connecting with Google to virtually transport my classroom—"flatten its walls," so to speak.

I worked with Google+ Connected Classrooms to connect my class with Lincoln's Cottage and Jefferson's Monticello. I couldn't believe that there were companies out there so willing to work with teachers in small pockets of society such as the one I was working in (something that inspired me to connect and work with my ambassadorship companies to partner with my classroom and sponsor my professional development). But it wasn't just buildings my students ventured to; it was other countries… halfway across the world.

I wrote a convincing proposal to Google when they posted a possible connection with Solar Impulse, a foundation building a solar-powered airplane that has since flown around the world. Google accepted me out of thousands of other classrooms that applied around the country; I talked to the people at Google, and a date was set. I then got extremely excited and brought the proposal to two other fifth-grade general education teachers. One loved technology and was in her late twenties and the other was a veteran teacher who a was self-confessed technophobe in her fifties. The day came, and I set up all the tech details in the veteran teacher's classroom, and she loved it! The students got to live video chat with scientists in Switzerland and the pilot/creator of the plane who was in the middle of a seventy-two-hour virtual cockpit flight to test his endurance. It was one of the most brilliant experiences of my career, and I thought I had the technophobe convinced to not be scared and begin to utilize technology.

The next day she went back to her old sit-and-practice routine and only asked for my help when a student Chromebook broke down or to fix her printer. Even after my trainings, websites designed to help noobs, etc. She was permanently resistant. She would talk to me as the months went on in the school year about how "amazing the virtually trip [sic] was" and how we should do it again, but when I would email (a little too frequently) about new technology opportunities, she would not take me up on them.

A couple of years later, I was offering other opportunities such as livestreams of comets and eclipses along with robotics and coding electives, and she would be one of the biggest (and sometimes only) supporters in terms of sending students to my classroom to reverse mainstream; and that is when it dawned on me: She was being smart about it. She realized her shortcomings and utilized the talent around her to fill in the gaps in her knowledge. Instead of trying to learn something that was either too difficult for her to understand in a reasonable amount of time or was of no interest to her, she was able to give her students something that would help engage them and give them skills for future careers. She was working smarter, not harder.

Of course, being the over-sharer that I am, I finally wore her down. She had me come over to teach her and her class the basics of coding! It was so fun! I can't wait for her to finally ask me to run a VR expedition…maybe this school year. ;)

Christopher Menhorn
@MrMenhorn
Zanesville
c. 2014

When I began my teaching career in 2008, many forms of technology and communication were still spreading. Not all of the families with whom I worked had email, online assignments for students weren't a consideration yet, and paper newsletters for home were still created, if time allowed. In fact, teachers were often discouraged from using social media.

Fast forward ten years and all of that suddenly changed. Most families seem to prefer email for communication, completing homework on a computer is often an expectation, and many teachers maintain their own websites, easily updated each day. We can access information just about anywhere, which can be useful when you're always on the run. As social media has evolved it has become an incredible source for information and ideas that teachers can access in a busy world. Groups on Facebook allow teachers to share ideas, like the latest research on how to help students learn. After I joined a group that focused on math instruction, my eyes were opened to new ideas from educators around the world. I found numerous recommendations for resources that could improve my work in the classroom. I was suddenly not afraid to try new things because I knew I had the support of all these educators and could turn to them with questions if needed.

Using Twitter has also been a game-changer for me. What may seem like a one-way form of communication is really some of the most powerful two-way communication I have experienced in the social media world. I joined with the intention of pushing out what my students were doing in the classroom to their families, as well as providing other news and information. As I started following my colleagues and other education professionals, my feed was suddenly filled with articles on current research and numerous strategies to try in the classroom. Participating in Twitter chats not only gave me new ideas but also allowed me to see that my struggles are similar to those of other educators and we now have the ability to problem-solve together. One of the most powerful things to me has been connecting with "celebrities" in the education world as they share their research. I'll never forget the day that I tagged a well-respected individual from the world of math education in a post, only to find that they "liked" and commented on my post. It only fueled my passion to engage more on social media, try new things with my students, and work to improve my practice each day.

If two heads are better than one, then an unlimited number of ideas must be the best situation. And all of this information can be accessed at any time from anywhere. While it may seem overwhelming with the endless information that can come from social media, engaging with other educators can transform the work you do. I saw the learning in my classroom go from mostly teacher directed to mostly student driven. Sharing ideas with others from around the world can be some of the best professional development in which you can participate!

BRAIN STRETCHERS

1. What social media tools do you use to further your own professional learning?

2. How can you use social media in your trench to engage parents and students?

3. What new social media tools are you hoping to explore?

4. What does it mean to be a betta vs. a goldfish? Which one are you?

Visit TeachinglandTheBook.com
to access the links and resources
in this chapter.

🔲 Scan me

CHAPTER 9
Warm Bodies in Action: For the Love of Learning

Perry: What the hell are you doing here? Are you actually dreaming right now?

R: I'm not sure.

Perry: You can't dream, corpse. Dreaming's for humans.

Julie: Chill out, Perry. He can dream if he wants to. [Julie approaches R]

Julie: What about you, R? What do you want to be?

R: I don't know. I don't even know what I am.

Julie: Well you can be whatever you want. Isn't that what they say?

—*Warm Bodies*

R and J: A Lesson on Collaboration

If you take away anything from this book, we hope it's that collaboration, rapport, choice, and communication with your students are critical. Even more important is letting them socially construct knowledge together. Some of the relationships our students build during the year and between the walls of our classrooms will transcend their time with us and last a lifetime. The impact of friendships, interactions, and the knowledge that comes from collaborative communities will ripple out and permanently stretch their brains. If you don't want to take our word for it, check out *Warm Bodies*, a modern and dark comic take on Shakespeare's *Romeo and Juliet*. In this film, one of the two star-crossed lovers is alive and well while the other has recently joined the ranks of the undead. This zomcom is not like any of its zombie predecessors and defies the rules we have learned from past movies. The story begins from the perspective of the protagonist, R, a teenage zombie struggling to come to grips with his new reality. R meets J, a local girl that he literally can't get out of his head—especially since he ate her boyfriend's brains—and he saves her from being eaten. In this movie, much like in *iZombie*, when a zombie eats the brain of another person, they experience memories and tendencies from the other person's life.

Over the course of the movie, their friendship kindles into something more romantic. After each encounter with J, R's heartbeat gets a little stronger, and by the end of the movie, he is restored to a warm-bodied human, teaching us that love and relationships are at the heart of humanity—and also the building blocks to true learning.

In the quote at the beginning of the chapter R is dreaming, though he is told that is reserved for the living. Julie defends his right to dream and inquires of R what he wants to be. She follows up with what we should be telling all our students: You can be anything.

As a teacher, the most important thing you can let your students know is that they are loved, and they matter. The best way this can be achieved is by creating a culture where they feel safe to use their voice...and then listen-to their dreams, their interests, their struggles. It may be the only time or place they feel a sense of belonging. In Chapter 3 we discussed building rapport by fostering relationships first and everything else after. Even the toughest students who have resigned to apathy or who are reserved from interacting can be won over. Even R, our existential protagonist dealing with the crisis of being dead, desires something more of life. J becomes the catalyst that reverses zombieism.

You can be the catalyst for your students. They may come to you with a drill-and-practice indoctrination as their frame of reference, but that doesn't have to be their manifesto. They want more; they just might not know it yet. And they will kick, scream, and bite at in the face of change, but changing that culture and transforming their hearts to love learning can transform their lives. As we learned from watching R and J, our students are the true catalyst that have the power to change the world for good. We just need to create conditions ripe for learning and let them interact authentically and often. This chapter was specifically designed for students to talk about what they yearn for in education and times when teachers truly led their trench. Here we leave you with some wise words from students.

Tales from the Trenches: Warm Bodies Speak Out

JW
St. Louis
c. 2010

I entered Ladue High School in the fall of 2006. It was my first time in the district, actually my first time in public school, and as most freshmen, I was awkward and nervous. Unlike most of my classmates, however, I didn't have any history with the people around me. I knew nobody.

Broadcast journalism allowed me to build an identity within the high school, to pursue my passion for filmmaking and to find my place in the social ecosystem of high school, which can be admittedly intimidating. I can think of countless others who similarly used broadcast technology to craft their identities, exploring areas of interest and telling stories which mattered to them in an effort to define their ethics and personal narrative.

In the LHWHS broadcast program, once you've mastered the basics, you build the curriculum. What Don Goble and Marteana Davidson have created is a framework, an evaluative and guidance system that helps students as they explore projects they conceive, and thus are personally meaningful. This also means there is a vast amount of personal responsibility, and many students have learned the hard way that nobody is going to push them to be accountable if can't take care of themselves. This is a critical nudge that many who find themselves taking the broadcast elective need, and many who've signed up for an "easy" elective end up discovering an aptitude and engagement, taking the course again and again.

When you look at the alumnus of the Ladue broadcast program, you see Pulitzer Prize-winning Journalists, Emmy-winning TV makers, lauded filmmakers, and innovative technicians and storytellers. It is indeed astonishing that such a crop should grow from such small harvest. As you well know, the broadcast program is niche, but it builds critical confidence and creativity that have yielded some of Horton Watkins alumnus' most prestigious accomplishments. These will only multiply, as the program is still young and many of its graduates are still in the early part of their careers.

Of my own journey I can only say that I would not be where I am today, working in Los Angeles in the music, film, and television industries without the mentorship and encouragement of Don Goble and Marteana Davidson and the flexibility and artistic freedom that the broadcast technology program allowed me.

David Paul McCahon Linares
Reynoldsburg
c. 2018

My school is really unique because it has activities called Design Challenges. Design Challenges are when the teacher gives you a problem about what you are working on in class, and you have to solve it. There are many different possibilities for correct solutions, instead of just a test where there is only one correct answer. One example of a design challenge I liked was when we learned about Reynoldsburg history. We researched changes from our city's past and used them to predict what changes might happen in the future. We showed our learning by using materials to make a miniature city on a coordinate grid of what Reynoldsburg might look like in the future. I love design challenges. Would you rather take a boring test on paper with one correct answer, only work by yourself, use memory, not ideas, and not have fun? Or would you want to use designing materials to be creative, work with your friends, have many diverse answers into one big kaleidoscope of answers and fun? I thought so!

My school is also unique because we use blended learning every day. Blended learning is digital work. We use learning programs that let the students learn at their level. We are given lessons at our level and we can earn token rewards that let you play games. Sometimes I save up a lot of lessons and have a game rally. There is also a program where the teacher assigns digital work for the students, and the students can show what they know by making videos, using emojis, drawing, take pictures, or we can record. The parents can see from a different device what you are working on. For example, if you were making a main idea review you could either make a "100% BORINGFEST" test, or you can make a digital scramble of ideas in one area of the screen and have the details to support the ideas in another part of the screen, and have the students match them!

My school is also awesome because we use programs for students to learn how to code on computers. Computer coding is helpful in many ways. One way it is helpful is because it can help you later on. Many jobs use technology and have coding embedded in it. For example, if you wanted to work at Apple, the machines would make the computer, but you have to program it. Even if you don't want a STEM job, then it would help in situations with troubleshooting for challenging problems. Another way computer coding is helpful is if you do not code correctly, you can watch the code you make and see how you can correct it.

One reason all that stuff, design challenges, blended learning, and computer coding…well, it all comes together and helps, is that the world itself is becoming more digital every second. We can use this to infer that it is becoming less and less traditional every second. So, we can learn to do things the digital way, the way that will be used more and more. I want to be a miner when I grow up, so maybe when I grow up they will need people like me to make mining safer and easier. If that does not work out I would be a computer coder. The only code language I completely know is LOGO, but that is changing. When I understand a lot of code languages, then I will find a coding job and make something! (After orientation and all those boring things to fill out.) Hey, my school may not be traditional, but I wouldn't want it to be.

Ethan Finney
Savannah
c. 2015

When I hear STEM, multiple subjects typically come to mind; primarily science, technology, engineering, and mathematics. Alone, these subjects are valuable; but what really makes these subjects flow and appeal to me is the connectivity between each subject. My teachers taught me that how subjects like English and history connect with technology and science is equally as important as teaching the subjects. It's in this realization that STEM education truly shines above regular education, as it gives students the tools necessary to gain intelligence and become wise decision makers while also teaching them how and when to use those tools to succeed in their endeavors.

When I was a STEM student at The STEM Academy, the school acknowledged that, in order to yield the best results from STEM education, they needed to have a class dedicated to using the talents we learned from our science, math, English, history, and engineering classes. This class manifested in the form of a research class. With limited curriculum, the teachers, together with students, were free from the bureaucratic requirements and able to genuinely participate in real-world applications of certain skills. In this research class we had no specific "lane" to stay in; for example, we had projects ranging from holding a mock trial to give a hands-on look at our judicial system, a project involving creating a new invention, and subsequently pitching that invention to the class. We became forensic scientists where we analyzed a "crime scene" outside of the school and used clues to solve what happened; and, finally, we were given a project to write a short story involving the decreasing bee population.

All these projects involved innovation, creation, and investigation; which may not directly link with STEM principles, but it connects with STEM in that all the projects centered around the scientific method. This method of procedure consists in observation, measurement, experiment, testing, and modification of a hypothesis. The trial project taught how to observe, formulate a hypothesis, and argue the validity of that hypothesis. Inventing and marketing a product taught how to measure, experiment, test, and modify a hypothesis (final product). Examining a "crime scene" taught us to methodically observe and modify a hypothesis based upon discovering facts. And our final project, to write a short, fictitious story about the declining bee population—having to write a multi-page story about a topic not many seventh-graders were truly aware of.

This was the most rewarding project I did. While it sounds dull compared to a trial, a crime scene, and pitching an invention, in the long term I benefited so much more from this project than any other. With this bee project, three things occurred: Number one, I tied together all my skills—English, science, and research. Number two, it allowed me to put to the test my ability to research a topic to the point of no return and develop all the information into an appealing format that brought in readers of all grades and ages. And number three, it showed me what STEM truly was meant to do: to teach different sects of knowledge and give students the ability to differentiate between and connect every single subject learned to create the best final product and future possible.

For me, especially at fifteen years old, if I don't see how a subject or a curriculum can benefit me in the short or long term, I adamantly refused to learn it; like most STEM students I would, admittedly, rather shut down than learn something that isn't strictly obvious in how it benefits me as a student. Thankfully, I had my bee project, which legitimized and epitomized what STEM education intended to do and was meant to do. I finally understood, that STEM education was about the collaboration of learning, not the competition of curriculum. This collaboration between teacher and student, subject and student, and student and student is what is inherent in this approach to learning and what allows for STEM to yield such tremendous students. In a constant, fast-paced world full of competition, teaching students to collaborate and not compete is one of the underlying truths and inherent pillars of STEM; teaching students to collaborate is preparing students for their future, whatever it may be.

Grant Boone
Reynoldsburg
c. 2017

The adventure began on January 6, 2017. The entire robotics team, including parents and alumni, crowded into Mr. Coley's room, and at 10:00 exactly, along with thousands of teams from around the world, we received our challenge. From that moment on, it was crunch time. For the next six weeks, we would be designing, building, prototyping, testing, wiring, and programming our creation. The process of build season gives invaluable lessons, from things as simple as how to accurately cut aluminum on a bandsaw, to things as intense as learning to design and picture mechanisms in your mind, and them bring them into reality. FIRST teaches students skills that they can use for the rest of their lives, like teamwork, solving problems under pressure, and how to learn new skills quickly. Through robotics, I have learned to use industrial-grade machinery, design and problem-solve as a team, and see the feats of engineering all around us in everyday life in a whole new way. Also, one of the greatest things about this team is that it allowed me to shadow and interact with professional engineers and geniuses every day. On the robotics team, there are "mentors" or adults who are not coaches that help students in a teaching capacity. Our mentors include many skilled professionals, from electrical engineers, to some of the best engineers at Battelle, some of which have patents to their names. Through robotics, I have the privilege of being taught by these amazing people every day. They impart invaluable knowledge and wisdom and motivate my teammates and I for future careers.

Through FIRST, my friends and I have learned to interact with corporate sponsors, create business plans to manage tens of thousands of dollars, do community outreach, code, design complex mechanical systems, align mecanum wheels, use machinery and work as a team to achieve a common dream. This year alone, each person on the team has put in over one hundred hours of work to achieve our goal. Our robot's name is Reboot, and we will see this challenge through to the very end.

FIRST provides a fun and engaging experience for students, while also teaching them valuable life lessons, inspiring them for the future, and connecting them with professionals in STEM fields. My teammates and I can use this experience well into the future. Robotics has motivated me to pursue a STEM career and connected me to professional engineers and companies. Last year, we made it to the robotics world championship. There, amazing companies showcased their work and encouraged us to come work for them in the future, giving us peer connections and wisdom that will help guide us for years to come. Companies that had achieved amazing feats of engineering were there like Boeing, BAE Systems, BELL Labs, the Air Force, and Qualcomm. FIRST robotics also makes over fifty million dollars in scholarships available to students.

This year we had a great and productive build season, and I have learned a ton. The only way to make this experience more valuable this year is to help my team make it to worlds again and pursue the connections that I have received through this amazing experience.

Robotics has given me a way to express my creativity and passion through hands-on, real-world experience that allows me to work with amazing people and learn new things every day, and to gain inspiration, connections, and memories that will help my teammates and me to become the leaders and innovators of the future.

Hailey Martin
Pembroke
c. 2013

An assignment I still remember that truly shaped the way I feel about writing is one that was given in my seventh-grade English class. As a middle schooler, I was still in the beginning stages of becoming who I am as a writer. I was unsure of myself often and felt as if my writing was not up to par with the rest of my peers. When trying to put pen to paper, my mind would wander all over the place. I couldn't set my mind on a way to write or how to go about starting. Once I entered the class of Mrs. Fox, she challenged our brains in ways that we'd never been introduced to before. I remember she was always enthusiastic about incorporating technology into our everyday assignments that usually teachers would have demanded with paper. This project was to use the app Storybird to create a story using only the pictures provided. This gave us students a free way to write, but also in a way that demanded creativity and fun. I thoroughly enjoyed the process of brainstorming my story with the photoset that I was given. I could feel my brain finally begin to work in a way that it was never made to before. After a day or so, I finally had my story written, and I was proud of writing! Using the iPads to do this assignment allowed me to write farther than a normal seventh grader would have been expected to.

My story involved a young child that used her imagination to escape to a world that was far greater than the one she had. Her home life was rocky at best and the only way she could feel true happiness was by creating this universe that involved talking animals and friendship that she had never experienced before. In some way, I was able to create a story that reflected my personal homelife at the time, and I wasn't aware of it. If it were not for the Storybird website, and my teacher allowing us to bring in technology to the classroom, I might have never discovered my love for writing fiction!

At the end of the year, I was presented with an award by Mrs. Fox at Honor's Day for this project. This gave me the courage to go on and write passion projects of my own from my family's computer and break into a world online that encourages those like me to write from the heart. I am forever grateful for the opportunity to have written the story, and I know that the way I view education changed afterwards.

Cami Lowry
Savannah
c. 2017

Knowledge is an incredible thing that can open your eyes to solve almost any problem related to school or life. But I have found that standard facts learned in the classroom are not enough to solve every obstacle that crosses your path. Collaboration with your peers and teachers are the factors that truly define how successful a solution can be.

I recall several times in middle school and my first year in high school where we worked on a project that required several different perspectives to discover a plausible solution. A series of projects that comes to mind are assignments called grand challenges. Grand challenges are worldwide problems that we attempt to solve. I remember when our teacher first explained the objectives of these grand challenges to us, I was slightly overwhelmed with the fact that we were going to have to attempt to solve a problem that was negatively impacting the entire world. I was relieved to hear that we were going to be assigned groups, because I would have other people to bounce ideas off of. When we began the projects, the ideas we created turned out better than I could ever have hoped for because not only were we all able to bounce ideas off each other, but our eyes were also opened to tons of new perspectives. Our groups were not self-assigned, which meant that I got to hear the ideas of people that I might not always talk to or collaborate with. Even though it was sometimes hard to adjust to working with people that might not be as motivated as yourself, it was extremely rewarding. Working with different types of people exposed me to concepts that I might never have even considered and allowed the creation of some amazing ideas, and this was all due to collaboration.

Collaboration is such an essential aspect to problem-solving because it opens your eyes to new perspectives that you may have never even considered by yourself. Lou Ludwig stated, "Knowledge opens doors, but you have to step through." This quote is one that I believe truly highlights the importance of collaboration. Knowledge is like the kindling used for a fire, but a fire requires a spark, and that spark comes from collaboration. Knowledge creates opportunities for success that you can only fully grasp through collaboration and communication with your peers.

Relationships are one of the key components that make for successful collaboration. Relationships made throughout your lifetime are the things that can truly differentiate how well you work with others and therefore how well a job gets done. When students are given the opportunity to work with others, the outcome can have an impact bigger than any outcome that could ever come from just one person. Having the knowledge to solve a problem and actually being able to solve it are often two completely different things, and the difference between them is collaboration.

BRAIN STRETCHERS

1. What personal interests do your students have?

2. How can you create opportunities for students to contribute and reflect on their classroom experiences?

3. What opportunities do you give your students to collaborate and work together?

4. What was your main takeaway from these student accounts?

Chapter 9 Badge Challenge

Instead of experiencing a Metaverse AR Formative that we have created, we challenge you to create one for your students or to create an AR experience on Teachingland. Share it with us on Twitter using the hashtag #Teachingland. We will add it to our Teachingland collection in Metaverse and send you the badge for Chapter 9.

CHAPTER 10
World War E

"I'm not great at farewells, so uh . . . that'll do, pig."
—Tallahassee, *Zombieland*

Don't worry, everything's going to be all right.
—Dr. Kwang Jingshu, *World War Z*

Dear Columbus,

The past year has been quite the journey, as we have traversed the classroom apocalyptic landscape—the nights have been long, and the dawns tiring—I have looked for messages from you on social media, but with grids down a physical tweet from a carrier finch will have to do. Sometimes the life we choose is a ride those dear to us have to get on—and in venturing through the zombie genre my kids boarded, too. The zombie puns have been an epidemic and watching *Zombies* the Disney musical is a favorite past time. My daughter Rowan sends regards to Amelia, and I have attached a drawing she has requested I include.

This journey started with *Zombieland* and its rules, so I am going to conclude with a *Zombieland* quote to bring my message around full circle…"I'm not great at farewells, so uh …that'll do, pig." Like Tallahassee, I also find myself not so great at farewells—in writing or in person—and wrapping up this odyssey is no different. Maybe because I'm optimistic that goodbyes are just temporary or are more of an "until the next." Maybe because like most humans, letting go is hard to do. Whether it's letting go of a tradition, a school, a decade, a city, a person, or inking the last page (all of which this year has brought me),…"goodbye," in the grand scheme of things, seems so finite.

But that is not why I put ink to this paper. I'm writing to remind you that similar to World War Z, goodbyes also mean a time for renewal, ushering in new ways of life and rebuilding society, culture, and a new normal. And through all the hardships if renewal, support, and positivity is what our book brings, then authoring this survival guide was all worth it.

I have spoken a lot about our education system being in a state of transition, but the truth is, each generation is constantly transitioning from one way of doing things to another. As technological advances, new ideas, and innovation turn the page of time into new epochs and new generations with new needs professional evolution is a necessary attribute regarding not only the vehicles that take us to our bunkers but those that drive our instruction. Whether in Columbus…Savannah….Louisville, or somewhere in LA. or Australia, we are all driven by wanting the best for our kids, and future generations.

Columbus, the battles that you face daily are the same battles this entire generation of teachers face. They will always exist in some form or fashion, much like the threat of another outbreak in a zombie movie. I mean…Have you seen a legit zombie film where the virus is completely eradicated? Whether the external factors that cause outbreaks in our classrooms are policy, leadership, conflict with colleagues, or time, challenges are something that are the bedrock of society, and though this is goodbye, through the collation of words and experiences our legacy will live on. Some of these battles may be out of our control individually, but collectively we can share, support, and rise up to be the change we want to see. Though here is where we part ways, I know you will keep on fighting the good fight.

We must also keep in mind that external battles are not the only ones we face. Every one of us is fighting our own silent internal battles. So I know I need not remind you to be kind. Don't let the adversity of the landscape bring out the worst of human nature; help those around you band together to weather the storm and through numbers you will find support. Each of us has the power to fight for our students and the future of the world in our daily actions. As we both travel the Teachingland landscape remember, Bethel, Vermonts, like in I am Legend, sanctuaries—are not found…they are made. They are built with dedication, passion, love, and kindness, which are far more infectious than any figurative zombie virus.

So for my conclusion, I can promise you and the rest of Teachingland, as Dr. Kwang Jingshu promised his daughter in World War Z (though that didn't end well for him)… that everything is going to be alright. When things are overwhelming, and you find yourself re-thumbing the pages of this letter looking for some secret sauce to survival, dog-ear this page, repeat this manifesto I have written for myself, and make it your own…for survival, success, and growth all start within. Believe it or chant it until you do.

Here are my personal takeaways from our journey and survival guide that I have turned into mission statements at times, and other times they're the reminder I need when the profession is getting the best of me—which it does.

My Teachingland Manifesto

1. I know there will be highs and lows, and for each low it will be met by a peak. Lows will grant me humility, while highs will give me drive to continue on. For everything else, there are Teachingland Rules!

2. I understand my struggles aren't isolated to me, and I will approach my students, colleagues, and peers with kindness and empathy.

3. I will be the best teacher I can be today by ensuring I set actions in motion to grow professionally and personally so that tomorrow I am a better version of myself.

4. When I get overwhelmed, I will remember the little things that count…and breathe!

5. When I fail, it is not fatal. I will use my defeat as a launchpad to fail forward and rise up.

6. I will be my students' biggest advocate, and I will try to help them feel loved, safe, and find their purpose in this world.

7. *I will share not only my professional successes widely but also my failures so others might learn from both while understanding we are all human.*

8. *I will lead by motivating and highlighting the strengths in others and let them shine. Like the moon, I will be illuminated by those I have helped shine and not just my own success.*

9. *I will collaborate like a goldfish and innovate like a betta.*

10. *I will say goodbye (when I need to) to things that don't work, to ideas, to colleagues, to anything that needs to be let go. I will then have space for renewal.*

While I have enjoyed riding this writing roller coaster ride of a book, it's time to say goodbye. So...that'll do, pig. Until the next!

Warm regards,
Savannah

"Fasten your seatbelts. This is going to be a bumpy ride."
—Columbus, Zombieland

"That's the worst goodbye I've ever heard, and you stole it from a movie."
—Columbus, Zombieland

Dear Savannah,

Thank you for your note. I am pleased that finches seem to finally be trained, though Little Rock and Tallahassee seem exhausted. I gave them some bread crumbs, and they are now resting in their cage. Hopefully Bill Murray and Wichita will deliver this message safely.

When we first embarked on this journey, we knew that it would be a wild ride. In all of our correspondences from our bunkers, our homes, and sometimes even shady hotels, we have learned so much about zombies, survival tactics, and what teachers need in order to survive this apocalyptic landscape. But this important work has not been easy, and everyone has had to pitch in and show understanding. Amelia sends her regards to Rowan and has asked that I send a zombie drawing for you to pass along. Please make sure that she sees it.

I was moved by the depth of your wisdom in your letter, as well as your manifesto. I've attached mine below.

Surviving the classroom apocalypse is not for the faint of heart. The original Columbus said it best when he said, "Fasten your seatbelts. This is going to be a bumpy ride." As we know, there's a battle going on out there to save impressionable souls from becoming casualties of this virus. However, if teachers use the rules of Teachingland, learn to collaborate with all of the Colleagues and Parents of the Apocalypse, leverage the tools we have provided for their arsenals, and are willing to share what they have learned with the world, I have every confidence that humanity will reign.

My Teachingland Manifesto

1. I will make every effort to promote the rules of Teachingland in every bunker and trench I encounter—and try to understand any unique rules that they may have—to help ensure harmony and inoculate others against the infection.

2. I will always make every effort to actively and empathetically listen, find value, and learn from others, even if they hold beliefs that are vastly different from mine, as there is so much that I still have to learn.

3. I will make every effort to ensure that my bunker feels warm, safe, and supportive so that teachers and students are able to thrive knowing that they are secure and cared for while they are at school. To this end, I will err on the side of love and compassion always, because as we know, frustration and anger leaves us all vulnerable to infection.

4. I will make every effort to remember the lessons of the Pedagogy Players that have gone before us. I will make every effort to stay current on the latest research and trends so that my bunker never goes stagnant and starts smelling like death.

5. I will make sure that my bunker is always outfitted with a robust arsenal, and that my teachers always have access to the R.E.M.E.D.Y., to ensure that we keep the infection at bay.

6. I will make sure that my teachers have a well-equipped survival kit to keep both students and teachers engaged and excited about learning.

7. I will encourage my teachers to use a variety of meaningful assessment types to ensure that we measure all aspects of student progress and spare the bunker from the chains of the grade-and-groan assembly line.

8. I will make sure that I create an environment where my teachers feel safe to take risks and share their successes (and lessons learned) with

the world through social media, and that I serve as a model for them by leading in beta as well.

9. I will be honest with myself when something is not working, and model the art of failing fast and forward, so that we can focus on what does work.

10. I will celebrate the successes of all of my teachers (and their students), so that they will continue to maintain trenches that foster innovation, collaboration, and a love of learning.

As for your goodbye, in the wise words of Columbus #1, "That's the worst goodbye I've ever heard, and you stole it from a movie." So, my friend, this is goodbye for now. You have been a kick-ass partner, and I can't wait until we can team up again. Stay safe, Savannah.

Much love,
Columbus

Teachingland Trivia

Think you have what it takes to become part of the #walkingread tribe? Then test your Teachingland knowledge with Augmented Reality trivia. Download the Metaverse app, and scan the QR code to test your knowledge and earn a badge!

Bibliography

INTRODUCTION

Wong, Harry and Rosemary Wong. The First Days of School. Mountain View, California: Harry K. Wong Publications, Inc., 1994.

Miranda, Lin-Manuel. "Hamilton: An American Musical." Edited by Jeremy McCarter. New York: Grand Central Publishing, 2016.

Polone, Gavin, Rhett Reese, and Paul Wernick. Zombieland. Directed by Ruben Fleischer. Los Angeles, California: Columbia, 2009.

The National Commission on Excellence in Education, "A Nation at Risk: The Imperative for Educational Reform." Washington, DC: U.S. Department of Education, 1983.

CHAPTER 2

Covey, Stephen R. The 7 Habits of Highly Effective People. New York, New York: Rosetta Books, 2013.

CHAPTER 3

Whannell, Leigh and Ian Brennan. Cooties. Directed by Jonathan Milott and Cary Murnion. Santa Monica, California: Lionsgate Premiere, 2014.

CHAPTER 4

Robinson, Ken, Future of Education Technology Conference (FETC), Orlando, FL, 2018.

Dweck, Carol, Mindset: The New Psychology of Success. New York, New York: Random House, 2006.

CHAPTER 5

Madison, Alan. Kathleen Cormley, and Matt Sharp. Doomsday Preppers. TV Series. New York, New York: Sharp Entertainment NGC Studios.

CHAPTER 6

Singh, Awinash, iZombie. The Series. Burbank, California: Warner Brothers Entertainment, 2015.

CHAPTER 7

Garland, Alex. 28 Days Later. Directed by Danny Boyle. London, England: DNA Films, 2002.

CHAPTER 8

Protosevich, Mark and Akiva Goldsman. I Am Legend. Directed by Francis Lawrence. Burbank, California: Warner Brothers Entertainment, 2007.

CHAPTER 9

Levine, Jonathan. Warm Bodies. Directed by Jonathan Levine. Santa Monica, California: Summit Entertainment, 2013.

CHAPTER 10

Pitt, Brad, and Matthew Michael Carnahan. World War Z. Directed by Marc Forster. Santa Monica, California: Skydance Productions, 2013.

Acknowledgments

First and foremost we would like to thank our families for being supportive and encouraging us from start to finish. When you sign up to write a book, you sign the whole family up whether they want to be signed up or not, and we are happy everyone jumped in and buckled up for this marathon of a roller coaster ride and put up with the highs and lows of the writing process.

Patrick, thank you for not only buying into my delusions of grandeur, but also allowing me the space and time to make this happen. Also, for putting up with the endless late-night binge sessions of *iZombie* and turning date nights into research sessions. Rowan, Bridgit, Connor, and Finnick—I couldn't ask for better cheerleaders. This book was ultimately for you. I hope it is a symbol that anything, no matter how challenging, is possible if you persevere—and writing a book is challenging!

Steve, thank you for being my rock and my encourager through this whole experience. I would not been able to do this without you. I am so very grateful for you and our amazing kiddos. Amelia, Eli, and Alice thank you for being patient with mama through the times when writing had to take priority due to deadlines. The three of you are amazing, and I am so proud of you. My prayer this process is that this is a lesson for you in the value of patience, dedication, and hard work.

Dave and Shelley Burgess—where do we start? When this book was just a vision and we were full of hesitation on which direction we were going, you had faith in it. It wasn't until your show of confidence in us, that we were confident enough to fully tackle this crazy topic of zombies and education. Thank you for being our compass and the wind in our writing sails. We are so fortunate to join the DBC family. A special thanks to your incredible editing team that took our words, diamonds in the rough—sometimes outright coal, and polished them into sparkling prose.

Also, this book would not be as meaningful without all of our amazing Tales from the Trenches contributors who were willing to share their stories of survival. We hope these resonate and empower up-and-coming educators. Special thanks goes out to Carl Hooker for not only being willing to write the foreword for this book, but also sharing our same infectious love for the undead metaphor.

Additionally, we would like to thank Tim Childers, Peter Ulrich, Benjamin Creasey, Steven Sato, Brian Costello, Isabel Bozada, Brett Salakas, and Mia Brower who served as our sounding boards and offered meaningful feedback and support throughout the writing process.

Finally, we want to thank George A. Romero, Max Brooks, Chris Roberson, Rhett Reese, Paul Wernick, Rob Thomas, and Diane Ruggiero-Wright for writing and producing media that has such a profound impact on the metaphors and parallels in our book. Rose McIver—you are our zomcom hero. And to Jesse Eisenberg (Columbus) and Woody Harrelson (Tallahassee)-your characters are the Twinkies of all zombie films—timeless—we can't wait for the sequel.

Bring the R.E.M.E.D.Y. to Your School or District

Teachingland Workshops

As new and seasoned teachers return to start another year, classroom preparations are in place to survive another year! In this fun, hands-on session, teachers will put *Teachingland* rules like Bare Hands and Zombie Zips into practice through team building and design thinking challenges to reshape the way they design activities in their classroom, and check the pulse of their students. Our R.E.M.E.D.Y. Model helps teachers reimagine and rectify the role of student voice and personalized learning. Amanda and Mary Ellen can customize this workshop to meet the needs of your school or district.

Teachingland Keynote

In this dynamic and engaging keynote, Amanda or Mary Ellen will share the rules of *Teachingland*, the R.E.M.E.D.Y. Model, classroom management strategies, and all other components of classroom survival. Leveraging design thinking, problem-based learning, and a multitude of technologically driven integration strategies, *Teachingland* spans all grades and content areas. Teachers will leave with a better grasp of designing lessons and engaging their warm-bodied learners. This keynote can be tailored to address a specific chapter or multiple concepts within the book!

Teachingland Book Study

Love *Teachingland* and want to bring a book study to your school or district? Amanda or Mary Ellen can lead readings and assignments through webinars, virtual reality meet-ups, or video sessions, with customized assignments based on your school or districts goals. Teachers are asked to work through each chapter via call to actions and AR experiences to immediately apply content through the submissions of authentic learning artifacts. Upon completion, digital badges are awarded. Looking to purchase more than fifty copies? Contact us for a discounted quote.

More from
Dave Burgess Consulting, Inc.

Since 2012, DBCI has been publishing books that inspire and equip educators to be their best. For more information on our DBCI titles or to purchase bulk orders for your school, district, or book study, visit **DaveBurgessconsulting.com/DBCIbooks**.

More from the *PIRATE*™ Series
Teach Like a PIRATE by Dave Burgess
eXPlore Like a Pirate by Michael Matera
Learn Like a Pirate by Paul Solarz
Play Like a Pirate by Quinn Rollins
Run Like a Pirate by Adam Welcome

Lead Like a *PIRATE*™ Series
Lead Like a PIRATE by Shelley Burgess and Beth Houf
Balance Like a Pirate by Jessica Cabeen, Jessica Johnson, and Sarah Johnson
Lead beyond Your Title by Nili Bartley
Lead with Culture by Jay Billy
Lead with Literacy by Mandy Ellis

Leadership & School Culture
Culturize by Jimmy Casas
Escaping the School Leader's Dunk Tank by Rebecca Coda and Rick Jetter
From Teacher to Leader by Starr Sackstein
The Innovator's Mindset by George Couros
Kids Deserve It! by Todd Nesloney and Adam Welcome
Let Them Speak by Rebecca Coda and Rick Jetter
The Limitless School by Abe Hege and Adam Dovico
The Pepper Effect by Sean Gaillard
The Principled Principal by Jeffrey Zoul and Anthony McConnell
The Secret Solution by Todd Whitaker, Sam Miller, and Ryan Donlan

Start. Right. Now. by Todd Whitaker, Jeffrey Zoul, and Jimmy Casas
Stop. Right. Now. by Jimmy Casas and Jeffrey Zoul
Unmapped Potential by Julie Hasson and Missy Lennard
They Call Me "Mr. De" by Frank DeAngelis
Your School Rocks by Ryan McLane and Eric Lowe

Technology & Tools

50 Things You Can Do with Google Classroom by Alice Keeler and Libbi Miller
50 Things to Go Further with Google Classroom by Alice Keeler and Libbi Miller
140 Twitter Tips for Educators by Brad Currie, Billy Krakower, and Scott Rocco
Block Breaker by Brian Aspinall
Code Breaker by Brian Aspinall
Google Apps for Littles by Christine Pinto and Alice Keeler
Master the Media by Julie Smith
Shake Up Learning by Kasey Bell
Social LEADia by Jennifer Casa-Todd
Teaching Math with Google Apps by Alice Keeler and Diana Herrington
Tech with Heart by Stacey Roshan

Teaching Methods & Materials

All 4s and 5s by Andrew Sharos
Ditch That Homework by Matt Miller and Alice Keeler
Ditch That Textbook by Matt Miller
Educated by Design by Michael Cohen, The Tech Rabbi
The EduProtocol Field Guide by Marlena Hebern and Jon Corippo
Instant Relevance by Denis Sheeran
LAUNCH by John Spencer and A.J. Juliani
Make Learning MAGICAL by Tisha Richmond
Pure Genius by Don Wettrick
Shift This! by Joy Kirr
Spark Learning by Ramsey Musallam
Sparks in the Dark by Travis Crowder and Todd Nesloney
Table Talk Math by John Stevens
The Classroom Chef by John Stevens and Matt Vaudrey
The Wild Card by Hope and Wade King
The Writing on the Classroom Wall by Steve Wyborney

Inspiration, Professional Growth & Personal Development

Be REAL by Tara Martin

Be the One for Kids by Ryan Sheehy

Creatively Productive by Lisa Johnson

The EduNinja Mindset by Jennifer Burdis

The Four O'Clock Faculty by Rich Czyz

How Much Water do We Have? by Pete and Kris Nunweiler

P Is for Pirate by Dave and Shelley Burgess

A Passion for Kindness by Tamara Letter

The Path to Serendipity by Allyson Apsey

Sanctuaries by Dan Tricarico

Shattering the Perfect Teacher Myth by Aaron Hogan

Stories from Webb by Todd Nesloney

Talk to Me by Kim Bearden

The Revolution by Darren Ellwein and Derek McCoy

The Zen Teacher by Dan Tricarico

Through the Lens of Serendipity by Allyson Apsey

Children's Books

Dolphins in Trees by Aaron Polansky

The Princes of Serendip by Allyson Apsey

About the Authors

Amanda Fox, creative director of FoxBrite LLC, is an educational pioneer. She has taught English language arts, social studies, film, journalism, and now leads STEAM programs via her startup STEAMPunksEdu in Louisville, Kentucky, with plans of expanding to Dallas in 2019. Recipient of the 2016 ISTE Emerging Leader Award, recognized as a PBS Digital Innovator for her initiatives in enhancing student learning with technology, Fox has also served as president of the Young Educator Network for ISTE, and received the President's Volunteer Award. Her current project, the Zom-Be kids book series, sees her introducing design thinking to elementary students, and is to be released in 2019. She has an affinity for coffee mugs, nerdy T-shirts, and can always be found in heels. Check out the *Teachingland Podcast, The Virtual Reality Podcast*, and *The STEM Capeless Crusaders Podcast* to learn more or connect with Amanda on Twitter @AmandaFoxSTEM.

Mary Ellen Weeks is the proud principal of Herbert Mills STEM Elementary School, a globally focused STEM school in Reynoldsburg, Ohio, and unapologetic advocate for STEM education and innovative best practices. In 2015, she was selected as an ISTE Emerging Leader, and served as ISTE Young Educator Network President from 2016-2017. She also wears many other hats including wife to Steve, mother to three awesome kids: Amelia, Eli, and Alice, and a goldendoodle named Gus. She enjoys cooking, traveling, and reading in her (very limited) spare time.

CPSIA information can be obtained
at www.ICGtesting.com
Printed in the USA
BVHW010129210619
551552BV00023B/142/P